DELIVERED UNTO LIONS

A novel by

DAVID AUSTIN

To Debbie

Good luck in your new post,
and very many thanks for all your
help and support over the last
few years

David Austin

Delivered Unto Lions
ISBN-13: 978-1-906628-21-5
Published by CheckPoint Press, Ireland

CHECKPOINT PRESS, DOOAGH, ACHILL ISLAND, CO. MAYO,

REPUBLIC OF IRELAND

TEL: 098 43779

EMAIL: EDITOR@CHECKPOINTPRESS.COM

WEBSITE: WWW.CHECKPOINTPRESS.COM

NOTE TO THE READER

This novel is inspired by fact. The historical existence of children's psychiatric units in Britain, of the kind described in this book, is not generally well-known. Upon entering my teens in the 1970s, I had some personal experience of such a unit, and so this book is based on that experience.

All of the characters in this book – including the main character, Daniel – are fictional. They may represent some general tendencies that were apparent in real people, but any personal details have been substantially altered. This is similarly the case with events, though given the nature of the setting, readers familiar with circumstances of this kind could well observe some resemblance to incidents in their experience. It is certainly the case that everything represented here, though portrayed from a particular point-of-view, would have been possible. And so I believe *Delivered Unto Lions* conveys a good impression of the reality.

David Austin

Table of Contents

PROLOGUE..7

CHAPTER ONE...9

CHAPTER TWO...27

CHAPTER THREE..39

CHAPTER FOUR..51

CHAPTER FIVE..65

CHAPTER SIX..79

CHAPTER SEVEN..95

CHAPTER EIGHT...109

CHAPTER NINE...121

CHAPTER TEN...137

CHAPTER ELEVEN..151

CHAPTER TWELVE...165

CHAPTER THIRTEEN..177

CHAPTER FOURTEEN...189

CHAPTER FIFTEEN...201

CHAPTER SIXTEEN...217

CHAPTER SEVENTEEN...227

EPILOGUE...241

PROLOGUE

The damp from a light drizzle settles in my hair as I walk through a newly-built housing estate lined with young trees. Almost everything in this new village, Hawkins Down, looks as though it was constructed or grown within the last five years. There are hardly any signs of a previous history, the only exceptions I can make out from my current position are a few common oaks, the modest spire of a nineteenth century chapel, and part of a granite façade of similar vintage.

I come to a minor intersection at the end of St Anslem's Road and pause. There's a signpost indicating directions to various local amenities: Woodland Lane Medical Centre, Hammer Pond Civic Hall, Mannings Heath Golf Club, and Grouse Road Leisure Centre. I turn onto another residential street, and suddenly my blood runs cold. I've noticed the name of the street: Oakdale Drive.

Rooted to the spot, my eyes scan the immediate area. There are a few people around: an elderly woman carrying a shopping bag, a young couple hand-in-hand, and parents walking with their children. I feel decidedly queasy upon seeing the children, because I realise they are walking on the very same ground that I knew when I was young. It's all very different now, however – quite unrecognisable. Only the name, Oakdale Drive, gives it away – that and the basic contours of the land on which it has been built.

I am back. After having left this place so long ago, way back in my teens, I now find myself standing where I once knew such utter desolation and horror. And yet, all trace of such things is gone, razed to the ground and buried under smart starter homes and attractive apartments, green saplings and shrubs. Hawkins Down in general, and Oakdale Drive in particular, conceal a dark secret.

Having recovered somewhat from the initial shock, I slowly begin walking again. As I place one foot in front of the other, the memories bubble up from where they have been hiding, the truth of this place no longer content to lay silent.

CHAPTER ONE

And that was it. My mum and dad – together with my younger brother, Mark – drove off out of the car park in their pale grey Morris 1100, leaving me behind at Oakdale Children's Unit.

It was a dull, cold February day when it happened, when I crossed the line from near-normality into the totally aberrant. Without realising the full significance of what had just happened, I found myself left behind by my parents, a patient in a children's psychiatric facility.

Yesterday – Monday – I had gone off to school as usual, more-or-less like any other twelve-year-old boy. It was true that I had been unsettled and unhappy for some time, and that I found the daily experience of school extremely miserable. But I wasn't doing badly at my lessons, and although I was a bit withdrawn, I did have a handful of good friends.

But now it was Tuesday, and all that was behind me. However, I was feeling excited at the prospect of this new and unusual adventure, and optimistic that Oakdale would sort out all my problems. And in any case, or so I thought, I would be back at home in Loxton, and back at school, in just a few short weeks. But, as I would eventually learn, it wasn't going to work out that way. Soon I would find myself looking back on my experience prior to Oakdale, troubled though it was, as if I had been in paradise!

It was late morning when I found myself undergoing a medical examination. I was lying down on the bed they had given me in the boys' dormitory. As I lay there, I took in my new surroundings. There were twelve or so beds in the room, lined up regimentally against the two longer walls. Each bed lay beneath a double-hung sash window, and was accompanied by an ash-veneered locker (I had just been given the key to mine). I was to learn later that these windows were fixed so that they could not be fully opened; both lower and upper sash could only be shifted by a few centimetres.

Through the wedged-open double-doors I could hear the sound of a radio. The radio was playing 'Mamma Mia', a song which had just dropped from the Number 1 spot; whenever I was to hear that song in the future, it would instantly bring back the memory of that morning.

Dr Ibrahim barely spoke as he mechanically carried out the examination, and the only time he looked me in the eyes was when he was shining his ophthalmoscope into them. Two nurses stood by the bed while this was going on. Neither of them was in uniform – in common with all the staff at Oakdale, as I was to discover. The more senior of the two was a middle-aged woman called Mrs Causton, while the other was a younger and rather more casually dressed man called John Webber. Both of them tried engaging me in friendly conversation as the examination progressed.

'What's your favourite TV programme, Daniel?' John asked. 'Do you like *Doctor Who*?' he added.

'Yes,' I answered.

'Well, you'll be able to see it in colour here.'

This alarmed me. *Doctor Who* was on Saturday evenings, and I'd been expecting to be allowed home at the weekend.

Then, Dr Ibrahim asked me to lower my trousers and underpants.

'It's all right,' said Mrs Causton, apparently noticing my discomfort. 'We've seen it all before.'

I felt awkward and embarrassed as the doctor inspected my genitals. The embarrassment became almost unbearable as I caught Mrs Causton's eye and found myself smiling at her, all because, just at that moment, this part of the examination had become extremely ticklish.

And then, the indignity was over. Dr Ibrahim packed-up his medical bag, washed his hands at one of the sinks by the double-doors and walked out.

'It's nearly lunchtime,' said Mrs Causton. 'John will take you to the dining room and introduce you to some of the other children.'

I got up from the bed, tucked my nylon shirt back into my trousers, and followed John as he led me out of the dormitory.

Just outside was an unoccupied nurses' station, which was where the sound of the radio was coming from. As we walked past it, I noticed, for the first time, the distinctive smell of disinfectant. This unhomely odour underlined the fact that I was in a strange place, and I felt a sudden stab of sadness penetrate me. But I fought it off, remembering that this was supposed to be an exciting adventure, while also recalling what Dr Rajasimha, the Child Guidance psychiatrist, had told me before I came here. He had said that I would probably be in Oakdale for only six weeks, that I would be given effective treatment for my problems, and that I'd *enjoy* my time here – especially as there were so many great facilities, including (he had particularly emphasised) a well-equipped art room.

John escorted me through another set of double-doors and along an extended stretch of corridor. As we walked, I heard a telephone ringing, but the sound seemed to be coming from every direction.

'The 'phone rings out across the whole Unit,' John explained. 'During the day, Miss Bishop's secretary answers it, but after she goes home we can pick it up in the nurses' station or in the kitchen.'

'Who's Miss Bishop?' I asked.

'She's the nursing officer,' John explained. 'She runs the place. You'll get to meet her later.'

As we continued walking I noticed a succession of closed doors leading off from the corridor, hiding rooms that I could only guess at.

Rather than heading through the next set of double-doors, we took a sharp turn left at the corridor's end, and I found myself being ushered through another corridor, this time with windows to either side. As I was discovering, this passageway connected parts of the building which must have been separate at one time.

Once through yet another set of double-doors and entering the main body of the Unit, my nostrils were again assaulted by that soon-to-be-accepted smell of disinfectant. Indeed, in the space of just a few short minutes the smell had already become so familiar that the sadness it provoked in me had become more of an empty ache than a sudden, sharp pain.

John guided me along another corridor, until we passed through an open door into the dining room.

On either side of the room was a row of Formica-topped tables, and at each table there were four plastic chairs. Apart from that, the room was empty, though I could hear voices coming through the serving hatch from the adjoining kitchen at the far end.

'The kids will be coming in from school in a couple of minutes,' John told me. 'You'll get to see the school after lunch; your key worker on the afternoon shift will take you over.'

I stood in the centre of the room and looked around me. To one side there was a row of steel-framed windows through which I could see an expanse of grass leading towards the car park where I had waved off my parents; there was another row of windows to the other side looking out onto an asphalted play area. But what struck me most was how *green* the dining room was; apart from the tabletops, which were orange, almost everything – walls, ceiling, floor tiles – seemed to be an alarming shade of luminous green.

And then I turned round towards the door we'd come through, and just as I noticed the time on the clock above the door – it was just after twelve – I heard the sound of children approaching.

They came streaming into the dining room like a swarm of bees, nosily darting towards their places at table. Although they were accompanied by a number of adults, that didn't seem to especially regulate their clamour, and I felt myself becoming anxious in the midst of the turmoil. I guessed that there must have been about thirty kids in all, ranging in age from about four to seventeen. And there was considerable variety in their dress too; some were clothed quite fashionably, while others were wearing what appeared to be ill-fitting hand-me-downs.

As the noise began to subside, John led me over to a table with two vacant seats.

'You can sit here, Daniel,' he told me, gesturing towards one of the empty chairs while he seated himself in the one opposite me.

The table was already set for lunch, with knives, forks, spoons, glasses and a Perspex jug filled with water.

To my left was a boy who appeared to be about a year younger than me.

'Daniel, this is Gary Jameson,' John introduced us.

Across the table, next to John, was another, slightly older, boy.

'And this is Sean Townsend,' John said.

'Daniel's just joined us,' he told the boys. 'He's from Loxton. Gary, as your home is quite near Loxton, I'd like you to help Daniel settle in.'

'Okay,' Gary answered, with cheerful compliance.

John then changed the subject. 'Sean's a big Liverpool supporter,' he told me.

'Liverpool are crap!' Gary chipped in.

'Who do you support, Daniel?' John continued.

I had no interest in football at all, and the question unnerved me, so I didn't immediately know how to answer.

'I don't really like football,' I replied eventually.

'What sport *do* you like?' Sean asked.

Again, I was nonplussed, as I simply wasn't that keen on sport. I struggled hard to think of a suitable answer – it would have been just too awkward to say I didn't like sport *at all*.

'Well,' I began tentatively, 'I suppose I quite like swimming.'

'We go swimming on Thursdays,' Gary remarked.

'Ah, yes,' John explained. 'Every Thursday morning there's a school visit to the new swimming pool over in Haywards Heath.'

While this conversation was going on, an older female member of staff, an auxiliary called Rose Boyd, was telling each table in turn to join the growing queue for the serving hatch.

'Okay, go on,' she said, as she came to our table.

The four of us got up and began queuing, and I found myself standing behind a girl of about fifteen. She turned round to me and gave me a look I couldn't quite work out.

'So, you're the new kid,' she said, a little abrasively. 'What's your name?'

'Daniel,' I replied.

'Welcome to the mad house, Danny,' she said. 'I'm Sharon. Sharon Gillan.'

'It's Daniel,' I corrected her, 'not Danny.'

'You're a stuck up little bastard, aren't you!' she mocked.

She turned away from me and giggled as she said something to the girl in front of her, and although I didn't actually hear it, I could tell it was an unpleasant remark about me.

A strange numb feeling came over me, but before I had time to yield to it, I was at the head of the queue.

From the serving hatch I was handed a bowl of thin, gravy-like liquid.

'It's oxtail soup,' said Mr Jones, the staff member who served me.

'Thank you,' I mumbled, returning to my seat.

The soup tasted like warm salty water, and the main course that followed it was just as flavourless.

'We don't actually do any cooking in our kitchen,' John explained to me, perhaps seeing how unimpressed I was. 'All the food comes over from the main building. We just dish it up.'

'What main building?' I asked, not having realised that Oakdale was, in effect, just part of a much larger complex.

'The hospital: St Anselm's.'

'That's where they put the grown-up mental patients,' Gary added, speaking through a mouth overfull with boiled cabbage.

I must have been daydreaming when I arrived at Oakdale, as I simply hadn't noticed any of the surroundings. I certainly hadn't observed the imposing nineteenth century granite building that was St Anselm's Psychiatric Hospital, a building that completely dwarfed the much smaller 1950s-built Oakdale Unit. Neither had I noticed how isolated this place was, standing as it did in the midst of the rural countryside, somewhere between the villages of Mannings Heath and Colgate.

'We're generally quite separate from the main building,' John went on, 'but we rely on them for some things, like dental and chiropody services, as well as for catering.'

'Some of the kids from here end up in St Anselm's when they're too old for Oakdale,' Sean commented darkly.

'Sean!' John took him to task. 'That hardly *ever* happens. Most kids,' he said, turning back to me, 'go back to their homes and their old schools as soon as they're better. It's only a few of the really seriously ill ones who get transferred to St Anslem's when they get older.'

Although I'd barely been at Oakdale for two hours, it was already starting to seem like an extremely grim place, and my initial excitement was rapidly evaporating. But I was determined to stay positive; after all, I was only going to be here a few weeks, and more importantly, I was going to get better.

'So, Daniel,' Gary began, 'which doctor are you under? Is it Rajasimha or Collins?'

'Dr Rajasimha,' I answered.

'Me too,' Gary replied. 'He's rubbish.'

'Gary –' John started to admonish.

'Sean's lucky; he's under Dr Collins,' Gary continued undaunted.

After the dessert course, I saw Mrs Causton and another nurse called Robert King rolling a large oak-laminated trolley into the dining room. This was the medicine trolley. Mrs Causton unlocked it, while Robert began calling out children's names. As each name was called, a child would get up and go over to the trolley to receive medication.

'Daniel Kinsley,' Robert called out. It was my name! But I wasn't expecting any medication!

'That's not right,' I said to John apprehensively. 'I take my tablet at bedtime. I don't have one at lunchtime; just at night.'

'There's nothing to worry about,' he answered.

'Daniel Kinsley,' Robert called again.

'Go on,' urged John.

I stood and walked over nervously to the medicine trolley.

'There's been a mistake,' I said to Mrs Causton. 'I only have a tablet at night.'

'Amitriptyline: that's your prescription,' Mrs Causton replied.

'Yes,' I said, 'but not *now*; I take it in the evening. You can check with my mum and dad.'

'*We're* looking after you now, *not* your mum and dad,' said Robert.

'Hold on a minute,' Mrs Causton said, looking at what I presumed was my prescription card. 'You're right, Daniel. You'll have your dose at supper time.'

I was allowed to return to my seat.

After the last child had been given her medication, Mrs Causton locked up the medicine trolley and Robert called out, 'Cigarettes!'

'– And whiskey, and wild, wild women!' Mrs Causton cackled.

A number of children – including Sean – rose from their seats and lined up to receive cigarettes from Mrs Causton.

Sean returned to the table.

'How old are you, Sean?' I asked him.

'Thirteen.'

'How come you're allowed to smoke?'

It was John who answered, removing a Player's Number Six from his own packet and then lighting up. 'We allow the kids to smoke here, just so long as their parents have given permission. Do you smoke, Daniel?'

'No,' I replied, rather bewildered. 'I'm only twelve – *of course* I don't smoke!'

'Good for you!' John smiled.

At that point, Mrs Causton announced that we could leave the table, and the kids – apart from the ones smoking – began filing out into the corridor.

'I'll show you round,' Gary declared, getting up energetically and leading me out.

'This is the quiet room,' he said, pointing to a locked door on one side of the passageway, without actually explaining what the quiet room was.

'And this,' he said, indicating the next door along, 'is the TV room.'

He took me through into a fairly large room which was as blue as the dining room was green. The walls were painted blue, the carpet tiles were blue, and the foam-filled chairs were blue.

A set of French doors opened out onto the play area I had noticed earlier – which now had three kids in it kicking a ball about – while on the other side of the room was a glazed door which I could see leading out into another corridor.

At first I didn't notice the television set – which was odd, considering that this was the TV room – but then I spotted it behind a pane of glass, locked away in its own secure compartment.

'Where do you live, Gary?' I asked him. 'John said you live near Loxton.'

Gary suddenly became less animated. 'I'm from Rudgwick,' he answered. Then, he brightened up again. 'These chairs are amazing!' he enthused, stretching out his arms to grab the sides of a foam seat.

He lifted the chair above his head and hurled it across the room, where it bounced off one of the other chairs before coming to rest on its side. Seeing that no harm was caused by what Gary had done, I wondered if perhaps these chairs had been designed with disruptive behaviour in mind. This dazed me a little, as I grasped the fact that kids could run riot in here, flinging chairs in all directions, with little risk of damage or injury.

'You have a go,' Gary suggested.

'No,' I laughed nervously. 'I don't think I will, thanks.'

'Go on,' he urged. 'It's fun!'

'No, I don't really feel like it.'

But Gary was very insistent, so I gave up resisting and threw one of the chairs against the wall.

Just at that moment Robert King came in. He was the nurse who had been assisting Mrs Causton in dispensing the medicines.

'Just what do you think you're doing?' he bellowed at me.

My heart leaped at the sudden shock of hearing a raised voice.

'How would you like it if I came into your house and started throwing the furniture around?' he demanded.

'Sorry,' I said lamely.

'I can see you're going to be trouble,' he went on. 'First you question your meds, and now you're vandalising the place! We're obviously going to have to keep an eye on you.'

'I'm sorry,' I repeated, feeling decidedly crestfallen. 'But I was *right* about the tablets,' I protested timidly.

'I suppose so,' he said. 'But if I catch you doing anything like this again there'll be big trouble. Now, tidy these chairs up!'

15

With that, he walked out.

'Cheer up,' Gary urged. 'Come and see the rest of the Unit.'

'Okay, just let me sort the chairs out first.'

'You don't need to bother with that,' Gary assured me. 'They'll only get messed up again by someone else.'

I felt torn between the instruction Robert had given me and Gary's direction that I go with him. I don't know why, but I chose to obey the command of Gary, a younger boy, over that of a responsible adult, and I followed him as he hurried me through the glazed door into the next corridor.

'And this is the punishment room,' said Gary, pointing to another locked door just off a foyer-like area at the corridor's end.

This particular door had a small porthole window in it, so I went up to it and peered through.

I could see that the room was fairly small, and that its only contents were a number of PVC-covered foam wedges and bolster rolls. The walls were smeared with several unpleasant stains, and the linoleum floor was similarly grimy.

'That's where they put you if you've been really bad or too lively,' Gary explained. 'They take away your clothes, but they give you a sheet, so you can make yourself a bed with the foam shapes.'

'It looks disgusting,' I remarked, feeling a little nauseous.

'Come on, I'll show you the playroom,' he said as he swiftly led me back down the corridor.

'Daniel?' a female voice called out to me from the other end of the passageway. 'Are you Daniel?'

A nurse I hadn't seen before came running in our direction.

'Hi,' she said, as she caught up with us. 'I'm Sarah Dawes. I'm your key worker on Mr Taylor's shift.'

She was a moderately attractive woman, and although I guessed she must be in her mid-twenties, she really wasn't very much taller than I was.

'What does that mean?' I asked.

'It's my job to look after you, and I'll be keeping a special eye on you for your first few weeks, just until you get used to things around here. I'm basically doing the same thing that John is doing on Mrs Causton's shift.'

'Oh,' I said, just as a number of children started trooping towards us and on towards the foyer.

Sarah looked at her watch. 'It's nearly half-past one; time to get to school.' She turned to Gary. 'You go on ahead with everyone else,' she told him. 'I'll bring Daniel along in a minute.'

Gary joined the procession of children as they made their way into the foyer and continued on through a set of doors leading outside.

'I'd hoped to catch up with you earlier, but not to worry, I'll see you again after school.'

Sarah seemed very likeable and friendly – just like John had been friendly. They'd both obviously been given the job of being nice to me.

'I see you had a run in with Robert,' she commented. 'I'm afraid he's just written a bad report of you in the Cardex.'

'I didn't mean to do anything wrong,' I said.

'We all make mistakes sometimes,' she said. 'But you really should have tidied up the chairs in TV room like he told you.'

'I know, I'm sorry,' I said, feeling ashamed.

'It's all right,' she smiled. 'Now, let's get you over to school.'

She led me outside, steering me through another play area – a grassy space with a climbing frame, a slide and some swings – towards a small flat-roofed building.

She took me inside, where a much older woman, Mrs Nakamura, the headteacher, greeted us.

'Mrs N., this is Daniel,' Sarah said to her.

'Hello, Daniel,' Mrs Nakamura greeted me. 'We've been expecting you.'

'I'll see you when you get back from school, Daniel,' Sarah smiled as she stepped back outside.

Mrs Nakamura put a hand on my shoulder. 'Welcome to Oakdale School, Daniel. Basically, we're a special school for the children in Oakdale Children's Unit.'

She directed me along a short hallway. 'We're a very small school,' she said. 'We only have about seven or eight children to a class. And you're going to be in Mr Baker's class,' she announced as we entered a classroom.

Mr Baker came over to us as we entered.

'You must be Daniel,' he said. 'Your old school has sent over some English and maths books, so you won't get left behind.'

'It's *not* my old school,' I corrected him, trying not to sound argumentative. 'I'm going *back* there.'

'Of course you are,' Mr Baker smiled. 'But until you do, they've sent over some books to keep you going.'

Mrs Nakamura placed her hand on my arm briefly. 'Well, I'll leave you to it, Mr Baker,' she said. 'See you later Daniel.'

Once she was gone, Mr Baker showed me to my place at one of the room's informally arranged tables.

What especially surprised me was the fact that the children in the class didn't all belong to the same age-group. Sean and Sharon were both in this class, as were another four children; at fifteen, Sharon was probably the oldest, while I was probably one of the youngest.

My first afternoon at the school was spent drawing.

'We mainly do English and maths in the morning,' Mr Baker explained, 'which leaves the afternoon free for other things.'

This seemed remarkably undemanding – the whole afternoon spent drawing. But I certainly wasn't going to complain, so I just got on and did what I was told.

And then, before I knew it, it was half-past three, and I joined all the other children, plus Mrs Nakamura, Mr Baker and three other teachers (who I later learned were Mrs Sutton, Mrs Conway and Miss Evesham) as we made our way back over to the Unit and into the dining room.

The teachers joined a couple of the higher-ranking Unit staff – Mr Taylor, the shift leader, and Miss Bishop, the nursing officer – at two pushed-together tables in a corner near the serving hatch, and they proceeded to chat over cups of tea and cigarettes.

Meanwhile, I joined a line of children queuing for tea and coffee, served from a trolley by a male auxiliary, Gerry Binstead.

'Tea or coffee?' he asked me when my turn came.

'Tea, with milk, no sugar, please,' I said.

'The tea's already made-up; everyone has milk *and* sugar,' he said, as he poured me a cup from a tarnished metal jug.

Slightly discomforted by this encounter, I made my way, with cup and saucer in hand, over to the place where I'd sat at lunchtime. However, I noticed that most of the other children were sitting more informally now, many of them pulling up chairs to join their friends at different tables. And, once again, I was startled to see that several of them were smoking.

Shortly after I sat down, I was joined by Gary.

'So, who's class are you in?' he asked.

'Mr Baker's.'

'He's all right,' Gary remarked. 'I'm in Mrs Conway's class. She's okay too.'

I took a sip of my tea, and finding it far too sweet for my taste, I didn't bother drinking any more.

'I still haven't shown you the playroom,' he reminded me. 'I won't show it you now 'cause the babies will be going in there after tea. I'll show you later, after supper.'

'What babies?' I asked, confused.

'The young kids,' he explained. 'Most of 'em are just babies really.'

As we were talking, a handful of nurses, including Sarah Dawes, were approaching children in different parts of the room and, apparently, giving them instructions. Finally, Sarah came to our table and said, 'Gary, As soon as you've finished your tea, go and sit down in the TV room – there's going to be a meeting. Daniel, you wait for me; we'll go in together.'

'Oh, no,' Gary groaned, as Sarah moved on to the next table.

'What's happening?' I asked.

'Trouble,' he said. 'There must be. The only time we have a meeting after school is when there's trouble.'

We took our cups back to the trolley as most of the kids started to amble out in the direction of the TV room. Gary joined them, leaving me to glance around the room looking for Sarah. When I spotted her, she was already coming over towards me. She put her arm round my shoulder and we followed the others.

As we entered the TV room, I saw that the foam chairs had now been arranged in a wide circle. Some kids were already seated, while others were shoving each other, laughing and shouting. Although it was still quite early, the daylight was just beginning to fail, and so the room was now illuminated by the glare of fluorescent tubes.

'Come on, settle down,' Sarah called out to the room in general.

At that moment, Mr Taylor came in and yelled more forcefully. 'Shut up and sit down, everyone!'

The room went quite as Sarah and I took seats next to each other.

I felt extremely apprehensive as the room continued to fill up with a few more staff and the remainder of the kids – excepting the younger ones who had been siphoned off to the playroom. Finally, Miss Bishop arrived, took her seat, and the meeting began.

'All right, everyone,' she announced severely, 'there are going to be some changes around here.'

Apart from the sound of a few kids shifting in their seats, there was absolute quiet as we all waited for her to go on.

'Some very disturbing reports have come to me from the night staff,' she said. 'Quite honestly, everyone's behaviour has been appalling!'

Now, even the sound of shifting in seats was gone as the room took on an air of stunned silence.

'There have been boys sneaking into the girls' dorm, girls sneaking into the boys' dorm, kids running in and out of the younger children's dorm and disturbing them. The fire doors have been opened, showers and baths have been left running –' Miss Bishop continued with an unremitting litany of offences. 'Well, *this is going to stop!*'

I vaguely heard two or three children whispering to each other that *they* hadn't done anything wrong.

On hearing these whispers, Miss Bishop very nearly exploded. 'You are *all* responsible for this atrocious behaviour! There isn't a single child in this room who doesn't share the blame.'

I felt rather aggrieved at this, having only arrived that morning, but Sarah gently squeezed my arm, and I was grateful for the reassurance.

'Well,' Miss Bishop declared. 'You are *all* going to face the consequences of your actions.'

Miss Bishop proceeded to explain that, from now on, by half-past seven each evening all children had to be in their dormitories, changed into their night clothes, and standing by their beds ready for inspection. First, members of the afternoon shift would inspect them, while also dispensing night time medication (little more than an hour after the supper time meds had been dispensed). And then, after the hand-over to the night shift, there would be a second inspection. Finally, if the night staff were satisfied, the kids who were allowed up beyond eight o'clock could return to whatever they were doing before (albeit now in night dress).

There were groans of dissatisfaction from around the room as this was announced – and not just from the kids.

'It's no good moaning,' Miss Bishop chided. 'You kids have brought this on yourselves, and the staff have every right to be unhappy as you've given them more work to do.'

With that, Miss Bishop called the meeting to a close and the majority of children and staff began to drift away.

I rose to my feet, and so did Sarah.

'I'm sorry about that, Daniel,' Sarah said. 'It's just bad luck this happening on your first day.'

In front of us, kids were rearranging the chairs around the glass-fronted compartment containing the television.

'I'll just go and sort out the TV,' Sarah remarked as she went over to the compartment and, having unlocked a door to the side, reached in to switch it on.

'What channel?' she called out to the handful of kids who had seated themselves in front of the glass.

There was no consensus, so Sarah went with the majority vote, and then relocked the compartment.

The kids settled themselves in front of *Jackanory* as Sarah came back over to me.

'Do you want to watch TV? Or is there something else you'd like to do?' she asked me.

'Dr Rajasimha said there's an art room here. Can I go in there?'

'No, not today, I'm afraid,' she said apologetically. 'It's only open when the art therapist, Fridgerd, is here – she comes over to lead her group sessions on Mondays.'

'Oh,' I said, feeling that Dr Rajasimha had, perhaps, misled me over the art room.

'Come and watch TV for a bit,' she said, giving me a friendly nudge.

I went over with Sarah and we both found seats, though not together this time.

I sat through what was left of *Jackanory*, and found the experience of watching television a little disconcerting, as the sound didn't come directly from the set – as it was enclosed behind glass – but from a wall-mounted speaker some distance from the screen. This continued to bother me as I sat through the subsequent children's programmes.

Then, just before twenty-five past five, six more staff members came in, five female and one male. One of them changed the channel, at which point most of the kids I'd been sitting with wandered off, leaving seats free for the staff.

Moving over to the now-vacant seat next to me, Sarah joked, 'This is the time when the TV room gets taken over by the soap addicts; my esteemed colleagues have come for their *Crossroads* fix.'

I didn't really want to stay glued to the television any longer, but neither did I want to leave the comparative security provided by Sarah, so I decided to remain where I was. It wasn't until the regional news programme, *Day By Day*, began at six o'clock that I finally got up. In fact, this was when *everyone* got up, as it was time to return to the dining room for supper.

We joined the horde in the corridor as it trailed into the dining room. I quickly found my place at table next to Gary, who was already there, and we were soon joined by Sean. As I expected, Sarah now occupied the place opposite me where John had sat previously.

Somehow, the dining room seemed far more bleak than it had earlier. This was probably a result of the darkness outside set against the harsh dazzle of the strip lighting.

Supper was fairly uneventful, as I already knew pretty much what to expect at meal times. First there was the queuing, and then, assisted by the occasional gulp of water, there was the eating.

One thing that was different this time was that Barbara Heaton, another auxiliary, made her way round the tables with a jug of tea. While both Gary and Sean held out cups to be filled from the jug, both Sarah and I declined.

'Mike will be coming round with coffee in a minute,' Barbara said as she moved on to the next table.

While Sarah accepted coffee when it arrived, I declined this as well – I didn't like coffee, with or without sugar – and just helped myself to more water.

And then Mr Taylor came over and beckoned Sarah to go with him. They disappeared together out of the door, but returned a few minutes later with the medicine trolley. And once again, after a succession of children had been called to receive their medication, I found my own name being called.

'I gather you tried to refuse your medication at lunchtime,' Mr Taylor said as I stood at the trolley.

'Not really,' I responded diffidently.

'Well, you must take your meds,' Mr Taylor stressed as he dropped a small yellow amitriptyline pill into my hand from a 30ml plastic medicine cup.

I released the pill into my mouth and swallowed. Then I turned to go back to my seat.

'Wait!' Mr Taylor called after me. 'Come back.'

I was trembling as I returned to him.

'You need to take some water with it,' Mr Taylor said, lifting a jug and pouring water into the 30ml cup.

'That's all right,' I said. 'I don't need any water, thank you.'

'You *will* take some water with it,' he said sternly, handing me the medicine cup.

I downed the water with one gulp, and handed the cup back.

I noticed Sarah give me a sympathetic look; at least it seemed I had *one* person on my side.

'Just let me check – open your mouth,' Mr Taylor instructed.

Not having been treated this way since I was a toddler, I was feeling quite shaken, but I did as I was told and opened my mouth. With one hand either side of my jaw, Mr Taylor rocked my head from side to side as he peered into my mouth.

'All right,' he said in a rather doubtful tone. 'But I'm going to be keeping an eye on you. Go and sit down.'

At last I was able to return to my seat, and I sank into it, relieved that the confrontation was over, but feeling deflated.

Once the ritual of the cigarettes was out of the way (I was little disappointed to see that Sarah smoked too), and we were given permission to leave our tables, Gary took me to see the playroom – just as he had promised earlier.

The playroom was almost identical in size to the TV room – indeed, it too had a glass-fronted television compartment. And if it hadn't been for the presence of a few foam chairs with tan-coloured coverings, it would have been just as blue as the TV room as well. What was different, however, was the presence of a pool table and a table tennis table.

'The babies come in here after school to play with their toys,' Gary explained. 'But after supper the playroom's ours. Do you want a game of ping-pong?'

'I'm not very good at it,' I said.

'That doesn't matter.'

Gary found a ping-pong ball and a couple of bats and we began to play. But my coordination was poor and I failed to return most of Gary's serves, and on the occasions when I got to serve, I either sent the ball straight into the net or propelled it across the room, missing the table completely.

'You'll get better with practice,' Gary assured me, but I wasn't at all convinced.

'I think I'll go and watch television,' I said, not willing to attempt a game of pool, and not knowing what else to do with myself.

Before long it was nearly half-past seven, and the staff began herding all the kids up to their dormitories.

Sarah came into the boys' dormitory briefly, just before we all started to undress, and said good night to me.

'I'm off duty in a minute,' she said, 'but I'll be back tomorrow afternoon.'

Once she was gone I began to feel uneasy. Mr Taylor and two other male members of staff stood in front of the now closed double-doors, supervising us as we changed into our pyjamas and dressing gowns. Undressing under the watchful eye of three men, in a brightly lit room full of other children – many of whom were rather noisy – was something I simply wasn't used to, and I found the experience quite upsetting. Needless to say, I got on with the task as quickly as I could while being sure to avert my eyes from the naked and semi-naked forms of the other boys around me.

'Okay then,' Mr Taylor announced loudly. 'You all know the new rules. As soon as you're ready, stand by your beds.'

Gradually, the dorm quietened and we took up our positions as we had been told.

Slowly, Mr Taylor began to walk the length of the dormitory, stopping to look at each boy in turn on the left-hand side, before doing the same on the right-hand side as he made his return journey. While he was doing this, the other two nurses – Mike Kirby and Jeff Knowles – briefly left the dorm, only to return a few moments later, Mike with a jug full of water and Jeff with a tray laden with plastic medicine cups, each containing a nitrazepam tablet.

'Everyone, stay where you are,' Mr Taylor instructed, now back by the doors.

Mike and Jeff approached several of the boys – though not all of them – with the pills. I was shocked and surprised, though perhaps I shouldn't have been, when they came over to me.

'Hold your hand out,' Jeff said, giving me a rather large white tablet.

'What's this?' I questioned him.

'It's Mogadon,' he said, using the drug's brand name.

'Am I meant to have this?' I asked, the name being unfamiliar to me.

'Daniel has a tendency to refuse his meds,' Mike commented to Jeff.

'That's not true,' I argued guardedly.

'Come on now,' Jeff urged me. 'Don't give us any trouble, just swallow it down.'

Although I was disturbed at the thought of having to take a drug I'd never heard of before, I did as I was told, and this time, given the size of the pill, I was more than willing to take the small cup of water Mike offered me.

After the distribution of Mogadon to those deemed in need of it, Mike and Jeff joined Mr Taylor back by the double-doors.

'Now,' Mr Taylor began, 'I want you all to stay exactly where you are until the night staff say you can go. And if I hear any noise coming from this dormitory in the meantime, there will be consequences.'

The three of them exited the room, leaving us for the time-being without staff supervision.

A gentle murmur began to rise as kids started grumbling to each other about being left standing.

'Dan!' came a stage-whisper from the boy to my right. 'Dan! What are you in here for?'

'It's Daniel,' I corrected him.

'Okay,' he said. 'I'm Andrew. But what *are* you in here for?'

Andrew Ramsey was just a few months older than me, but he somehow seemed very mature, very authoritative, and so I felt compelled to offer some kind of answer, even though I wasn't exactly sure what the answer was.

'Depression, I think. What about you? Why are you here?'

'It's a mistake,' Andrew replied. 'I shouldn't be here at all, there's nothing wrong with me.'

I was about to question him further when the doors opened again and a large man on the younger side of middle-age, Mr Barry, came in.

'Right, you lot,' he said. 'It seems I've got to inspect you.' He paused for a moment. 'All right, then, consider yourselves inspected. You can push off now, if you want.'

Mr Barry went back out through the doors, shortly followed by around two-thirds of the boys.

I threw myself down on my bed, as I just didn't feel like venturing into the Unit's corridors in my dressing gown.

'Aren't you coming, Daniel?' Andrew asked as he made his way towards the doors.

'No, I think I'll stay up here and read for a bit.'

With Andrew gone I reached out to the locker on my left and retrieved a paperback book from one of the drawers: *Arthur of the Britons* by Rex Edwards.

I lay there on top of the continental quilt (as we referred to such things in those days) trying to focus on the printed pages. Somehow, I found it a great struggle, and although I made it through several pages, the sheer effort of concentration meant I couldn't remember a single word I'd read. My attempt at reading was made even harder by the sound of T. Rex coming from a cassette tape recorder at the other end of the room. And, if that wasn't enough, a couple of boys were chattering away about sexual matters. Having had a fairly sheltered upbringing thus far, I found some of this talk quite disturbing, and it contributed to a significant lowering in my mood.

Just before nine o'clock (bedtime for the under-thirteens) I went over to one of the sinks and brushed my teeth. I then got into bed just as a few boys – including Andrew – returned to the dorm, and the main lights dimmed to a muted glow.

I lay there staring at the ceiling. This continued until ten o'clock, when the lights went out completely.

And so my first night in Oakdale began.

CHAPTER TWO

Laying there in the dark I could hear the sound of the other children breathing.

I don't know what time it was when Mr Barry came in, but a harsh stab of light pierced through the open doors as he entered. As the doors swung shut again and the light died away, I could just about see him pushing some foam-filled chairs together to make a bed for himself near the sinks.

Though feeling somewhat drowsy by now, I just couldn't get to sleep. As I continued to lie there in this unfamiliar setting, I found myself beginning to sob. The sobbing became uncontrollable, and it was beginning to disturb some of the other kids.

'Shut the fuck up,' hissed Nigel Green, a fifteen-year-old boy in the bed to my left.

Mr Barry got up from his make-shift bed and came over.

He spoke to Nigel first. 'Leave him alone, he's new here.' Then he turned to me. 'It's Daniel, isn't it?'

'Yes,' I managed to respond through my unrestrained weeping.

'Come with me,' he said.

I got up and followed Mr Barry out the dorm.

The light dazzled my tear-filled eyes as he led me into the nurses' station. The station was already occupied. Seated at a small desk was a woman, Carrie Hancock. I didn't know how many staff were on the night shift, but I guessed it was probably Carrie's job to supervise the girls' dorm, and that there would be someone else already in with the younger children.

Carrie looked up as we entered the confined area and, seeing my tears, she gave me an understanding smile.

'You're Daniel, aren't you?' she said. 'Are you feeling homesick?'

I wasn't sure what I was feeling, but I guessed it might well have been homesickness.

'Yes, I suppose so,' I answered, still weeping.

'Sit down here,' Mr Barry said, directing me to one of two vacant chairs squeezed into the restricted space.

'I'm Carrie, by the way,' the woman introduced herself.

'Kids often find their first night here rather strange,' Mr Barry commented.

'It won't be so bad once you've got used to it,' Carrie added, getting up from her seat and unlocking a steel cabinet mounted on the wall above the desk.

The cabinet contained various medicines, and Carrie selected from it a bottle of Mogadon tablets.

Sitting back down as she opened the bottle, she said, 'Take one of these.'

'I've already had one,' I said, recognising the pill now in her hand.

'It'll help you get to sleep,' Mr Barry encouraged.

Feeling uncertain, I took the pill from Carrie and swallowed it as she reached to grab a glass from a nearby shelf. Taking water from a jug on the desk, she filled the glass and offered it to me. With the large tablet wedged uncomfortably in my throat, I hurriedly took several swigs to help it on its way.

'Now just let that go down for a minute, and then you can get back to bed,' Carrie smiled.

I was still crying, I just couldn't help myself.

'Come on, Daniel,' Mr Barry said. 'Try and stop crying; things'll look much better in the morning.'

I don't know how long I sat there in the nurses' station, but my tears eventually began to run dry and Mr Barry led me back to my bed. Once there, I remained awake for a little longer before finally slipping into a disturbed sleep.

'Wake up, you lot!'

A discordant male voice ruptured my troubled sleep. I rubbed my eyes as I struggled to come to. The unforgiving blaze of the electric lights made the dull morning light from the windows seem especially dismal, and I wondered if the struggle was really worth it.

'Come on!' Mr Jones's voice sounded another jarring note. 'Get with it! Rise and shine!'

I fought to raise my head from the pillow, and I was taken aback by how great an effort it took. Somehow I managed to swing my legs out of the bed as I brought myself to a sitting position.

Mr Barry and his make-shift bed were now gone from the dorm, leaving Mr Jones and John Webber to rouse the boys into wakefulness.

John came over to me. 'Good morning, Daniel. How are you feeling this morning?'

I looked up, and found I couldn't quite focus on his face. I felt terrible; my head was like lead, my mouth was dry, and all my muscles were aching and drained of energy. But worse still, I desperately wanted to be out of this place.

28

I wanted to be back home, in the comfort of my own bed with familiar things around me. And I realised that I was crying again – or maybe I'd never really stopped.

John knelt down to bring his face level with mine, and he gave me a comradely slap on the arm.

'Come on, Daniel,' he said. 'It's really not that bad. Get up, get washed, get dressed – then you'll start to feel better.'

He rose and began walking around the dormitory, just as Mr Jones was doing, checking on the progress of the other boys.

'You kept me awake all night, you little runt,' Nigel complained aggressively from behind me.

I couldn't find the strength to turn round and answer back. But from in front of me I heard Andrew say, 'If anyone gives you any trouble, Daniel, just verbally kick 'em in the teeth.'

'Piss off, Ramsey!' Nigel barked at Andrew.

'Piss off yourself, moron,' Andrew shot back at him. And then, turning to me again, he repeated, 'Just verbally kick 'em in the teeth – and that goes for staff as well as kids.'

Looking up towards Andrew I simply nodded at him, while Nigel's belligerent grumbling continued from behind.

Three of the four sinks were now in use as kids started to go about their morning ablutions. I tried to get myself up to wash, but my limbs weren't yet ready to cooperate.

'Come on! Come on! Get moving!' Mr Jones yelled at me, seeing my failure to rise to my feet. 'And stop that snivelling.'

Finally, I managed to force myself to an upright position. As I did so, I suddenly felt dizzy and faint, and for a moment I thought I was going to drop back down onto the bed – but I just about managed to hold myself steady.

Another boy had now taken the one vacant sink, but a moment later another two became free, so I started to slowly shamble over.

The first thing I did was to stoop down and fill my dry mouth with water from the cold tap. I was exceptionally thirsty, and I guzzled the water impatiently. Then, with that done, I began to wash.

Getting washed required an enormous exertion, and when Mr Jones shouted at me to hurry up, I realised that I was taking a very long time over it. I looked up at the mirror above the sink, and found I still couldn't quite focus properly. But what I managed to make out in the glass was not entirely recognisable. It was my face, certainly, but the eyes were bloodshot and the skin sallow. Shaken by this, I was almost glad that my vision was a bit blurry.

Somehow I made it back to my bed, snatched some clothes out of my locker, and began dressing. This time I wasn't so embarrassed about performing this normally private task with so many others around; all my concentration was required for the arduous chore itself. And then, having dragged my clothes on, I fell back onto the bed, exhausted.

John came and sat with me on the bed. 'Daniel,' he said with some compassion, 'you really must try and pull yourself together. Breakfast is at half-past seven, so you've got ten minutes to get yourself going.'

It seemed obvious to me that the problem was down to the drugs I'd been given – two Mogadon pills. I opened my mouth to explain this, but I couldn't quite bring myself to say anything.

'Did you hear me, Daniel?'

I strained to murmur an acknowledgement.

It was as though I had sleep-walked to the dining room, as I had so very little awareness of how I got there. But there I was, seated in my place, with my heard buried in my arms. Realising that I was still troubled by the dryness of my mouth, I briefly looked up, poured a glass of water, and then knocked it back with urgency before once again burying my face.

'Cheer up,' Gary said with grating buoyancy.

John Webber and Sean, on the other side of the table, said nothing, but I was aware that John was watching me closely.

Rose Boyd, the auxiliary, breezed past, inviting us to join the queue for cereal. Gary Jameson and Sean Townsend got up instantly, but I stayed where I was, my buried face doused in tears.

'Daniel, don't you want any cereal?' John asked, as he stood to join the queue.

'No,' I mumbled.

'You must eat something,' he persisted.

I couldn't motivate myself to answer again, and after a short pause, John got in line, leaving me alone at the table.

After John had returned with Gary and Sean, I heard them chatting to each other and occasionally referring to me – quite sensitively – but none of them addressed me directly until Rose came by a second time and called us to get in line for the cooked breakfast.

Gary and Sean eagerly joined the queue once again, while John urged me to join them.

'No, I'm not hungry,' I blubbered into my hands.

'Sooner or later you're going to have to eat,' John told me.

He held back for a moment, presumably to see if there was any chance I might drag myself to my feet and get a cooked breakfast, but I didn't shift, and so he went on without me once again.

Throughout breakfast I didn't raise my head once to see what was going on around me, but I heard the medicine trolley being wheeled in, and I heard children's names being called as their medication was dispensed.

Following this, I remained in my place with my head buried in my arms. I didn't shift, even after several of the other kids had left the room. Indeed, I was still there fifteen minutes later, by which time almost *everyone* had wandered off.

John stayed behind, however, sitting opposite me at the table, cigarette in hand. 'Daniel, it really isn't that bad here,' he said. 'You must make an effort to brighten up.'

I tried to force myself to say something in reply, but it was such an incredible effort. 'I want to go home,' I eventually slurred. 'It was a mistake coming here. Please, let me go home.'

John didn't answer me immediately, but after a pause he said, 'You haven't been here twenty-four hours yet. You don't really know what it's like here, the different things you can do, all the fun that you can have. You need to be here a bit longer to find out what it's like.'

I raised my clouded head to look at him through streaming eyes. 'I don't want to know. I want to go back home. I want to go back to Worthing Road Comprehensive.'

'You *will* go back,' John said. 'You'll go back as soon as you're better. You're not here forever, you know. But while you *are* here, you need to make the best of it.'

'I don't think I should be here,' I argued, trying to put some energy into my voice. 'It's all been a mistake. I need to go home now.'

'Well,' John said, 'you're here for the time being. Now, I'm not promising anything, but I'll see if I can arrange for you to 'phone your parents later – let's see what they have to say.'

'Thank you,' I said, brightening just a tiny fraction at this thought.

'In the meantime, though,' he continued, 'we have our morning meeting at ten-past nine, which you have to go to, and then at half-past nine it'll be time for school. So, you need to get yourself into gear.'

The morning meeting took place in the TV room, just like the meeting the previous afternoon. As before, the chairs were arranged in a wide circle. Both kids and staff were rapidly finding themselves places to sit.

I had wandered in with a handful of others, and although I wasn't sobbing quite so profusely now, that didn't stop Mr Jones from coming up behind me and clipping me round the ear. Shocked, I just stood there open mouthed as he slated me.

'I'm getting sick of your bawling!' he exclaimed. 'Now, sit down, and for

God's sake, shut up!'

Stunned at having been so unjustly reprimanded, I didn't immediately set about finding my way to an available chair, but simply stood there.

'Over here, Daniel.' It was John. He was already seated, and he signalled for me to join him.

As I sat down, I asked somewhat hesitantly why Mr Jones had hit me.

'Mr Jones is usually a bit prickly in the mornings,' John half-smiled. 'I'd just forget about it if I were you.'

Miss Bishop had come in and assumed her place, and she called for everyone to be quiet. 'It's time we made a start,' she said.

The room began to settle. I looked around me and noticed that, as well as the nursing staff, there were various other adults present. Dr Rajasimha was there – this was the first time I'd seen him anywhere other than at the Child Guidance Clinic – and seated next to him was the other consultant psychiatrist, Dr Collins. Also present was Mrs Fox, the social worker, and Bridget Fitzpatrick, the occupational therapist.

'I hear from the night staff,' Miss Bishop continued, 'that things were a lot better last night. So, let's hope the new system continues to work over the coming weeks.'

Then, Miss Bishop seemed to notice me for the first time. 'Now, I'm sure we'd all like to welcome Daniel Kinsley to Oakdale.' Looking at me directly, she added, 'It's unfortunate that you arrived just as we started the new bedtime regime, and that yesterday afternoon's meeting about it was so awkward. Hopefully you'll find this morning's meeting more pleasant.'

But as the meeting continued, I thought that it wasn't so much pleasant as just extremely dull. It also seemed rather futile. Various staff members raised a number of minor and tedious issues, and while the kids were allowed to make comment here and there, very often Miss Bishop cut them off. Seemingly, this was because she thought their remarks inappropriate, irrelevant, unimportant, or just too time-consuming to deal with.

Just before half-past nine, the meeting looked like it was going to be adjourned, as we were all sent on our way to school. John Webber and a couple of the other nurses accompanied us, but most of the staff remained behind – the meeting was obviously going to continue without us.

I was now sitting in my first assembly at Oakdale School, and like so much here, it was quite different from anything I'd known at any previous school. For a start, the assembly wasn't being held in a hall, but in Mr Baker's classroom. Unlike the previous afternoon, however, the room was filled, not just with the other members of my class, but with all the school's pupils –

except for, that is, the very young ones (those aged seven and under) who'd been shepherded off to a separate annex.

With the room full, though not over full, I found myself sharing my table with another child, a fourteen-year-old girl called Jennie Saunders from Mrs Sutton's class. Rather than saying anything to acknowledge me, she just nodded, and I nodded back. Though my eyes were almost dry now, I still didn't feel much like speaking.

Glancing around me I saw that all the tables had at least two children sitting at them, while there were also a few, mostly older, kids seated at the back of the class away from the tables.

The teacher's desk at the front was unoccupied, as Mr Baker was sitting to one side with Mrs Nakamura and Mrs Sutton – plus Mrs Burrows, the school secretary. Mrs Conway (Gary's teacher) was seated at a piano in the corner. Almost the entire teaching staff was present, with the exception of Miss Evesham, who was with the younger children in the annex.

There was some chattering and general shuffling as we settled ourselves, and then Mrs Nakamura said, 'Good morning, everyone.'

'Good morning, Mrs N.,' all the kids answered – all the kids apart from me, that is, as I hadn't been aware of the proper response.

Mrs Nakamura announced that we would sing a hymn. In front of me, on the table, was a dark green, hardcover hymnbook, and I picked it up and started thumbing through the pages in anticipation. 'Please turn to Number 14,' she said, and Mrs Conway struck up an introduction on the piano. We remained seated as we sang, rather feebly, 'God of concrete, God of steel' – I didn't think I'd ever heard this hymn before; it certainly wasn't one we sang at Worthing Road.

After the hymn, Mr Baker read some prayers. While this was going on there was a bit of shifting about and whispering, and this led Mrs Nakamura to rebuke us.

'I know you may not all be believers,' she said, 'but you must respect those who are. So I don't want to hear any chatter or messing around while a teacher is leading prayers. Now, I want you all to bow your heads again and close your eyes as we say together the Lord's Prayer.'

I don't know how many of us actually joined in with the words, but it certainly wasn't all of us – there were some quite obvious dissenters.

Once the assembly was over, Mrs Nakamura called for a volunteer to collect up the hymnbooks, and then she led Mrs Conway, Mrs Sutton, and their pupils, out of the room.

That left Mr Baker with us, his class, and the first thing he did was to instruct us to get out our English books. The others made their way to the back of the room to rummage in drawers, extracting from them assorted schoolbooks.

'You've got a drawer too,' Mr Baker told me. 'You'll find in it the books your other school has sent over for you, and some new exercise books for you to use here.'

I found the drawer labelled with my name, and looking in it I saw, on the top, an SMP maths book. Delving underneath I found my English textbook, and then groping further towards the back I located a fresh exercise book.

There was nothing for me to write with, so after placing the books on my table, I approached Mr Baker.

'I didn't bring my cartridge pen,' I told him. 'It's still at home.'

He pulled a graphite pencil from a desk drawer and gave it to me.

'Here you are,' he said. 'We don't allow the children to use ink here anyway, it makes too much mess.'

Having started to use a pen after going up to Worthing Road from Loxton Junior School, reverting to a pencil was yet another contribution to my sense of despair. Still, I assured myself, I'm going to get myself out of here soon; as soon as I talk to my mum and dad, they'll take me home.

It was break time.

We all hurried back over to the Unit, and most of the children began queuing in the dining room for coffee or orange squash. I had other things on my mind, so I searched around to find John Webber, and I found him at a table with another, much older, male nurse called Ted Trowbridge. Both of them already had coffees, with John also smoking a cigarette while Ted was making several attempts to light a pipe.

'John,' I said to him, calling him by name for the first time. 'You said I could 'phone my mum and dad.'

'Children are only allowed to use the telephone after supper,' Ted said abruptly, probably more annoyed with his pipe than with me.

'It's all right, Ted,' John said to the other nurse. 'Daniel's been very distressed, and I said I'd try and arrange for him to 'phone home.' Turning to me, he said, 'Will anyone be at home if you call now?'

'My dad will be at work,' I said. 'But my mum should be home.'

'Okay.' John drained his coffee cup and stubbed out what was left of his cigarette. 'Come with me.'

As we left the dining room, he asked, 'Have you got money for the 'phone?'

'Yes, in my locker.'

'All right,' he said. 'You run and get it and meet me in the foyer – you know, by the doors you go out through to get to school.'

A few minutes later, having run from one end of the Unit to the other and back again, I found John in the foyer.

He unlocked a door adjacent to the exit, and led me into a small empty room. It was fairly dark in there, as the curtains were drawn, but rather than open them, he flicked a wall switch. But the glow of incandescent electric light made very little difference to the room; it was still extremely dingy.

'There you go,' John said, pointing to the tall grey payphone mounted on the wall.

I balanced a two-pence piece in one of the coin slots, lifted the black receiver, and after learning from John that I didn't need an STD code, I dialled my home number. I heard my mum answer, followed by the rapid pips demanding I insert money. Pushing the coin home, the connection was restored, and at last I could speak to her.

Then the call was over.

I was frustrated that my mum wasn't about to drop everything and come and collect me that minute. But I was reasonably satisfied by her promise to visit me that evening. I was fairly confident that once she was here, I would be able to get her to take me home.

'All right?' John asked.

'My mum's coming to get me tonight,' I answered.

'Are you sure?' he said, sounding sceptical.

'Yes,' I insisted. 'She's coming tonight.'

For the remainder of the morning at school I buried my head in maths. It wasn't my favourite subject, but I applied myself to it thinking that if I threw myself wholeheartedly into everything I did for the rest of the day, time would pass more quickly and then, before I knew it, I would be in the car with my mum heading home to Loxton.

Lunchtime came – with John Webber commenting that it was good to see me eating again – and then the shifts changed and Sarah Dawes was back on duty.

When Sarah found me, I was with Gary in the playroom again, trying without much success to give him an adequate game of table tennis.

We stopped playing and Gary wandered off.

'Hello, Daniel,' she smiled. 'I hear you mum's coming to see you later.'

'Yes,' I smiled back at her. 'I'm going to go home.'

Sarah came nearer. 'Don't get your hopes up, Daniel,' she said gently. 'It's only a visit. After you 'phoned home this morning, John called her back to make sure we knew what was happening. She's just coming to visit you – that's all, I'm afraid.'

'But she *will* take me home,' I maintained heatedly, feeling tears starting to well up in my eyes once again.

Sarah put her arm around me and drew me close to her. Although I didn't really want to reject the comfort Sarah was offering me, I pushed her away, upset by her words of caution. I hurriedly left the room and ran to the boys' dorm, where I flung myself on my bed and cried. I cried at the knowledge that Sarah was probably right, that I wouldn't be going home tonight, and I cried at being unable to accept the consolation she had offered, consolation that I so desperately needed.

With my head still feeling cloudy – as it had done all morning – I almost dozed off as I moaned into my pillow. But I was instantly brought back to wakefulness by the voice by Mike Kirby. I hadn't heard him come into the dorm, so I gave a start when he laid a dispassionate hand on my left shoulder and told me it was time I got back to school.

Grudgingly, I dragged myself up from the bed, rubbed my eyes, and headed out of the dorm. Mike followed me along no less than three corridors before breaking off in another direction once I'd joined the parade of children *en route* to the foyer. As I continued on my way, Sarah caught up with me.

'I'm sorry if I upset you earlier, Daniel,' she said.

'It's all right,' I mumbled, without actually looking at her.

She put her hand on my shoulder – just like Mike had done a couple of minutes ago, only *her* touch was less clinical, less detached. She gave a supportive squeeze as I glanced at her and smiled weakly. I was thankful for the physical connection.

She continued walking with me until we reached the school.

After school I avoided tea and settled for a glass of water. Sarah Dawes pointed out Gary to me as I looked for somewhere to sit. He was with a small group of boys at one of the dining room tables; had it not been for Sarah's encouragement I probably wouldn't have braved pulling up a chair and joining them.

Andrew was one of the boys in this small group.

'How are you doing, Daniel?' he asked.

I gave a rather noncommittal reply.

'*The Tomorrow People*'s on at ten-to-five,' he said. 'You gonna watch it with us? It's the last part today.'

'Yes, I've been following it,' I answered.

'We'll need to get into the TV room early,' Gary added, 'to make sure we bag the right channel.'

I nodded, but I didn't really manage to join in with their conversation after that, and once they started drifting off, I just made my way back to the dorm to read some more of my Rex Edwards paperback.

Although I tried very hard, every little distraction, such as the occasional boy entering or leaving the dorm, had a major effect on my concentration. Just as when I'd tried to read the previous night, the pages went by virtually unseen. My concentration was no better when I joined the others in the TV room. I sat through the second half of *How*, followed by *The Tomorrow People*, then a five-minute cartoon, and finally *Crossroads* – but they all pretty much washed over me.

By suppertime, however, I was becoming less robotic and more restless. The meal seemed interminable as I waited for it to end and for my mum to arrive. Eventually, after my dose of amitriptyline I joined the gradual exodus from the dining room. I made my way to the dormitory once again, where I decided to retrieve my suitcase from under the bed and start packing.

I began turning out my locker and transferring clothes to the open case now resting on the bed. It was partially packed when Sarah came in and told me my mum was here – though she also cautioned me that I probably wasn't going home tonight. She led me out of the dorm and down the corridor to a small visitors' room where, upon seeing my mum, I burst into frantic, unrestrained tears once again.

And then my mum was on her way.

I howled and screamed outside the visitors' room, pleading with my mum not to leave me. Hearing the commotion, Sarah ran to me just as my mum disappeared through a nearby exit leading to the car park. Sarah fervently tried to calm me down. But I darted out into the car park after my mum, though she didn't even look back as I desperately begged her not to go. Sarah was trying to reason with me when I suddenly found myself tackled to the ground by Mr Taylor and Mike Kirby. I hadn't noticed them coming towards me, and so I tumbled awkwardly, my distress turning to panic as I found myself winded by the fall.

'Ross! Mike!' Sarah hollered at them. 'Don't be too rough with him – he's very upset!'

'Sarah!' Mr Taylor breathed heavily, jabbing his knee into my back while Mike held one of my wrists in a vice-like grip. 'We need to get him sedated. Go and make up a syringe – you know what to do.'

'But, Ross…!' Sarah began to protest.

Having got my breath back, and knowing what they were planning to do, I unreasoningly struggled all the harder. 'You can't do this to me!' I wheezed, battling to resist them.

'Sarah! *Do as I say!*' Mr Taylor shouted, apparently responding to some hesitation on her part.

I couldn't be sure of the exact sequence of events that followed, or even if Sarah obeyed her instructions. All I knew was that somehow I ended up back inside being thrown face down onto my bed, my half-filled suitcase sent flying. Several strong, rough hands were holding me down with significant force when someone – I didn't see who – administered a syringe to my left buttock. The solution began to take effect quite quickly, and my consciousness poured away as though someone had pulled the plug from a bath.

CHAPTER THREE

I'm not really sure when I came round. Whatever solution had been administered to me cannot possibly have left me unconscious for the next day or so – unless, of course, they'd given me some further doses while I was already under. But apart from odd fragments here and there, I wasn't really aware of anything much until the Friday morning, and that was more than thirty-six hours after I'd had the injection!

I was lying in my bed in the boys' dormitory. If I had felt groggy and dry upon awakening on the Wednesday morning, that was nothing compared to how I felt now. I was queasy, my head was spinning, my tongue was stuck to the roof of my mouth, and I could barely move without my muscles complaining. I just about managed to turn my head to see Mr Jones sitting in a foam chair by one of the sinks reading the *Daily Mirror*. Apart from him, there was no one else in the room.

One of the double doors was wedged open, and once again I could hear the radio in the nurses' station. This time it was 'Love Really Hurts Without You' making a bid to become another entry in the unforgettable soundtrack to my wretchedness.

Beneath my bedclothes I suddenly noticed that I wasn't wearing my pyjamas – I was completely naked. I tried to speak, to ask Mr Jones what was happening, but all I managed to do was grunt incoherently.

'So, you've finally stopped fighting us, have you?' he said, putting down his paper and walking over towards me.

I wasn't sure what he meant, and I didn't have the strength, or courage, to ask.

'Your behaviour, young man, has been absolutely unacceptable,' he went on. 'You should thank your lucky stars that you're still here and not in the time-out room – or worse still, in a police cell.'

I tried again to speak. 'Water,' I begged hoarsely.

'Thirsty, are we?' Mr Jones teased. 'All right, I suppose you can have some water.'

He disappeared from the dorm for a moment, and then returned with a full plastic jug and a small glass. He then filled the glass, but rather than handing it to me, he suddenly threw its contents in my face.

'That's for treating me like your slave,' he said, before filling the glass again and then, at last, handing it to me.

Though it was a struggle to move, I took the glass and downed the water without hesitation.

'Better now?' he said indifferently, as he took back my glass and placed it, along with the jug, on my locker.

'My pyjamas…?' I exhaled shakily.

'We've taken them away; we've taken *all* your clothes away.'

I wanted to cry again, but I couldn't even do that. I tried to raise my head from the pillow, but that failed too. I was powerless.

'You're stuck in here,' Mr Jones explained, 'until we say otherwise. If you need the toilet, you'll have to go out with your sheet wrapped around you.'

That's when I became concerned that I was indeed quite desperate to urinate, and I was not at all sure I could make it out of the bed.

With a tremendous effort of will, I shifted myself towards the edge, hoping that once my feet touched the floor I'd be able to propel myself up. I dragged the top sheet and quilt with me as I moved, nearly toppling to the floor as I groped for firm ground on which to stand. Then, as the quilt fell away, I looked imploringly at Mr Jones, hoping that he would lend me a hand.

'Don't for one second think that *I'm* going to help you,' he said.

Now in a sitting position, I managed to precariously drape the sheet around me. I staggered to my feet, and for a second I thought the momentum was going to send me falling headlong into the carpet. But slowly I edged one foot forward, and then the other. My progress was painfully slow.

'If you've gotta go,' Mr Jones said, 'you'd better get on with it. I'm not clearing up after you if you wet yourself.'

Absorbed in the task of moving forward while simultaneously keeping the sheet in place, I barely heard what Mr Jones was saying.

After what must have been about three minutes of struggling – the radio played an entire song – I got to a lavatory cubical located just outside the dorm. And then, after relieving myself, I was faced with the strenuous return journey.

'You made it then?' Mr Jones said, rather mockingly, back in his chair with his *Daily Mirror*.

As 'Miss You Nights' began issuing forth from the radio, I stumbled back into bed, and after clumsily arranging the sheet and quilt on top of me, I drifted into sleep once again.

40

*   *   *

Thankfully, when I next woke, Mr Jones had been replaced by John Webber. Apparently they had swapped over during the morning break, but somehow I'd missed it, even though there must have been quite a few comings and goings in the dorm during that time.

As soon as John noticed I was awake, he put aside the magazine he was reading and got up from the chair. He carried the chair over with him as he made his way towards me, setting it down next to my bed.

'How are you feeling?' he asked as he sat back down.

'Not very good,' I uttered dimly.

'I'm not surprised,' he said. 'You could've knocked out a horse with what we had to give you.'

I must have looked at him rather blankly, as he then asked me, 'Do you remember what happened?'

The last thing before that morning that I could be sure of was my mum leaving, and how desperately upset I had been. I knew I had resisted Mr Taylor and Mike Kirby as they prevented me from running after her, and I knew I'd been given an injection to subdue me. Beyond that, all I had were isolated flashes of memory, of being here in the dorm, of kids and staff coming and going, and of periods of darkness and periods of light.

'You were so disturbed after your mum left that Mr Taylor had no choice but to have you sedated,' John said. 'And then, every time you began to wake up, you started thrashing about again. You were even thrashing about in your sleep half the time.'

'What happens now?' I asked.

'Well, I'm afraid you won't be able to go home this weekend.'

Inevitably, I began to whimper.

'You probably wouldn't have gone home on the first weekend anyway,' John said. 'We usually keep new kids here for their first weekend, so there's no interruption to them settling in.'

'I don't *want* to settle in,' I complained. 'I just want to go home. What do I have to do to get home?'

'You need to let us help you get better,' John said. 'If you cooperate with us, do your best to settle down, then you'll start to improve. You'll probably find that this can actually be quite a nice place. You may even miss it once you're gone.'

Not only was I sceptical at this, I wasn't convinced that John completely believed it either. But John's words led me to think more carefully about my circumstances and how I was going to change them. My goal, naturally, remained unaltered: to get back home and back to Worthing Road Comprehensive and my friends. The question was, what was the best way of achieving this?

Of course, I was still dumbfounded that my mum hadn't taken me away as soon as I'd asked. After all, my mum and dad had asked for my agreement before bringing me to Oakdale, and I'd given it – though I didn't fully realise what I was agreeing to. Therefore, I reasoned, if I changed my mind, my parents would accept it and allow me home. But clearly I was mistaken about that.

I didn't believe for one minute that my mum and dad would just abandon me here – which is what it felt like – so I assumed that in failing to collect me promptly they were simply acting on some very credible advice from the Oakdale powers-that-be. My parents obviously had no idea what it was really like here; if they had, they would never have allowed me to be admitted.

When she had come to see me on Wednesday evening, I had tried to explain to my mum why I thought I shouldn't be in Oakdale. While certain that she didn't think I was lying, I imagined that both she and my dad found the arguments of important psychiatric professionals more persuasive than those of a twelve-year-old boy. In letting me stay here, my parents were simply making a mistake – but it was an *honest* mistake. I could still try to convince them of their error, of course, but I mustn't allow myself to bank on them being persuaded.

Acknowledging all this, I came to the conclusion that to achieve my goal of returning home and getting back to my school, I needed to get a clear idea of what help Oakdale was going to give me, what was expected of me in return, and how best I could hurry this process along and so get it over with as rapidly as possible.

While these thoughts had been flashing through my head, John had sat there quietly observing me.

'What are you thinking about?' he asked.

'I was wondering what, *exactly*, you're going to do here to help me get better.'

John didn't have a chance to answer. All of a sudden, Mrs Causton came bursting into the dorm. She looked very agitated and impatient.

'John!' she said urgently. 'You're needed over at the school!'

'What's going on, Mary?' he said, getting up.

'It's Julie Wilson; she's having an episode. Bill and Robert are over there already, but they need help. She's completely out of control!'

John sprinted from the room.

Turning to me, Mrs Causton said gruffly, 'Just you make sure you behave yourself while John's away – I can't spare anyone else to keep an eye on you for the moment.'

And then she hurried out as well, leaving me alone.

Even though my head was decidedly foggy, I was able to recall that Julie

Wilson was a chubby sixteen-year-old with a reputation for violent behaviour. She was retarded (to use the language of the time) but no one would ever dare say so in her hearing, or make any reference, however indirect, to her educational limitations. She was known to have an extremely short temper, and Gary had mentioned to me that almost anything could set her off. The kids were frightened of her, and it was the general consensus that she was best avoided. Where that wasn't possible, it was apparently good practice to treat her as superior to oneself in every conceivable way. But the sad fact was, of course, that Julie was extremely challenged, and it was unimaginable that she would ever be able to maintain her fantasy of superiority as she entered adulthood.

As I lay there, I wondered how bad this incident could be. If two well-built male nurses were finding it so hard to contain her that they needed John for reinforcement – and possibly other staff as well – then Julie's outburst must be absolutely extraordinary.

Not for the first time I found myself reflecting on what sort of place Oakdale really was. I was here, so I understood, because I was depressed. But Julie obviously had a major behavioural problem – she was *dangerous*. I wondered how many of the other kids might be dangerous too. Was Oakdale really set up to deal with emotional problems like depression, or was it more like a borstal?

Around half-an-hour passed, during which time I dozed rather than slept, allowing these thoughts to continue playing on my mind until John returned.

As he sat back down by my bed, I noticed that his face was scratched.

'What happened?' I asked.

'Julie had a bit of a turn,' he said.

It was clear he wasn't going to discuss the subject with me, so our conversation soon returned to the matter of what I needed to do to get myself discharged from Oakdale.

'Well, that's not really for me to say – not yet, anyway,' he answered, apparently ducking the question. 'We work as a team here: there's the doctor, the social worker, therapists, nurses – and your parents, of course. We're all working together, and it's the team who will decide how best to help you.'

'But you're *part* of the team,' I said.

'Yes, I am. But the first thing we need to do is observe you for a bit, then gradually we'll start to get an idea of what to do, and after a few weeks there'll be a case conference involving everyone in the team, and then we'll make some definite decisions about what's best.'

'And when will I be allowed home for a weekend?' I asked.

'Well,' John replied, 'hopefully you'll be able to go home *next* weekend, just so long as we don't have a repeat of Wednesday night.'

My eyelids were becoming heavy again, but despite the threat of sleep crashing in on me once more, I asked, 'When will I be allowed to get up?'

John smiled, clearly noticing how fatigued I was. 'Do you think you're strong enough to get up yet?'

'Not really,' I admitted.

'The situation is this,' John began, 'as a consequence of your actions you've been confined to bed and your clothes have been taken away. It's not really a punishment, but it *is* because of your behaviour. Fortunately for you, we decided not to send you to the time-out room – which is just as well as that's where we've had to put Julie.'

I recalled Mr Jones mentioning a time-out room. What *was* the time-out room?

'The kids call it the punishment room,' John explained. 'I'm sure you've had a look through the window, haven't you?'

'Yes,' I said, remembering Gary's guided tour.

'You really wouldn't have wanted to end up in there,' John said, perhaps as some kind of warning. 'We don't actually ever punish kids here – it's not *really* a punishment room – but bad behaviour always has consequences, and they're not usually very pleasant.'

I thought of Julie shut away in that bleak room with nothing but foam bolster rolls and wedges. She would have had her clothes taken away, as I had, but while a warm quilt protected my modesty, all she would have – remembering what Gary had told me – would be a thin sheet.

'Anyway,' John went on, 'you'll probably be in bed for the rest of today, and then we'll see how things are tomorrow.'

I nodded drowsily.

John smiled. 'It'll soon be lunchtime, so just a get a few minutes sleep now, and then someone will bring you up a tray.'

I was woken by the arrival of my lunch. The radio in the nurses' station was playing 'I Love to Love' – 'Currently Number 3 in the charts,' the DJ enthused, 'after a massive leap from 23.'

John Webber had left, and it was Ted Trowbridge who now sat with me by my bed while I attempted to eat.

'I can't stand that racket any longer,' he announced, marching off to kill the radio.

Meanwhile, I was finding the effort of chewing and swallowing surprisingly tiring, and I only managed to eat about half of what had been served up.

'I thought you'd have been really hungry,' Ted remarked genially, evidently happier now the radio was off. 'You wouldn't wake up to eat at all yesterday, and you didn't have any breakfast this morning.'

Quite apart from the sheer hard work that eating seemed to require, I was still feeling nauseous, so no, I *didn't* really feel very hungry, and I more-or-less said as much.

'I expect you'll get your appetite back in due course,' Ted said.

'I suppose so.'

'You've not got off to a good start here, have you?' he commented.

'Not really,' I had to agree.

'Just give us a chance,' he said. 'You won't find us so bad if you behave yourself.'

It seemed to me that they were constantly going on about behaviour! Earlier, Mr Jones had told me my behaviour had been unacceptable; Mrs Causton had warned me to behave myself while I was left alone in the dorm; and John had told me I was confined to bed because of my behaviour. Could it be that they saw me, not so much as a sufferer of depressive illness, but more as a potentially disruptive offender? If that was so, then I might find I had to work extremely hard at managing their impression of me. It wouldn't be enough simply to follow Ted's advice and 'behave myself'; I had to make sure I was *seen* to behave myself.

After a while a few boys came into the dorm. One of them, a fourteen-year-old called Michael Davey, went and rummaged in his locker, and finding his cassette recorder, started playing his T. Rex tape again. And so the status of these tracks became further established in the songbook of my current experience.

Gary dashed into the dorm briefly. He came over, sat on my bed, and chatted excitedly to me to me, while Ted disappeared with my empty tray.

'Did you hear about Julie?' he asked breathlessly.

'Yes – but what actually happened?'

'She went completely mad!' he said at great speed. 'Mrs Sutton just couldn't control her. We could hear *everything* in Mrs Conway's class. Julie was screaming her head off, and it sounded like she was throwing the tables and chairs about! Mrs N. had to run over to the Unit to get help. And it took *five people* to hold her down!'

I looked at him in horrified fascination, as I'd never heard of anything like this happening at Worthing Road.

'And you should see Mrs Sutton's classroom!' he went on just as rapidly. 'She's wreaked it. I had a look through the door just before we came over for lunch, and there's ripped-up books and broken chairs and stuff *everywhere!*'

'Why did she do it?'

'I don't know,' Gary replied hurriedly. 'But someone said it was because Mrs Sutton laughed at her.'

And then, clearly unable to sit still any longer, Gary dashed off again.

However, Andrew Ramsey had entered by now, and planting himself in Ted's seat, he began talking to me.

'Long time, no see,' he said in a friendly way.

I mumbled a response.

'You've been in the wars – and you missed swimming yesterday,' he said. 'They're complete bastards, the staff here; you can't trust 'em an inch. But like I said before: if anyone gives you any trouble, you should *verbally* kick 'em in the teeth; don't let them get to you, and don't try and fight 'em physically. You *definitely* shouldn't try what Julie did this morning – and you shouldn't try what Donna did last night either. They'll have Julie in that punishment room, drugged up to the eyeballs, for days!'

Although Andrew wasn't speaking quite as swiftly as Gary had done, he was obviously eager to expand further on that morning's incident. And while I was curious to hear more, I also wondered what he meant when he referred to Donna. I didn't actually know who Donna was, but it was clear that something significant had happened to her.

'What about Donna?' I asked. 'And who *is* Donna?'

'Donna Bennett,' he answered. 'She's about the same age as us, I think. She got hold of loads of pills and took an overdose. They had to take her to Casualty in Horsham and get her stomach pumped out.'

I wanted to know more, such as how Donna had got hold of the drugs in the first place, but Andrew was keen to get back on to the subject of Julie.

'You should have seen it!' he went on. 'She's like a nuclear warhead on legs, that girl!'

'Did *you* see it?' I asked, not imagining that he could possibly have seen very much while in Mr Baker's class.

'You bet I did!' he exclaimed. 'As soon as we heard her go off we ran out of our class to see what was happening. It was unbelievable! She was flailing about all over the shop! Sutton didn't stand a chance! Baker tried to help, but she punched him to the floor too! You wouldn't *believe* the energy that girl's got – the Army could do with her as their secret weapon!'

Andrew then proceeded to recount how Julie was finally subdued.

'They had to call in the heavy mob,' he said, 'Bill Jones and Robert King. But even those buggers couldn't keep her down! I was glad to see her give them a run for their money!'

Despite the way I'd been treated by some of the Oakdale staff, I still respected adult authority, so I questioned Andrew's delight at the way Julie had briefly got the better of two male nurses.

'They're sadists!' Andrew exclaimed. 'They deserved everything Julie gave them. Unfortunately, Julie's going to pay for what she did. She'll be lucky if they ever let her out of that punishment room! And even if they do, she'll be so heavily drugged up on Largactil from now on that she'll be like a vegetable.'

Although I was alarmed at the reports I'd heard of what Julie had done, I was even more alarmed at how Andrew believed she was going to be treated.

'They'll really keep her drugged-up all the time?' I asked.

'I expect so,' Andrew replied. 'They try and keep most of us drugged-up to some extent, but they'll keep Julie *completely* out of it. As I said, the staff here are bastards! You need to know that, and you need to know how to handle them.'

Andrew went on with various nuggets of advice on how best to deal with the staff. Whether or not his advice would be of any help to me, I wasn't sure, but any information was welcome as I prepared to develop a strategy.

'They're not all bad,' he said, 'but some are real gits, and you need to know how to play them at their own game.'

By now, Ted had come back in, and he affected a mock cough in response to Andrew's last remark.

'Ah, I didn't see you there, Mr Trowbridge, sir,' Andrew said mischievously.

'Just you make sure you don't lead Daniel astray,' Ted warned. 'He's in enough trouble already. Oh, and by the way,' he added, 'I believe you're in my chair.'

Andrew made a play of deferring to Ted. 'All yours, sir,' he said.

Ted lowered himself into the seat while Andrew sat down on my bed.

Despite the mild, and possibly artificial, antagonism between Ted and Andrew, the three of us chatted quite agreeably for a while. Not surprisingly, given that the current hot topic was Julie's incredible outburst, Andrew made attempts – some subtle, some not so subtle – to pump Ted for more information. Ted, however, managed to skilfully steer the conversation away from Julie whenever that happened.

Participating in this three-way conversation was draining, and I was becoming decidedly weary again by the time Sarah Dawes came in. Despite my weariness, I was very pleased to see her.

'If it isn't the lovely Miss Dawes!' Andrew announced.

Ted rolled his eyes. 'I'll go and write up the Cardex then,' he said, rising to allow Sarah to sit down.

'It's good to see you awake, Daniel,' Sarah smiled as Ted made his exit. 'How are you feeling?'

'Tired and groggy.'

'I'm not surprised; it'll take a while for that stuff to get out of your system.'

'I've told him,' Andrew began, 'not to use *actual* violence if anyone gives him any trouble, but just to *verbally* get his own back.'

'Daniel hasn't been violent – he *isn't* violent,' Sarah said. 'He just got understandably upset. It's not easy getting used to this place.'

I was reassured to know that at least Sarah didn't see me as a prospective offender.

'Well, anyway, I told him not to try what Julie did this morning.'

'Andrew,' Sarah censured him, 'I don't think there's any chance of that.'

'But you lot drugged him,' Andrew said curtly. 'Just like you've drugged Julie.'

'I think it's about time you were getting back to school,' Sarah cut him off before he could say anything further.

Andrew looked at his watch. 'No, we've got another five minutes yet.'

'It's time you were getting back to school, Andrew,' she repeated, more firmly. 'You too, Michael,' she called across the dorm.

Michael packed away his cassette recorder, and started to follow Andrew out of the dormitory.

'See you later, Daniel,' Andrew said.

Once they were gone, Sarah leaned forward.

'I'm very sorry about what happened Wednesday evening,' she said. 'If it had been up to me, I –' She broke off, before continuing. 'What I mean is, Mr Taylor did what he thought was best, but he didn't really know what was happening, he didn't realise that you were just a bit upset. Despite what Andrew said, there's no comparison between what happened with Julie today and what happened with you. From what I understand, Julie became so aggressive that she was a danger to others, so they had to do something to subdue her. But I'm sure Mr Taylor didn't think *you* were a danger to anyone; he was just worried you might hurt *yourself.* That's why he sedated you. I'm so sorry I didn't manage to explain to him what had happened before he did what he did.'

'I still feel really drowsy,' I said.

'I'm afraid you will for a while.'

'For how long? When will I start to feel normal again?'

'I'm not sure,' she said. 'You've been so disturbed, even in your sleep. I was with you all yesterday afternoon, and even though you barely opened your eyes once, you were very distressed, so they just thought it best to keep you under. But you've been a lot better today. Hopefully they won't give you any more injections now, so I expect you'll start to feel better over the weekend.'

'Will you be here?'

She broke eye contact with me. 'No. After today, I'm not on duty again until Monday morning.'

My heart sank.

'I'm usually only on one weekend in every four,' she said, looking back up, 'and unfortunately this isn't one of my weekends.

'The way it works,' she continued, 'is that one week we do afternoons and evenings, and the next week we do mornings. Mr Taylor's shift is on mornings next week, so I'll be here bright and early every day, probably before you're even awake.'

I shut my eyes for a moment, hoping that would ward off any tears before they started. Sarah was the one person here who I completely trusted, and I recoiled at the thought of having to spend the next couple of days without her. It was true that there were other staff members who had been good to me – like John – but I didn't feel that any of them were *completely* on my side, not like Sarah.

She placed a hand on my brow. 'You'll be all right, Daniel. It's very quiet here at weekends. There won't be very many kids or staff here. You're not one for crowds, are you? I know you've not found it easy adjusting to all the noise and busyness around here. Well, you'll be able to get a bit of space to yourself for the next two days.'

I didn't say anything, but it must have been apparent to her that I was fighting to stop myself from crying.

'Shh,' she whispered, starting to stroke my hair. 'Keep your eyes closed and get a bit more sleep. I won't let anyone else take over from me – I promise I'll still be here when you wake up.'

I accepted Sarah's comforting attention, and as it was such an effort to stay awake anyway, I soon edged back into unconsciousness.

Sarah was as good as her word, and she didn't leave me. She was there when I awoke later in the afternoon – as Andrew came in to say goodbye before going home for the weekend. She was there when they brought my supper to me. She was there when the two other boys remaining for the weekend stood by their beds for the first inspection of the evening. She was there while Jeff Kirby made sure I had my night-time dose of Mogadon – and she conspiratorially whispered that she didn't think I really needed it. And she was *still* there when Mr Barry came in to make his second 'inspection'.

With the dorm so empty, in the absence of the boys now on weekend leave, Mr Barry didn't even bother with his 'consider yourselves inspected' quip; he simply wandered out of the room. He was soon followed by the other boys – the surly Nigel Green and a younger kid called Jonathan Hunter. Then, in the evening stillness of the virtually empty dorm, Sarah prepared to leave.

'I'll be thinking of you,' she said, as Mr Barry wandered back in through the double doors. 'And I'll see you again on Monday morning.'

I was surprised, but not unpleasantly so, when she leant down and gently kissed me on the forehead.

After Sarah had left, Mr Barry came over to me. 'You're a bit of a one for the ladies, aren't you?' he joked.

'Of course, if you've got your sights set on our Sarah,' he continued to jest, 'I'm afraid you're wasting your time – *she's* a bit of a one for the ladies too!'

I was far too naïve to understand what this meant and I couldn't be bothered trying to make any sense of it anyway. Now that Sarah had gone, all I could feel was a sense of emptiness, and I was grateful for the assistance of the Mogadon – if any assistance were needed – in sending me off into my doleful sleep.

CHAPTER FOUR

My Saturday morning began by being stirred from sleep by Mr Jones. He was the only staff member in the dormitory this morning, presumably because there were so few boys in at the weekend. As I blearily observed the daylight sluggishly attempting to overcome the retreating night, I guessed that it must have been around seven o'clock.

'Wake up! Wake up!' Mr Jones bellowed with his customary morning irritability, before barging his way out of the dorm, leaving us unattended for a brief moment.

He was barely gone at all when he returned with a large fabric laundry bag emblazoned with the legend 'St Anselm's Hospital.' As he seemed to be coming towards me with the bag, which was only about an eighth full, I assumed that it contained my clothes.

'Here you are,' he said offhandedly. 'You can get up and dressed today.'

As on every other occasion when I'd awoken here, I felt decidedly groggy. I also felt just as miserable as I ever had, but I tried to hide my melancholy behind a neutral mask – a cheerful mask being simply too great a challenge.

I swung my legs out of the bed, rummaged in the laundry bag for underpants and trousers, and proceeded to clothe the lower part of my body. I then made for one of the sinks and started getting myself washed.

With only three boys in the dormitory, including myself, the hubbub of activity I remembered from Wednesday morning was greatly reduced.

Jonathan Hunter, who must have been only about ten, needed very close supervision as he washed. If left to his own devices he would probably have just splashed a little water around and then considered the job done. As it was, Mr Jones impatiently reminded him of every required action.

'Now wash behind your ears,' he demanded with irritation.

Meanwhile, Nigel Green had taken up position at the sink next to mine. He filled his basin with water before noticing that there was no soap to hand.

'Have you taken my soap, you little bastard?' he whinged at me aggressively.

Though extremely intimidated, I replied, 'No.'

This angered him. 'What did you say?' he glowered.

'I, er, I haven't got your soap,' I answered shakily.

'Then what is *that*?' he scowled, pointing to the bar of soap that I'd been using.

I swallowed nervously. 'It's just the soap that was there,' I said.

He advanced on me and gave a vigorous shove, causing me to lose balance and drop to the floor.

Mr Jones quickly withdrew from cajoling Jonathan and rounded on Nigel and me.

'Green and Kinsley!' he barked. 'What do you think you're playing at?'

'That runt took my soap,' Nigel complained, while I sat dazed on the floor.

'Kinsley,' Mr Jones snapped at me. 'Get up!'

As I dragged myself up from the floor, Mr Jones addressed us both. 'I don't want any more trouble from either of you.'

'But –' I tried to protest my innocence.

'I don't care whose fault it is or who started it,' Mr Jones cut me off. 'I want you both to behave yourselves.' Then turning to me, he added, 'Just give Green the soap, will you?'

I handed over the soap to Nigel – I'd finished with it anyway – and Mr Jones went back to coaxing Jonathan.

'Just you watch it, Kinsley,' Nigel hissed at me. 'I'll have you.'

I quickly towelled myself dry and returned to my bedside to finish getting dressed, after which I stowed my other clothes away in my locker.

The dining room, it seemed, had been rearranged for the weekend. The rows of tables at each side of the room had been broken up; six tables were now pushed together in the centre to make one large table.

I was seated between Jonathan and Mr Jones, while across the table from me were two girls seated either side of a female member of staff called Michelle Newbold. One of the girls was Sharon Gillan, who I remembered calling me a 'stuck up little bastard' on my first day. The other was a girl of around thirteen, Jane Sparrow, who looked disturbingly bony. Her paper-dry skin was extremely pallid, her eyes sunken and her hair slightly thinning. I was looking at her with dismayed fascination – she was so chillingly skeletal – when I realised I was staring and quickly looked away.

I looked around to see if there was any sign of Donna Bennett, the girl who had taken the overdose. Although I wasn't exactly sure what Donna looked like, it was obvious that she wasn't here.

'Cereals!' The voice belonged to Robert King, who was calling from the other side of the serving hatch.

We all got in line – nine kids in all, including two of the very young ones, plus a handful of staff.

Once back at my place with a bowl of corn flakes, I looked around the table, while taking care to maintain my impassive mask, scanning the kids and staff to see who was present. I noticed two empty places; one of these I assumed to belong to Robert, who was currently in the kitchen, but I couldn't immediately work out who was missing from the other one. Then I remembered Julie Wilson, who had been confined to the time-out room. Surmising that she couldn't possibly have been sent home for the weekend, I wondered if the vacant place was hers.

'Is Julie here this weekend?' I asked, not directing my question at anyone in particular.

'You concentrate on eating your breakfast,' Mr Jones said tersely.

'Yes, she is,' answered Michelle, a women of indeterminable age. 'We've already taken her breakfast to her.'

'Is she still in the punishment room?' I asked.

'It's called the time-out room,' Michelle corrected me. 'And yes, we've just put her back in there. She had to be in the girls' dorm last night so the night staff could keep an eye on her. They'd have been constantly running from one end of the building to the other if we'd left her there. But we've taken her back now, 'cause she still needs a bit longer to –'

Mr Jones interrupted. 'You ask too many questions,' he said to me. 'Just be glad we haven't put *you* in the time-out room.'

'When will she be allowed out?' I asked Michelle.

It was Mr Jones, once again, who spoke. 'Julie would pound you to a pulp as soon as look at you, Daniel, so why are you so worried about her?'

I didn't get a chance to answer as, all of a sudden, Jane was explosively sick.

'Oh, for fuck's sake!' complained Nigel, who had been sitting to the right of her.

'Watch your language!' Mr Jones demanded, standing up and reaching across the table to swiftly smack Nigel across the head.

Meanwhile, Michelle and another older female member of staff, Mrs Sampson, began attending to Jane, who was simply sitting there staring blankly at her foul-smelling vomit. It was astonishing that someone could have spewed up so copiously after eating just a few corn flakes.

Around the table, everyone gave up on their cereals – except for Jonathan who continued to hungrily wolf his down.

'Why did she do that?' came a little voice from the far end of the table. It was Sally Abiola, a six-year-old Nigerian girl.

'She's just feeling a bit poorly,' answered Glenys Dawson, the nurse sitting next to Sally.

'Come on, Jane,' Michelle urged. 'Let's get you cleaned up. Then we'd better see if you can keep some Complan down.'

Michelle ushered Jane out of the dining room, while Mrs Sampson disappeared into the kitchen to get a bowl of hot soapy water and a sponge. Then, with Mr Jones's help, she set about cleaning up the mess.

When Robert called for us to collect our cooked breakfasts, everybody was noticeably reluctant to line up – with the exception of Jonathan who was first in the queue.

I gazed at my over-cooked fried egg and grey-looking bacon for a good few seconds before I tried sampling them. But like almost everyone else at the table, I no longer had an appetite, so I gave up after a couple of mouthfuls.

'What's wrong with Jane?' I asked Mrs Sampson, leaning past Mr Jones.

'Go ahead, don't mind me,' Mr Jones remarked caustically.

'It's called anorexia nervosa,' Mrs Sampson answered. 'It means she's obsessed with losing weight.'

'But she's so thin already!' I said, astounded at how emaciated she was.

'She's a very stupid girl!' Mr Jones said bluntly. 'She's practically starving herself to death!'

I glanced from Mr Jones to Mrs Sampson and back again in bewilderment. I'd never heard of anything like this before.

'Just you remember how lucky you are,' Mr Jones told me. 'Whenever you bawl your eyes out and start complaining that you want to go home, just remember how well-off you are compared to Jane. *She* may never get better, but *you* will – if you stop acting up.'

I was a little stunned. 'So she isn't going to get better?'

'We're not giving up on her,' Mrs Sampson said. 'She'll get better if she wants to.'

By this time, Robert had come out of the kitchen with his own cooked breakfast, and sitting himself down, he tucked into it enthusiastically, not having been put off by seeing Jane throw up.

Once the dirty plates had been cleared away, Mr Jones and Robert took care of distributing the medication, followed by cigarettes.

'Right, then!' Mr Jones announced, getting to his feet. 'I need two volunteers to do the washing up.' And without waiting for any response, he said, 'Okay, you and you.'

He had pointed at me and then at Sharon.

'Git!' Sharon scoffed. 'I'm not your slave.'

'Just you mind your manners, my girl,' Mr Jones retorted. 'Go on, both of you, get on with it,' he ordered as the other kids and staff dispersed.

I meekly followed Sharon as she traipsed rather defiantly into the kitchen. A very large pile of dirty plates, bowls, cups, glasses and serving dishes greeted us. It came as a surprise to me that all this had to be washed-up by hand; I'd assumed that, being attached to a large hospital, the Unit would have had access to some heavy-duty dish washing machinery. Apparently that wasn't the case. And so we divided up the responsibilities between us as Sharon saw fit – that is, with Sharon washing and me rinsing, drying and putting away.

It took us some considerable time to complete the task, and throughout Sharon needled me with antagonistic remarks.

'See ya, Danny Boy,' Sharon taunted once we'd finished.

She made her way out of the kitchen, and I was left there alone, unsure of what I was supposed to do next.

Only yesterday I had been under constant supervision, but now there didn't seem to be anyone keeping an eye on me at all. For a fleeting moment I wondered whether I could just slide out through the kitchen's back door, meander out of the hospital grounds, and find my way to the A264. From there, maybe I could hitch a ride to Loxton…

But I dismissed the idea. Firstly, I wasn't sure what the chances were of getting out of the hospital grounds unobserved, and secondly, even if I could do that, I was doubtful of my ability to successfully navigate my way to the main road, let alone hitch a ride. And this was without even considering the possibility that Oakdale would call out the police, or the fact that my parents would send me back as soon as I got home.

Realising how hopeless it was, I let my mask slip, and I allowed myself to sob for a few moments. Then I took a deep breath and battled to regain my carefully composed façade of impassivity.

Not knowing what to do or where to go, I found myself walking in the direction of the time-out room. I was curious about Julie, and I wanted to see if I could find out for myself what was happening to her. I made it there without challenge and pressed my face up against the porthole window in the door.

Whatever I might have imagined, I wasn't prepared for what I saw. Julie was just lying there, apparently unconscious, resting partially on foam shapes and partially on the hard lino. I could see that, below the single sheet which inadequately covered her, she was completely naked, and I was horrified to see that she had badly soiled the sheet. Amidst the grime of the room, I could see against one of the walls a tray of breakfast things, untouched, while in one corner a bucket had fallen over spilling human waste onto the floor.

I turned away, appalled and nauseous.

'Did you see what you wanted?' Mr Jones gave me a start, having come up behind me silently.

'I – I – er,' I stammered.

Mrs Sampson came round the corner with a mop and bucket.

'Daniel, since you seem so interested in Julie's situation, perhaps you'd like to do the slopping out,' Mr Jones said, rattling a large bunch of keys and then selecting the one which opened the time-out room door.

'Leave him alone, Bill,' Mrs Sampson admonished mildly. 'He's just being inquisitive.'

Mr Jones made a tutting sound. 'Go on, off with you!' he commanded me.

I didn't need to be told twice. I bolted away down the corridor as quickly as I could, making it to the boys' dormitory at the opposite end of the Unit in less than a minute.

Once there, I threw myself face down on the bed, and breathlessly cried into my pillow. There was no way I could disguise my feelings any longer.

I assumed that Robert must have heard me, as he came in from the nurses' station and sat himself down on my bed.

'What is it now, Daniel?' he asked, clearly irritated but trying to sound patient.

'This place is disgusting!' I gasped.

'Why? What's happened?'

I tried to catch my breath. 'I've seen Julie. Locked up in the punishment room. It's horrible!'

'We'll let her out as soon as she's cooled off, Daniel,' he said calmly.

I couldn't believe what he was saying, or the way in which he was saying it. 'Cooled off? You've knocked her out and left her in her own –' I struggled to finish the sentence, knowing it needed a far stronger choice of words than I would normally use. 'You've left her –' I tried again '– you've left her in her own, er, her own *shit*!'

'Daniel!' Robert spoke sharply. 'That kind of language is not acceptable!'

The revulsion and despondency I was feeling gave way to pure rage. I turned over, pulled myself up to a sitting position, and faced Robert with absolute anger.

'Not acceptable!' I seethed. '*Not acceptable*! What *you* lot have done to Julie is not acceptable!'

He looked at me open-mouthed.

'You've drugged her up till she doesn't know what she's doing,' I continued to fume, 'and you've left her lying in filth. And *you* think it's unacceptable that *I* said "shit"!'

Robert just looked at me, and I looked back at him, neither of us saying anything.

In the end, Robert broke the loaded silence and surprised me by saying, 'You might be right.'

He stood up, his whole demeanour having become less certain, less self-confident. 'You *are* right. What we've done to Julie is –' he paused. 'Well, maybe it *shouldn't* be acceptable.'

*   *   *

56

That morning I had been left with two grotesque images burned into my brain: that of Jane, wasted and frail, and that of Julie, insensible and squalid. Unable to erase those impressions in my mind, I drifted aimlessly through the Oakdale corridors for a while, not knowing where to go and unable to determine any purpose to the morning.

I passed Nigel walking in the opposite direction, but I barely noticed as he elbowed me aggressively as our paths crossed.

Passing the TV room, I heard that the television had been switched on and that the morning start-up routine was reaching its climax – 'Good morning,' came the announcer's voice. 'This is Southern Television.'

I drifted in and planted myself in a foam chair next to a girl named Wendy Cole who, at seventeen, was currently the Unit's oldest patient.

'Any idea what's on?' she asked me in a glum monotone, looking every bit as miserable as I felt.

I hadn't, and after sitting in front of the TV for the next hour or so, I still had no idea what was on; two or three programmes coasted by without my seeing them – all I could see were those troubling afterimages of Jane and Julie.

'Come on, you two,' Mrs Sampson called to us from the door. 'You can't sit in front of the TV all day.'

She came further in and, after unlocking the door to the TV compartment, reached in and switched the set off.

'It's just about time for coffee,' she added. 'Are you coming?'

Wendy and I made our way through to the dining room, where Jill Cooper, one of the younger nurses, was standing by a trolley serving coffee and squash. I accepted a squash and sat myself down at the central assemblage of tables.

I was somewhat relieved to see both Jane and Julie sitting there. My relief wasn't particularly great, however, as Jane still looked hideously shrunken while Julie looked like a zombie.

With a great effort of courage, I overcame my reticence – and, to be honest, my revulsion too – and asked Jane if she was feeling better.

She may have been attempting to smile, but it looked more like a pained grimace. 'Yes, thank you,' she said. 'I just ate too much; I was a complete pig!'

I looked at her dumbfounded, remembering how very little she must have eaten before she was sick.

'But you hardly had anything,' I said.

'Good, Daniel.' It was Michelle who spoke, having just joined us at the table. 'Jane never believes us when *we* tell her that, but maybe she'll accept it from you, a new kid.'

'He's wrong,' Jane complained to Michelle. 'I completely stuffed myself. I *deserved* to be sick.'

It was obvious to me that there was nothing remotely useful I could say; this was all far too complicated and serious. I lowered my gaze to the orange surface of the table, clamming up as I told myself this girl might well be dying.

Then Mr Jones came striding in, settled himself in the seat next to me, and lit up an Embassy Regal.

'For God's sake, Daniel, stop looking so miserable,' he said tetchily. 'You've got what you wanted – you should be happy.'

I looked up, confused. 'What?'

'We've let Julie out of the time-out room, cleaned her up, got her dressed,' Mr Jones said. 'That's what you wanted, isn't it?'

I glanced over towards Julie, who showed no response at all to the mention of her name.

It was true, of course, that I was gratified to see Julie out of that awful room, but seeing her so diminished and docile still struck me as wrong. I knew that Julie was extremely volatile, and that in her normal condition there was good reason to fear her, but somehow, seeing her so overpowered was just as fearful. I thought of what had happened to me the previous Wednesday, of how *I'd* been subdued – as Julie was subdued now – and I contemplated the thought that, at Oakdale, they could do anything they liked to any one of us. We were powerless to resist and we were powerless to protest – after all, who would ever believe us? The very idea that children could be treated like this, here and now in the 1970s, just wasn't plausible.

Mr Jones had made some sort of vague suggestion that, once the afternoon shift came on duty, Jeff Knowles might take us all out in the minibus, perhaps for a walk on the South Downs. But by late morning it had started to rain, and there was no sign that it would let up anytime soon.

So we were all stuck in the Unit with very little to do. As the morning wore on, Michelle tried to encourage a few of us to get involved in doing a large jigsaw. She emptied out the pieces on one of the currently surplus dining tables, but in the end it was only Wendy and myself – the two depressives – who persevered with it.

And then it was lunchtime. My thoughts returned to Jane and Julie, and I wondered how they were going to manage. As it happened, Julie didn't manage at all, slumped in her seat barely conscious. Robert King, who was seated to her left, and Jill Cooper, just around the corner of the table to her right, made a few attempts to get some mushroom soup down her. But Julie was completely oblivious to everything, and though Jill tried feeding her like a baby, she didn't even seem to realise she had to swallow, and the soup just trickled down her chin.

While I had worried how Jane was going to get on, given what had happened following just a few mouthfuls of cereal, I was reassured to see her doing rather better with the soup. While she was hardly lapping it up with pleasure, she did at least manage to make her way through about half of it.

The second course, however, proved more of a problem. Admittedly, the plateful of liver, mashed potatoes and broad beans looked overly dry and decidedly unappetising, but Jane reacted to it as though she'd been presented with a serving of noxious effluent.

'I'm not eating *that*!' she declared.

'Jane, just try *some* of it,' coaxed Michelle Newbold.

'No way, it's putrid!'

Rather oddly, I found myself fixating on the word 'putrid' – I didn't have a clue what it meant, but it sounded so marvellously peculiar – and so I didn't even begin to anticipate where the growing tension might lead. Perhaps that was why I was so shaken when Jane raised her plate high in the air before smashing it back down on the table. Ceramic shards flew in all directions, along with the food, prompting a callous round of applause from Nigel and Sharon.

'Why did she do that?' asked Sally once again.

'Right, that's it, my girl!' Mr Jones shouted angrily at Jane. 'I'm taking you into the quiet room where I will personally force feed you.'

'Bill –' Michelle sounded as though she was going to object.

Mr Jones got up, stormed around the table to Jane, grabbed her by the wrist – while calling to Robert to fetch another plate of food – and then marched her out of the dining room. She struggled, albeit rather feebly, as Mr Jones navigated her towards the closely adjacent quiet room.

'I'll take it,' Michelle said to Robert, collecting the freshly laden plate from him as he emerged from the kitchen.

Mrs Sampson and Robert cleared away the debris Jane had left behind, while Michelle made her way to the quiet room with the plate.

The rest of us resumed eating. However, the atmosphere was decidedly unsettled, as we could clearly hear Jane shouting and screaming. Occasionally, Mr Jones's voice would rise above Jane's as he gruffly scolded her, and I anxiously worried that she might not be able to withstand the physical force I imagined him using; in my mind I could see her matchstick arms snapping in two as Mr Jones restrained them so determinedly.

I found I just couldn't eat any more as the sound of the ongoing struggle continued to distract and disturb me. Right the way through the dessert course, and carrying on as Glenys Dawson and Robert attended to our medication, Jane's agonising howls permeated into the dining room like some fearful siren.

Even after we had all left the table, and Wendy and I had returned to our jigsaw, Jane's pitiful cries endured relentlessly.

Members of the afternoon shift began to appear – Mike Kirby, Jeff Knowles and a few others – ambling into the dining room and helping themselves to coffee. They all seemed rather indifferent to the noise coming from the quiet room; all apart from Derek Ball and Mrs Hamilton, two nurses I'd seen very little of until now, who had the job of taking over from Mr Jones and Michelle.

Sometime after the morning shift had gone off duty, the sound from the quiet room gradually began to subside.

'How are you finding it here?' Wendy asked me in her mechanical tone, as she located a piece to complete the jigsaw's edge.

'It's like hell,' I said.

'Yes,' she agreed, without feeling. 'It is.'

This was the first time I'd had a chance to tell anyone what I really felt about Oakdale.

'I've seen things happen here, awful things, that I never knew went on,' I said. 'And things that have happened to *me* here –' I wasn't sure how to finish the sentence.

'You're still very young, aren't you?' Wendy said.

I told her my age.

'You're learning stuff the hard way,' she said, revealing a small amount of inflection in her voice at last. 'You look like you've come from a nice home and a nice school. You probably had no idea just how bad the world can be. It must have come as a big shock.'

'But I know about children starving in other countries,' I said. 'I just didn't think I'd see it happening here.'

'You're talking about Jane,' she said. 'I know; it's a nightmare.'

'And there are other things,' I went on. 'Like all the drugs, the way they –'

'The way they suppress us, subdue us, and control us – is that what you mean?'

'Yes.'

'I've been here over a year,' Wendy told me, 'and I've seen it all – several times. It came as a shock to start with, but now I've just got used to it.'

'I don't think I could *ever* get used to it.'

'Look, Daniel,' Wendy said purposefully, 'the only way you'll avoid getting used to it is if get out of here soon; stay here too long, and you *will* get used to it, just like I have. You'll stop noticing how mad everything is here. Only when some new kid comes along, and you see how shocked he or she is, only then will you remember that you used to be shocked too.'

'Why haven't you got out of here yet?' I asked.

'I'm going to,' she said. 'The only reason I'm still here is because my parents can't cope with me at home when I'm depressed. But as soon as I'm eighteen, it won't be up to them anymore. Either they'll have to put up with me, or I'll get my own place: lodgings, a bedsit, or something.'

This all sounded very scary to me, the idea of coming out of Oakdale and having to find your own accommodation because there was no one to look after you. What would you do? What would you live on?

Wendy and I continued working on the jigsaw until we'd finished it – apart from the three pieces that were missing.

It was beginning to get dark outside, so I went back to the dormitory to read for a while before going to the TV room to watch *Doctor Who*. But I only got to see the first fifteen minutes of it before we were called in for supper at six o'clock.

Back at the large central table, I sat in dread, trying to anticipate what might happen during the forthcoming meal. Across the table to my left was Julie, still looking every bit as comatose as before – it was obvious that they were still keeping her heavily tranquillised – while almost opposite me sat Jane. Although I felt genuinely sorry for Jane, I just couldn't bear the thought of eating at the same table as her once again. And so, for the first time, I set about trying to make myself insensible to everything that was going on around me. There had already been a few times during the day when I'd been so preoccupied with my unhappiness or some disturbing thought, that I'd found it difficult to focus on what was in front of me; but now I deliberately tried to dissociate myself from my present reality. Unfortunately, I wasn't wholly successful, as the staff sitting nearest to me – Mike, Mrs Hamilton and another nurse called Tracy Grafton – made incessant attempts to draw me out of myself. But somehow I managed to get through supper completely numbed to whatever was happening with Jane.

Shortly after supper, but before we were told we could leave the table, the sound of the telephone ringing echoed through the Unit. As it turned out, the call was for me. Jeff came to get me, telling me I could take the call in the kitchen.

The 'phone was on the wall near the serving hatch. I lifted the receiver, which was lying on the work surface below it, and found my mum on the other end.

We talked for some time, and then she put my dad on. I tried convincing both of them they must come and collect me, free me from this terrible place. I described all the horrendous things I'd seen and experienced here, hoping this would persuade them, but it was clear they thought I was exaggerating. The call ended with them wishing me well, passing on my brother's love, and saying they hoped to see me next weekend.

With the 'phone call over, all that remained was to kill the time left before going to bed. I think I may have watched some television, or maybe done some more reading; nothing made much of an impression on me – all I wanted was for the day to end.

Sunday morning. Dawn was making modest inroads into the dark as I awoke, muzzy and miserable, which I now realised had become my normal state. I reflected on how I'd been admitted to Oakdale for depression, but that my condition was now significantly worse as a result.

I began getting myself washed while, just as yesterday, Nigel took the neighbouring sink and stood there belittling and threatening me. 'I'm gonna get you, Kinsley,' he said. 'I'm gonna smash your fucking head in.'

The fear in me was beginning to escalate, as it sounded as if Nigel was going to carry out his threat imminently, and Mr Jones, who was attending to Jonathan once again, appeared to show no inclination to intervene.

It was after breakfast that the immediacy of Nigel's intimidation started to make a real impact on me. Finding the quiet room open, I decided to take my book in there and read.

The quiet room was of a moderate size, with around five or six of the vinyl-covered foam chairs occupying most of the floor space. I hadn't been in there very long when Jonathan darted in and started bouncing about on the seats. If that was distracting, I soon found I was going to be put off even more: Sharon and Nigel had appeared, apparently having chosen to come in here in preference to the dining room in order to smoke.

Nigel made some intimidating remark to me, while also threatening Jonathan with terrible consequences if he didn't stop bouncing about. Jonathan froze, and continued to sit absolutely still while Nigel turned his attention to Sharon.

I had assumed that Nigel and Sharon were friends as they had come in together and, of course, they appeared united in their hostility towards me. But it soon became clear that Sharon detested Nigel. Nigel, however, clearly had designs on Sharon. He moved in close to her, sidling over from his seat on to hers and putting a hand on her knee.

'Fuck off, Green!' Sharon spat at him.

I dropped my book, and looked on apprehensively.

Sharon's venomous rebuke hadn't stopped him, he moved in closer still, and shifted his hand from her knee to roughly grab one of her breasts. 'Come on,' he menaced. 'You know you want it.'

She stabbed her lit cigarette into his face. He yelled out, but instead of backing off, he closed in on her more forcefully, throwing his own cigarette aside and climbing on to her. Their combined weight squeezed the foam chair, lowering them closer the floor. Sharon tried to fight Nigel off as he kissed her ferociously on the lips, but though vicious herself, she wasn't as strong as him.

Jonathan was still rooted to the spot, terrified, so it was clear that it was up to me to do something. Though terrified myself, I leaped out of my seat and grabbed Nigel by his collar and began trying to haul him away from her. I couldn't shift him, but he reacted by rolling off Sharon and then springing up to attack me. His brutality was incredible; he repeatedly punched at my head and stomach until I fell to the ground, utterly unable to defend myself. Then, as I lay in a heap on the carpet, he began kicking me. I coiled myself into a ball, but this offered very little protection as he continued to put the boot in.

Someone must have raised the alarm – whether it was Sharon or Jonathan, I couldn't tell – because Mr Jones and Robert King eventually arrived on the scene and dragged Nigel away.

I had some vague awareness of Mrs Sampson and Michelle Newbold coming into the room.

'Daniel,' came Mrs Sampson's voice as she stooped down, bringing her face close to mine. 'Can you hear me?'

I murmured a detached response.

'Just keep still,' she said. 'We need to make sure that nothing is broken.'

I don't know quite how it happened, but somehow they managed to get me to the sluice room, close to the dormitories. Once there, Michelle applied antiseptic to a number of cuts on my face and upper body, while Mrs Sampson prepared a syringe.

'You're going to drug me again?' I complained dimly.

'You've had a very bad experience,' Mrs Sampson said.

'So this is another "consequence of my actions",' I said, having now learned the euphemism for 'punishment'.

'No,' Mrs Sampson laughed. 'It's not a consequence of your actions, but it *is* a consequence of you getting hurt. You're not in trouble, or anything like that. We're not stupid, you know, we realise what Nigel's like – *he'll* certainly have to face the consequences of *his* actions.'

'But I don't want to be knocked out again,' I said.

'Don't worry,' she said. 'We're not giving you a large dose – just enough to help you relax a bit. You'll definitely feel better for it.'

Once back in the dormitory, Michelle told me I needed to get into bed.

'It's just until the doctor gets here,' she said. 'Then, if he says it's okay, you can get up again.'

It was very awkward and painful, but I managed to get into my pyjamas and ease myself under the sheet and continental quilt.

Then Michelle walked off, and I was left alone in the dormitory for some time before Mr Jones came in with Dr Wanjiru.

Dr Wanjiru was very pleasant and sympathetic, but although he tried to be gentle as he inspected my bumps and cuts, my body objected quite painfully to his poking and prodding.

'You'll live,' he announced once he'd finished the examination. 'You'll be black and blue for a few days, and quite sore too, but you'll be all right.' Then, to Mr Jones, he said, 'Make sure he takes it easy for a while. He can get up, but he mustn't overdo it.'

Dr Wanjiru left, leaving Mr Jones standing over me.

'It's a good job we allowed Julie out of the time-out room,' he said sarcastically, 'otherwise we wouldn't have had anywhere to put Nigel.' And then, simulating sudden realisation, he added, 'Oh, but you don't approve of the time-out room, do you? You'd much rather we let Nigel roam free so that he could beat you up again!'

Despite what Dr Wanjiru had said, I remained in bed for what was left of the morning. I was given my lunch in bed, but once the afternoon staff came on duty, I was allowed up again. But I ached all over, and every slightest move resulted in a powerful stab of pain from some, often unexpected, part of my body.

Jeff Knowles, Glenys Dawson and Jill Cooper took most of the kids out in the minibus that afternoon. The walk on the South Downs that had been suggested for yesterday finally took place – but not for me. I was obviously in no fit state to go clambering about on wind-swept hills, so I was the only kid – apart from Nigel in the time-out room – to be left behind.

Just before going off on the trip with the others, Sharon came up to me as I sat in the TV room. 'I didn't need your help – I can handle Green,' she said. 'But, er, thanks anyway.'

As soon as Sharon had disappeared, Tracy Grafton, the nurse sitting with me, remarked, 'Well, Daniel, if I hadn't heard it with my own ears, I'd never have believed it! I don't know what you did, but it must have been quite something – *Sharon thanked you!*'

CHAPTER FIVE

A handful of children returned from their weekend leave on the Sunday evening. Gary Jameson came back to find his bed had been swapped with Nigel Green's – which was an enormous relief to me. Nonetheless, Nigel still seemed a very real threat. Though sedated, he managed to find the energy to curse and swear vigorously as he arrived in the dormitory having been conducted there from the time-out room. Jeff Knowles and Mr Köhler, a member of the night staff, persuasively directed Nigel to his new bed, which I was pleased to see located at the farthest corner of the dorm from me.

But it was on Monday morning that the majority of the kids reappeared, and so I found myself sitting in school assembly, still very sore and stiff, among the full complement of pupils – excepting, of course, for the younger ones in Miss Evesham's class.

While we were singing the hymn 'Lord of the dance' (Number 36 in the green book), I looked round and saw both of the miscreants who had been confined to the time-out room over the weekend. I was puzzled, however, to notice that they were in very different states of wakefulness. Nigel's sedation had clearly all but worn off, while Julie Wilson still seemed extremely drowsy. And yet, Julie's misdeed had taken place three days ago, while Nigel's had only been yesterday. What was more, the episode involving Julie had done very little harm to any actual person (aside from the minor scratches sustained by John Webber), whereas the harm done to me by Nigel would have been obvious to anyone at a glance.

After assembly, Mrs Nakamura asked to talk to me in her office. I was worried that I was going to be in trouble, possibly for missing school on Thursday and Friday.

'Come in,' Mrs Nakamura said as she led the way through the door to her office. 'Sit down.'

I seated myself opposite her desk, apprehension crowding in to join my existing sense of feeling miserable, groggy and physically sore.

'There's nothing to worry about, Daniel,' Mrs Nakamura said reassuringly.

I looked at her wondering why she wanted to see me.

'I understand from your other school, er –' she looked down at some papers on her desk for an *aide-mémoire* '– from Worthing Road, that you could do with a bit of help with your French.'

I nodded.

'Well, I'm going to try giving you a few French lessons myself, just twice a week,' she said, 'on Monday mornings and Friday afternoons. And then, hopefully, you'll be able to catch up.'

I had mixed feelings about this. French was not my favourite subject by any means, but if Mrs Nakamura really could help me with it, then maybe I'd find it a bit easier once I was back at Worthing Road.

'If there's time, we'll have our first French lesson this morning, before break,' she said. 'But I'd just like to have a bit of a chat with you first.'

I was pleasantly surprised by what she had to say.

'I'm not sure that you really belong in Oakdale,' she said. 'We've got all sorts of children here, as you've seen. Some have very serious mental illnesses, and others have major behavioural problems. A few are here because there isn't really anywhere else to put them, and there are a some who have been in trouble with the police and are here by order of the courts.'

I listened intently, and with growing excitement, as I realised that she seemed fairly certain I was in the wrong place. I started to think that, just maybe, she might be able to help me get out of Oakdale.

'You're not really like any of those other children,' she continued. 'It's true that quite a few kids come here just for a short while – which is obviously the intention in your case. Sometimes kids just have a few problems that we can help with, and then they get sent back to their normal schools after just a couple of months. But I can't help thinking that all you really need is a bit more support and encouragement. I'm not a psychiatrist, of course, but I've read all the notes Worthing Road have sent me, and I think you've just got into a bit of a rut. You've started to feel like it's normal to be miserable most of the time; all you really need is for someone to remind you what it's like to have a bit of fun, what it's like to be happy.'

'Can you help me to get out of here, to get home?' I asked, a little hesitantly.

'I'm afraid I can't promise anything,' she cautioned, 'but I'm going to see if I can hurry things up a bit, so that you get home sooner rather than later – and with the support you need.'

I managed a bit of a smile as I thanked her.

'That's better,' she remarked. 'You need to try smiling more – you've got out of practice.'

Mrs Nakamura then began her attempt at trying to teach me French. She found a book on one of her shelves, *Le Cheval Vilain*, and got it down. It wasn't a textbook for learning the French language as such, but rather it appeared to be a French equivalent of a learn-to-read book, similar to the more advanced of the *Janet and John* or *Peter and Jane* early readers I'd been taught from at primary school.

Mrs Nakamura opened up the book in front of me on her desk and stood over me as I tried to read out some of the French text.

'You're doing well,' Mrs Nakamura remarked. 'You've definitely got the makings. I can't see any reason why you shouldn't do really well at French.'

Then there was a knock at the door.

'Come in,' Mrs Nakamura called.

It was Sarah Dawes. 'Hello, Mrs N.,' she said. 'I was wondering where Daniel had got to. It's break time.'

'Sorry,' Mrs Nakamura said, closing the book and returning it to the shelf. 'We must have lost track of time. We were working on Daniel's French.'

Sarah laughed. 'I'm rubbish at French, I'm afraid.'

'Well, Daniel's quite good, actually,' Mrs Nakamura said. 'Or, at least, he *will* be if he puts in a bit of effort. That's the trouble with you English,' she joked, 'you're just plain lazy when it comes to languages.'

'I suppose that comes from being an island nation,' Sarah said.

'That's no excuse,' Mrs Nakamura smiled. 'I'm from an island nation myself, and we're not nearly so lazy as you.'

'All right,' Sarah giggled, 'I'll consider myself told off.' Then turning to me, she said, 'Are you coming, Daniel?'

I got up and went with Sarah over to the Unit.

Still aching following the previous day's encounter with Nigel, I walked unsteadily into the dining room and joined the tail end of the queue for coffee or squash.

All the tables were now returned to their customary positions following the weekend, and I spotted a group that included Andrew Ramsey, Jennie Saunders, and Gary Jameson seated at one of them. I went over with my glass of squash and pulled up a chair to join them.

'So,' observed Andrew theatrically, 'you've done battle with Nigel Green and lived to tell the tale. That's impressive.'

It didn't feel very impressive.

Sarah, coffee in hand, came over and added to our number.

'How's it going, you lot?' she asked affably, fumbling with the cellophane wrapper on a fresh packet of Consulate.

'We were just sitting here in awe of Daniel for taking on Nigel,' Andrew said.

'I think the less said about that the better,' said Sarah, still struggling with her sealed cigarette packet.

'You were lucky, Daniel,' Jennie said. 'Nigel's been convicted for GBH, but he got sent here instead of borstal 'cause he's so unhinged.'

I looked towards Sarah, who nodded confirmation. 'That's true – more-or-less. It would be best if you avoided him. I know it's a bit difficult at the weekend when there are so few kids here, but you shouldn't have too much trouble keeping out of his way now everyone's back.'

Andrew suddenly snatched the cigarette pack off Sarah.

'Hey!' she exclaimed.

'Here,' he said, handing it back after deftly removing the cellophane. 'I shouldn't have helped you really – it's a filthy habit.'

'Yeah, I know,' she agreed, lighting up anyway.

'Fridgerd, the art therapist, should be in this afternoon after school,' Andrew remarked.

'Ah, yes,' said Sarah. 'Daniel wanted to see the art room; Andrew, you can introduce him to Fridgerd.'

'All right,' he said.

'The art room's brilliant!' Gary enthused. 'There's paints, clay, all sorts of stuff.'

'Yeah,' said Jennie, 'it's pretty good, actually. And it's only open on Mondays, so you need to make the most of it when you can.'

'So,' Sarah said brightly, 'you'll all be in to see Fridgerd after school then?'

The art room was relatively large. It housed three potter's wheels and a number of tables. One wall was almost entirely taken up by shelves and cupboards containing a plentiful stock of art materials. Two of the other walls were dominated by substantial windows looking out onto a well-kept grass field. These windows had the potential to bring daylight flooding into the room; but as it was an overcast afternoon in February, their illumination had to be supplemented by the artificial 'sunlight' of fluorescent tubes.

Fridgerd Vogt turned out to be rather taller than I'd been expecting. She was probably in her late twenties, and had a very easy-going manner; she readily supplied me with assorted acrylic paints, artists' brushes and a large sheet of paper. If it hadn't been for the presence of Mr Jones in the art room, who seemed to be monitoring Gary, Andrew, Jennie and myself, then my first experience of group art therapy might have provided some diversion from my troubled thoughts and feelings.

Like me, Gary was busy applying paint to paper, while Andrew and Jennie were both working with clay, Andrew apparently attempting some sort of sculpture, while Jennie was seated at a potter's wheel.

'That looks interesting,' Fridgerd remarked, casting an eye over the rather

68

stormy seascape I was trying to create. 'Do you live near the sea?'

'Not that near – I live in Loxton,' I answered. 'But we do sometimes go down to Bognor Regis or Worthing, or one of the other beaches down that way.'

'That's a very *angry* looking sea you're painting there,' she said. 'Why is that?'

I didn't really know, and I found myself thinking quite carefully in order to come up with an answer. I also speculated that maybe part of the purpose of art therapy was to try and explore the meaning behind whatever I was trying to create, and so I reasoned that the answer I gave might be significant. With all this going on in my head, I didn't give an immediate reply.

Mr Jones came over and interposed. 'Miss Vogt asked you a question, Daniel,' he said coldly.

'I'm just thinking,' I said defensively.

'It's all right, Bill,' Fridgerd said. 'Actually, I think I can manage on my own as there are only four of them in this afternoon; there's no need for you to hang around – I expect there are other things you'd rather be doing.'

'All right then,' he said, a little uncertainly. 'If that's what you want.'

Mr Jones left the room, and the moment he was gone it felt as though there was a huge collective release of tension.

'That's better,' Jennie remarked from the potter's wheel. 'Now we can relax.'

Fridgerd suppressed a slight giggle.

My mood lightened appreciably, and while Fridgerd went to see what Gary was doing, I started adding some lighter shades to my painting. The scene remained stormy, but it was now somehow more spirited than angry.

I was just starting to think that Dr Rajasimha may have been right after all in commending the Oakdale art room to me, when the situation suddenly changed. Sharon Gillan, Michael Davey, and another boy called Clester Henry arrived, and with their arrival the satisfying recreation of the afternoon ended.

'So, what would you all like to do?' Fridgerd asked them.

'We just wanna bit of fun,' Clester answered in a broad West Indian accent.

'Yeah,' Sharon echoed.

While Michael was a little more restrained than either Sharon or Clester, it wasn't long before all three of them brought complete chaos to the art room. Even Gary got caught up in their mischief and joined in with their hastily devised clay-throwing fight.

Jennie and Andrew's efforts at modelling in clay were commandeered as projectiles, and in the ensuing battle all our creative efforts were completely destroyed.

Fridgerd tried frantically to restore calm, but was unable to make her voice heard above the commotion. Order did not return to the art room until after Mrs Causton, Mr Jones and Robert King came charging in to take control of the situation.

'Right!' Mrs Causton declared, angrily surveying the wreckage of the art room. 'I am appalled at your behaviour. We're lucky that Fridgerd can spare the time to come over to us on a Monday afternoon, but if this is the way you treat her, she'd be better off giving more time to the patients in the main building.'

Fridgerd went over to Mrs Causton and spoke to her in a low voice. 'Mary, it wasn't all of them. Andrew, Jennie and Daniel had nothing to do with this.'

'Well, Fridgerd,' Mrs Causton answered, ensuring her voice was loud enough for everyone to hear, 'they can *all* help clear up this mess.'

'You heard Mrs Causton,' Robert said. 'Get this place cleaned up – *now*.'

My mood having dropped back again to a more dismal state, I began to tackle my share of the cleaning-up operation.

'I thought you said you could manage,' I overheard Mr Jones goading Fridgerd.

'Bill,' Fridgerd objected in a quiet but penetrating hiss, 'I'm not an amateur. I know my job. Perhaps if you could just watch the more disruptive ones, maybe keeping them out of the art room when they're being unruly –'

'I bet it was Jones who sent those buggers in here,' Andrew whispered to me.

'– then I might be able to get somewhere with the others,' Fridgerd finished.

'Miss Vogt, they're *all* disruptive, and they're nearly *always* unruly. They're animals, every one of them, and they need to be treated like animals. They don't need art therapy; they need discipline.'

It was early Tuesday afternoon – I'd now been at the Unit for a week – and we had just finished lunch. John Webber and Ted Trowbridge, having now come on duty, took a group of us outside to play in the 'Adventure Camp'. The Camp was just a little distance past the school, sitting to the edge of the grass field I'd seen through the art room windows. It consisted of a collection of improvised apparatus, including a tree house lodged in the branches of a large winter-bare oak. A death slide ran from the tree house towards a raised wooden platform some five metres away, and standing nearby was a separate timber fort and pirate galleon.

Though cold, the late February sunshine had broken through the clouds to allow these few moments of outdoor activity before we had to get back to school for the afternoon.

Gary, Andrew and Sean threw themselves into their open-air pursuits with passion, clambering in the tree and on the fort, and zipping along the death slide at great speed. But I had to fight against my despondency, grogginess and soreness to participate as best I could. Had I felt better, I would have loved scrambling about in the Camp and sliding through the air suspended from a pulley. But as it was, my attempts to defy my low spirits and wooziness were especially inhibited by the objections of my body, still protesting in the wake of Nigel's assault on me.

I tried climbing the makeshift ladder leading to the tree house, but every part of me seemed to moan at the effort, and by the time I reached the top, Gary, Andrew and Sean were all clamouring impatiently at the base to make the ascent themselves.

Sitting on the suspended floor of the tree house, I wondered if I could manage the death slide across to the other platform.

'You'll need this, Daniel,' John said, running over to seize the handgrip hanging from the pulley resting at the centre of the overhead line. As I got to my feet, he swung the handgrip up towards me, and so I felt compelled to attempt the slide. I grasped it firmly and launched myself into the air. My arms stretched agonisingly as I dangled from the pulley. For a moment I thought I would fall, but eventually, driven by gravity – I'd achieved no real momentum when I set off – I arrived sluggishly at the other end, where I dropped to the platform in a painful heap.

If anything, this brief excursion into the Oakdale grounds made me feel more depressed, as I was unable to fully take part in something I should have enjoyed.

And so I returned to school in the afternoon feeling even more dejected than I would have done otherwise. Indeed, my emotional state was noticed by Mr Baker, which surprised me as I thought I must appear pretty grim most of the time.

'What's the problem, Daniel,' he asked, as I stared with disinterest at a geography textbook.

'I can't *do* anything,' I grumbled. 'Everything is just too hard. My eyes hurt from trying to concentrate, I'm wobbly from all the tablets, and I ache all over.'

Mr Baker put a hand on my shoulder, and I winced at the discomfort – that was one of the places where Nigel had kicked me. He quickly removed his hand and apologised, before saying, 'Things will improve, Daniel. Just do your best, and when you start to feel a bit better you'll find things will get easier.'

The school afternoon dragged and I almost began to think that half-past three would never come. But in the end it did, and we all trouped back over to the Unit for tea. It was over tea – or orange squash, in my case – that I learned I was to see Mrs Fox, the social worker, at four o'clock.

*   *   *

On my first day at Oakdale, John had guided me through a corridor leading from the dormitories towards the connecting passageway leading to main body of the Unit. On one side of the corridor I had seen a series of closed doors. I remembered contemplating what might be behind those doors. Now, a week later, I found myself on the other side of one of them.

Mrs Fox's office was fairly spacious. Against the wall behind her desk stood several heavily laden bookcases, bearing titles such as *Decision in Child Care, Residential Work with Children* and *Children, Courts and Caring*.

Mrs Fox sat to the side of her desk, facing me across the room without any intermediate obstruction. I assumed that her intention was to make the encounter less formal, but as I sat stiffly before her it seemed to me that the atmosphere was hardly casual.

'You've not had a good first week at Oakdale, have you?' Mrs Fox said.

'No,' I answered.

'You kicked up a fuss when your mum came to see you,' she said, 'and you got into a fight at the weekend.'

'The fight wasn't my fault,' I objected.

'That doesn't really matter, Daniel,' she responded. 'The point is that you need to try and reconcile yourself to your present situation. After all, we don't want your mum and dad anxious about you all the time. They need to know that you're getting on well, that everything's fine and that you're making progress.'

'I'm trying my best,' I said. 'I just want to be able to go home, and get back to my friends at school.'

'Of course. And my job is to find what kind of support your family will need to make that happen.'

'Mrs N. says she doesn't think I should be in Oakdale; she doesn't think it's the right place for me,' I said.

'Well,' Mrs Fox said doubtfully, 'that's as maybe. But while you're here, at least your mum will be able to get a bit of time to concentrate on your younger brother. He's only just started school, hasn't he?

'Mark started school last year, in September,' I said.

'Right,' she said, 'so he deserves a bit more of your mum's attention at the moment, don't you think? It's not fair that he should miss out because she's so concerned about you all the time.'

I couldn't think what to say.

'Daniel,' Mrs Fox leant forward, 'we hope you'll get better while you're with us, of course, but you're also here to give your parents a bit of a break. So even if this isn't exactly the best place for you, it will do your whole family good for you to be here for a while.'

Up until now I had been so focussed on my own condition that I hadn't considered that being at Oakdale might not be intended just for my benefit alone. But then, I couldn't help thinking, lots of families must have troubles of various sorts, but surely they can't *all* send one or other of their kids off to a psychiatric unit just to get a break.

Somehow I found the courage to voice my scepticism. 'I'm not here to give my parents a break,' I said. 'I *can't* be.'

Mrs Fox reclined back in her chair a little. 'Don't you think your parents need a break?'

'Maybe – but they wouldn't send me here just for that.'

'Don't forget your brother,' Mrs Fox said. 'He's quite a lot younger than you and he needs looking after. If you mum and dad are having to worry about you all the time – just when you should be old enough to start taking a bit more responsibility – then poor Mark is going to lose out. That's not fair, is it?'

Again, I couldn't think of anything to say.

'You love your brother, don't you, Daniel?' Mrs Fox said. 'And you love your mum and dad?'

'Of course I do,' I answered, resenting the suggestion that maybe I didn't.

'Then try thinking of them as well as yourself,' she said.

I conceded this, thinking that it was probably only fair that I should try giving some thought to my family's needs. But still there was a nagging feeling in the back of my mind that Mrs Fox was representing the whole situation in a slightly dishonest way. Until now, I'd been under the impression that I was at Oakdale because I was ill with depression, that I was here to receive treatment to help me get well. Although I had become convinced that Oakdale was really more of a hindrance than a help, it just didn't seem plausible that I was here because of my *family's* needs.

Or perhaps it *was* plausible after all. I thought of some of the other children I'd met here, and it occurred to me that many of them were probably burdens to their families in various ways. Maybe that was it then; I was here because I was a burden, and in order to get out I needed to learn how to become less of a burden.

'Hopefully,' Mrs Fox said, 'you'll be able to go home this weekend. If you are, I want you to be considerate to you parents and brother and not give them any worry.'

'I'll try,' I agreed.

'If all goes to plan, I shall give you a lift home myself, after school on Friday,' Mrs Fox continued. 'That way I can have a bit of a chat with your mum – I don't suppose your dad will be home from work, will he?'

'Not until just before six,' I said.

'Well, it'll have to be just your mum then,' she said. 'I'll catch your dad some other time.' She paused for a moment. 'In the meantime, Daniel, you do your best to stay out of trouble and keep cheerful. That's your ticket out of here: behaving yourself and keeping cheerful.'

Wednesday was rather uneventful. Thursday, however, brought with it the school trip to the swimming baths in Haywards Heath. A total of nine children, plus Mrs Conway from the school, and Jeff Knowles, Sarah Dawes and Derek Ball from the Unit, piled into the minibus. To the accompaniment of the radio, Jeff steered the Ford Transit on the twenty-minute drive, starting out along Grouse Road, Plummers Plain and Handcross Road, and then on to the B2115. Penetrating through the noise of a boisterous bunch of kids came part of the mid-morning DJ's playlist – including 'Convoy', 'It Should Have Been Me' and a Glenn Miller medley – thus increasing the content of the ever-growing cannon of tunes I would enduringly associate with my time in Oakdale.

Eventually we arrived in Haywards Heath, turned into Pasture Hill Road, and found ourselves a parking space at the pool.

There were three things that were worrying me about this swimming trip – or rather, there was the presence of three particular kids that bothered me. As it happened, I needn't have worried about either Nigel or Julie. I was terrified of Nigel, of course, but between them, Jeff and Derek were careful to keep him under very close supervision for the duration of our visit. As for Julie, I was anxious that someone still very docile from drugs might get into difficulty in the water, but she remained in the shallow end throughout, and both Sarah and Mrs Conway kept a watchful eye on her.

But no matter how carefully I had tried to prepare myself, I was not ready for the sight of Jane Sparrow in her swimming costume. She and I had emerged from our respective changing rooms at almost the same moment, and stepping out into a relatively crowded pool area, I not only caught sight of Jane but was reminded that this was a very public space; we were not the only users, and I was fearful of what other people might think of Jane.

She stood there at the edge of a pool, a frail reedy frame in blue nylon. The outline of her ribs projecting into the elasticity of her costume made for an unbearably macabre sight, while her bony cadaverous arms and legs looked as though they would splinter at the slightest touch. I couldn't help but stare as she tentatively descended the steps into the water, but I found myself comforted by the fact that, once she had submerged the greater part of her body, her appearance wasn't nearly so unsettling.

'Come on, Daniel,' Gary called out, diverting my attention. 'Let's see who can swim a width the fastest.'

I lowered myself into the water, and joined Gary in wading towards a slightly deeper part of the pool where we took up our positions at one side.

'Ready – steady – go!' Gary hollered, and we both pushed ourselves off.

I wasn't an especially skilled swimmer, but I was reasonably competent, so I just about managed to beat Gary to the other side of the pool. If it hadn't been for my bumps and bruises – they were still bothering me, even though they had started to subside – I would probably have beaten him by a much greater margin.

'How about another width, but under water this time,' I suggested to him.

'I don't think I can do that,' he said.

'I'm not sure *I* can,' I replied, 'but let's try anyway.'

I plunged towards the bottom of the pool with an inelegant dive, and thrust myself forward, challenging my aching limbs to the utmost as I tried to reach the far end before coming up for air. I didn't quite make it, as I broke the surface gasping for breath a couple of metres short of my target. But looking back, I saw that Gary hadn't even made it halfway, and so I was quietly pleased with my achievement.

Sarah had seen my attempt, and she swam over to say a few encouraging words.

'That was amazing!' she said. 'I didn't know you were such a good swimmer.'

'I'm not that good,' I said. 'I didn't make it all the way across.'

'All the same,' she argued, 'it was pretty impressive.'

'Thank you.'

Sarah, it seemed, could always be relied upon for support and affirmation. She was like a beacon of light in the dark shadowy world of Oakdale. It was all too tempting to reach out to her for affection, but at some level I realised I must not become dependent on her. She was not a substitute mother, and, at twice my age, she was not a potential girlfriend; she was a nurse dealing with several troubled children. Although she was obviously very caring, she would be making a mistake to risk being anything other than completely professional, and I would be making a mistake if I expected anything else. But all the same, in my emotional poverty I looked to her for warmth, and she, for her part, seemed to be giving it.

She began playfully splashing me, and I splashed back. Gary and an eleven-year old called Lisa Clayton swam over to join in. With them was Donna Bennett, who had been discharged from hospital in Horsham at the beginning of the week following her overdose. This was the first time I'd really seen anything of Donna, as she must have remained confined to the girls' dorm until today. But whatever had led her to take the overdose, she appeared fine now, as she was joining in with the energetic splashing.

And then something unexpected happened: I found I was laughing. I couldn't remember the last time I had laughed, and it felt rather strange. Sarah noticed, and she lunged through the water towards me and enfolded me in a spirited hug. I hugged her back, still laughing. I felt a brief moment of awkwardness at the closeness, but I suppressed it – I wasn't going to let it spoil this rare moment of laughter and empathy.

'Well, *that's* something I've never seen before!' Sarah exclaimed. 'You're laughing! I can't tell you how glad I am to see it.'

She gave me a tight squeeze while I was still in her arms, and just as she did it, Jeff came swimming over to us.

'Sarah,' he called, 'could you go and watch Julie for a moment?'

Sarah released me, and the laughter stopped.

'All right, Jeff,' she replied, and then, briefly touching my arm, she said, 'I'll see you later, Daniel.'

She swam off towards the shallow end, while Jeff made his way back over to Derek who had been left minding Nigel on his own.

The moment was over, and bleakness oozed back into my consciousness.

Gary, Donna and Lisa tried to involve me again in their mischievous splashing, but my mood had changed, drastically and completely, as though someone had flicked a switch.

I paddled off on my own, leaving the others to their enjoyment, and I spent the remainder of my time at the pool in quiet isolation at the side, passively allowing the water to lap against me.

When we were called out to get showered and dressed, I followed the others in silence and did what I had to do.

We returned to the Unit in time for lunch, and once again I was back at the table with Gary and Sean.

My unhappiness eased slightly when Sarah arrived at our table and sat down, but the effect was only marginal, as she appeared a little downcast herself. It seemed to me that either she or I – or, more probably, both of us – had crossed a line at the swimming pool. Maybe we now needed to retreat from that line, if at all possible. This knowledge greatly saddened me, as I so desperately needed affection, so desperately needed *love*. In truth, almost *anyone's* love would have done, but at the present time, my preference was for Sarah's.

She smiled at me across the table, but somehow her smile wasn't an especially happy one.

'It *was* good to see you laughing at the pool this morning,' she said. 'I hope it's something I'll see again.'

*   *   *

76

That afternoon, after school, I began – unnecessarily early – to prepare for my weekend at home. I pulled my suitcase from under the bed and emptied the contents of my locker into it. I was now ready, albeit twenty-four hours ahead of time. And so the first phase of what was to become a regular end-of-week ritual had been completed.

The second phase occurred on the Friday morning, between breakfast and the morning meeting. This was an event – which I had slept through the previous week – that involved all the children stripping their beds of sheets, pillow cases and quilt covers and depositing them in laundry bags. We were then required to collect clean bedclothes from a linen cupboard located near the dormitories, and make our beds afresh. The whole process should not have taken more than about ten or fifteen minutes, but it was considerably slowed by the inevitable pillow fights, arguments over who was to get what colour quilt cover, and by a general tendency towards procrastination. For my part, however, I just wanted to get the chore over with, because once done it would represent completion of a closing feature of the week, thus bringing me symbolically closer to the weekend, and closer to home.

Despite horseplay and delaying tactics, all the kids had finished changing their bedding in plenty of time for a humdrum morning meeting. And then it was over to school for the final assembly of the week.

The morning at school was unremarkable, but as I buried my head in English and maths, I looked forward to the afternoon when I was due to have another French lesson with Mrs Nakamura.

It was about half-an-hour into the afternoon school session when Mrs Nakamura called me into her office. Once we were both seated, at either side of her desk, she directed my attention to the already-open copy of *Le Cheval Vilain* lying in front of me. Once again I did my best to read the text, while Mrs Nakamura encouraged and occasionally corrected me. After having read the book from cover-to-cover, she started asking me questions about it.

'So,' she began, 'what was the book all about?'

'A horrible horse,' I said.

'A *horrible* horse?' she commented. 'You *could* be right – but do you think "horrible" is really the best English word to describe the horse?'

The questioning continued, while I offered answers – often after being fed various helpful clues.

'All right,' Mrs Nakamura said eventually. 'I think that's probably enough for now. We'll do some more on Monday.'

I was about to get up to return to Mr Baker's class when she indicated that I should remain for a moment.

'By the way,' she said, 'I've been thinking a bit more about what we talked about last time.'

I waited, remembering what the social worker, Mrs Fox, had said to me on

Tuesday, and wondering if maybe Mrs Nakamura had now changed her mind, that her views might now be closer to Mrs Fox's.

'When I talked to you before, I said I wasn't sure that you really belonged in Oakdale. The more I've thought about it, the *more sure I am* that Oakdale really isn't right for you.'

A little bit of tension in my body dissolved as I heard this.

'If I can – and I can't give any guarantees, unfortunately – I would like to see you get back home and back to your own school very quickly. But we have to find out what we need to do to make sure everything works out all right.'

I sat there thinking that all this was almost too good to be true.

'I'm going to think a bit more about this over the weekend,' she said, 'and then, on Monday, I'll talk to you again, and I'll also talk to some people over in the Unit, and at the Local Education and Area Health Authorities, and we'll try and get something sorted out.'

'Thank you,' I said, and then, not being able to think of anything else, I said it again. 'Thank you'.

Mrs Causton found me in one of the Unit's corridors carrying my suitcase; she handed me two small glass bottles containing a small quantity of amitriptyline and Mogadon tablets.

'You'll need these for the weekend,' she said.

I put the suitcase on the floor, partially unzipped it, and dropped the bottles inside.

'There you are, Daniel,' Mrs Fox called from the end of the passage. 'It's time we were on our way.'

'Have a good weekend,' Mrs Causton said. 'See you on Monday.'

I retrieved my suitcase from the floor and ran to Mrs Fox, who then led the way out into the car park and to her white Renault 16.

As we drove along the A281, Mrs Fox reminded me that I mustn't worry my parents while I was at home, that I must ensure that I didn't demand all their attention and so deprive my younger brother.

'Most particularly,' Mrs Fox went on, 'I don't want to hear that you've upset your mum and dad by begging them to take you out of Oakdale. We're all working together on this, we're all agreed on what's best, so you won't gain anything by trying to divide us.'

Though unsettled by Mrs Fox's instructions, I smiled quietly to myself, remembering that Mrs Nakamura had a very different opinion, and that she was going to help me.

CHAPTER SIX

My mum dropped me back at the Unit on Monday morning. Despite my attempts to maintain some sort of outward impression of self-control, I cried desperately as she left.

Together with a few other returning kids, I joined the trail of those leaving the morning meeting to trudge over to the school.

As I dried my eyes, John Webber walked with me as we all made our way to the foyer and then through the set of doors leading outside. There was a curious attitude of restraint among all the kids as we walked through the play area towards the school building – not only was there a lack of the usual lively interactions between kids, there was barely any talking at all.

John asked me, in a noticeably hushed manner, if I'd had a good weekend, but it was obvious that there was something else on his mind.

'We've had some bad news,' he said, putting a hand on my shoulder. 'You'll hear all about it at school. I'm just warning you about it now so that you'll be ready.'

We filed into the school and through the passageway leading to Mr Baker's class; once there we all took up our usual places for assembly. This time the younger children, who usually went off with Miss Evesham, also joined us – some smaller chairs had been set out for them specially.

John, together with two other nurses, Robert King and Mrs Sampson, didn't head back to the Unit as they would normally have done; instead they came into assembly as well, and stood just inside the door to Mr Baker's classroom.

Standing at the front of the class – not sitting, as was typically the case – were members of the Oakdale School staff: Mrs Sutton, Mr Baker, Mrs Conway, Miss Evesham and Mrs Burrows, the secretary. But there was no Mrs Nakamura. I started to wonder if maybe she was ill, or had been called away unexpectedly on some important, and perhaps unpleasant, business. My heart sank, as I'd been anticipating my Monday morning French lesson with her, together with the possibility of further encouragement in connection with her plans to help me.

'Good morning, everyone,' Mrs Sutton announced rather morosely.

There was obvious uncertainty among the kids about how to respond. A few started to reply, hesitantly, 'Good morning, Mrs –' but their words petered out into silence.

'As I think most of you – probably *all* of you – now know,' Mrs Sutton began in a slow measured tone, 'on her way home after school on Friday, Mrs N. was in a serious car accident. She was taken to hospital in Brighton, but she died later on Friday evening.'

I stared at Mrs Sutton. Although I was aware of my heart pounding forcefully in my chest, I couldn't identify what else I was feeling. Powerful emotions flooded in on me, but I couldn't distinguish them from each other, and I couldn't properly understand them. I was also weighed down by the realisation that Mrs Nakamura had been dead for the whole weekend that had just passed, and I had been completely ignorant of it. And so, not knowing what to do with these sensations that beleaguered me, I just went on staring.

Mrs Sutton continued speaking, but I didn't hear anything she said. She may have led us in a prayer, but again, I didn't hear it.

At some point Mrs Sutton must have announced that we would sing a hymn, as Mrs Conway was now at the piano, and someone – Jennie Saunders, I guessed, as she was sitting next to me – had opened my hymnbook at Number 22, 'Beyond the mist and doubt of this uncertain day'. But all of this passed me by as though part of a mostly-forgotten dream.

No doubt the assembly came to an end at some point, but I wasn't conscious of it happening. I didn't notice the three nursing staff from the Unit leave, nor did I see all the other children and their teachers depart for their own classes. I saw nothing and I heard nothing. I may as well have been like Julie Wilson, heavily dosed-up on Largactil, I was so far removed from what was going on.

I spent the rest of that day, and much of that week, in a daze. I also found a sense of guilt creeping in upon me. I was sad at the passing of Mrs Nakamura, of course, but I also felt betrayed by her. She had been the only one to openly state that I should not be in Oakdale, and she had said she would talk to some people in the Local Education Authority and the Area Health Authority on my behalf. This was not now going to happen; Mrs Nakamura had broken her promise.

My sense of betrayal, and the guilt that went with having that sense, was especially heightened when Mrs Fox, the social worker, asked me to see her in her office on the following afternoon after school.

'Well,' Mrs Fox began, sitting to the side of her desk in exactly the same way as before, 'you haven't quite kept your side of the bargain, have you?'

80

Facing her from the same chair as on the previous occasion, I wasn't immediately sure what she meant. This uncertainty must have made me frown slightly, as she commented on my reaction.

'Don't give me that baffled look,' she said. 'You know what I mean. You promised that you wouldn't upset your mum and dad, but I'm told that when your mum tried to leave you here yesterday morning, you made a big fuss again.'

'I just cried a bit,' I said. 'I couldn't help it.'

'That's not good enough,' Mrs Fox went on. 'And more importantly, that's not the *only* thing you've done to upset your parents. Over the weekend you got them all worried about your bruises. You led them to think that you might be in some sort of danger here.'

'When they saw my bruises I *had* to tell them what happened,' I objected.

'But you *upset* them – *and* you lied about what it's like at Oakdale.'

'No,' I said, 'I only told the truth.'

'But you *did* upset them,' Mrs Fox insisted, 'and you promised you wouldn't do that.'

I looked down at the floor. 'I did my best,' I said shakily, 'but when they asked about my bruises, I couldn't lie to them.'

'Well,' Mr Fox went on, 'you'll just have to do better next weekend. But if we get a repeat of this kind of thing, that'll be your *last* weekend home until you've convinced us you can treat your family with proper consideration.'

I looked back up at Mrs Fox and decided to brave asking her about what Mrs Nakamura had said to me on Friday.

'Mrs N. said she was going to talk to some people about me this week,' I said tentatively. 'She said she was going to see how to get me back home and back to school quickly, and she was going to find out what sort of help I would need for that.'

'How dare you!' Mrs Fox exclaimed. 'Mrs N. has just died very tragically, and all you can do is think of yourself! And what's more, I don't believe for one second that Mrs N. would go ahead and do anything like that unless we'd all agreed it.'

I felt tears tracing their way down my cheeks as shame took possession of me – I should have known that now was not the right time to mention this.

'Quite frankly,' Mrs Fox ranted on, 'I am shocked at your disrespect. Well, let me tell you something, Daniel: this sort of thing is not going to get you out of Oakdale any quicker. Stop looking for shortcuts; the only way you'll get out of here is by showing us over a period of time that you can behave in an acceptable way – and that means keeping out of trouble and staying in good spirits.'

*   *   *

On the Friday afternoon of that week I was delivered home by minibus, as Jeff Knowles did the rounds of the villages and towns to the west of Oakdale where some of the children lived.

'See you on Monday,' he said, dropping me at my doorstep in Loxton. I looked back, as my mum opened our front door, and saw some of the other kids waving me goodbye from the Transit.

Fortunately, once back at the Unit for the subsequent week, there was no recurrence of my last difficult confrontation with Mrs Fox. At first I assumed that, this time, there had been no bad reports of my weekend conduct to reach her. But by the middle of the week I realised there was another matter that may have been preoccupying her. On Tuesday, the Prime Minister, Harold Wilson, had unexpectedly announced his resignation, and this was *the* hot topic of conversation among several members of staff – some of them expending far more energy on it than on the kids supposedly in their care.

In the remaining weeks leading up to my case conference in early April, and the Easter holidays which followed soon after, two significant things happened. The first of these was Sarah Dawes being relieved of her responsibilities as my key worker on Mr Taylor's shift – though there was no equivalent change on Mrs Causton's shift. The second was my developing friendship with Andrew Ramsey.

Sarah, as always, was being a great support to me, and – with Mr Taylor's shift covering mornings again – she was one of the Unit staff accompanying us on Thursday's school trip to the swimming baths.

By now I was used to seeing Julie Wilson confined to the shallow end, thanks to the effects of Largactil; I was used to Nigel Green being under the firm control of two male members of staff; and I was even used to the terrible wasted appearance of Jane Sparrow. And so, for this brief period on Thursday morning, I could leave behind the wretchedness of life in the Unit, together with my mournful thoughts about Mrs Nakamura, and simply swim. I could challenge Gary Jameson to races across the width of the pool, which I always won, and I could be stretched by the superior swimming ability of Donna Bennett – and of Sarah.

Indeed, Sarah and I spent quite a bit of time together in the pool. Some of this was in the company of other children, but there were also occasions when it was just the two of us. Something of the experience of a fortnight ago returned as I found myself splashing and laughing in her presence, and again there were times when she apparently forgot herself and embraced me vigorously. I now felt no awkwardness at this intimacy, but I did feel awkward at it being seen by the other Oakdale staff, especially Jeff Knowles.

But whereas Jeff had intervened the last time I'd been at the pool with Sarah, calling her away to mind Julie, this time he left us undisturbed. However, I was very aware that he was watching. Every time I glanced over to where he was, tending to Nigel, I found my gaze meeting his. I was sure that Sarah must have noticed his attention too, but she seemed almost defiant in the way she ignored it.

As we made our way back to the Unit in the minibus, I sat next to Andrew, while from time to time Sarah would smile at me from her place a few seats further forward. Despite our destination, I felt moderately content and, to my own surprise, I even joined in with most of the others in singling along to the radio when it played 'I Love to Love' – though I had reached the age when my voice was starting to change, so I struggled with the falsetto phrases.

Although I felt an unsurprising sense of despondency in returning to the Unit, at least some small part of the delight and playfulness of the morning's swimming remained with me as I sat down to lunch. What I didn't know then, as Sarah joined Gary Jameson, Sean Townsend and me at our table, was that this would be the last meal we would share in her immediate presence.

I learnt of the change in Sarah Dawes's responsibilities in the afternoon after school, by which time she had been off duty for a couple of hours.

Having entered the dining room with all the other kids at just after half-past three, I obtained an orange squash and sat down with Andrew and Gary at one of the tables. Once we had finished our drinks we got up to leave. My intention was to go to the boys' dormitory and pack my bag for the weekend, but as I started for the door, Miss Bishop, the nursing officer, came over.

'Daniel,' she said, 'I'd like a quick word with you.' She indicated to Andrew and Gary that they should carry on without me.

It was a little unusual for Miss Bishop to approach one of the kids in this way. With the exception of exchanges within the morning meeting, she normally left all direct dealings with the children to others.

'Would you sit back down for a moment?' she said.

I resumed my seat while she placed herself in the chair opposite me.

'I've decided to make some changes to your oversight,' she explained. 'When Mr Taylor's shift is on, you will no longer come under the care of Sarah Dawes; Jeff Knowles will be looking after you from now on.'

The news hit me like a giant fist, leaving me momentarily stunned.

'Why?' I asked, rather unsteadily.

'Because reports have come to me that you've been trying to wheedle your way into Sarah's affections,' she said frostily. 'You've been preying on her good nature, perhaps trying to manipulate her into taking your side against ours.'

I was utterly shocked. 'What?'

'I think you understand me,' she said. 'I will *not* have you attempting to ingratiate yourself with my staff. For that reason, I've decided a firmer hand is necessary, and so that's why I've appointed Jeff as your key worker.'

Miss Bishop stood up and walked away, leaving me devastated. I tried to maintain my mask of self-control, but it just wasn't possible. And so, trying very hard to suppress my sobbing, I walked as briskly as I could to the dorm, where, once again, I flung myself onto my bed, burying my head in the pillow.

In the space of less than a fortnight I had lost the only two adults at Oakdale whom I completely trusted; first Mrs Nakamura, and now Sarah. It was true that there were others here who were friendly and relatively sympathetic – like John Webber – but in every case my faith in them was conditional; none of them inspired my full confidence. With dread I realised that, unable to call upon any real ally from among the staff, I now had to rely almost entirely on my own resources to survive my day-to-day existence at Oakdale.

I consoled myself with the knowledge that by this time tomorrow I would be on my way home once again, that for three nights and two whole days I would be free of this ongoing trauma. And so I dragged myself up from the bed, and began the simple task of packing my suitcase.

'Wake up! Wake up!' came the voices of Mike Kirby and Jeff Knowles, rousing the boys' dormitory to wakefulness.

Still having to face the morning rather muzzy-headed – though less so now that I was becoming more tolerant of my medication – I hauled myself to a sitting position and swung my legs out of the bed.

As I stood up, Jeff approached me.

'Daniel,' he said, 'for my sins, I'm now your key worker on Mr Taylor's shift.'

'I know,' I replied bleakly. 'Miss Bishop told me.'

'Well, I'm no happier about it than you are,' he said. 'Just make sure you don't give me any trouble. All right?'

'All right,' I echoed as he strode off to check on some of the other boys.

This didn't seem like a very promising start to the new arrangement, and the general atmosphere at our table over breakfast was rather tense as a result of Jeff's presence.

While queuing for my cereal, I cast an eye around the dining room to see where Sarah Dawes was, and I saw that she was currently sitting with Jane Sparrow, Donna Bennett and Lisa Clayton, at their table. She seemed to notice straight away that I was looking in her direction, as she glanced up and gave me a sad smile.

Back at our table, we all – Jeff included – consumed our breakfasts quietly and efficiently without any real attempt at conversation. Although Jeff remained with Sean as they had their cigarettes afterwards, I got a definite impression that he was as relieved as the rest of us that the strain of breakfast was now over with.

Gary and I made our way to the dorm to start changing our bed linen. Once all the kids had completed this unnecessarily lengthy process, Gary ran off to do whatever it was he liked to do – something or other in the playroom, probably – while I remained in the dorm.

I decided to lie on my freshly-made bed and read – I was now working my way through an Edgar Rice Boroughs fantasy – but, as always in Oakdale, it was difficult to concentrate with everything that was going on around me.

Several kids were rummaging around in their lockers or talking noisily with each other. And Michael Davey, of course, had started his habitual playing of the T. Rex tape, the opening bars of 'Venus Loon' boring into my brain at the expense of the printed page before me.

Then, unexpectedly, Sarah came in and sat down next to me on my bed.

'I'm afraid I can only stay for a second,' she said, as I put my book to one side. 'I just wanted to say I'm so sorry about what's happened. You know it wasn't my choice, don't you?'

'Yes,' I answered, sitting myself up.

'I'm sure you'll find Jeff all right, though,' she continued, 'once you get used to him, and once he gets used to you.'

'Maybe,' I replied, unconvinced.

Standing up, she said, 'I've got to go now.'

She looked at me before turning to leave, holding the look as though there was something else she wanted to say. Then she took a step towards me and quickly kissed me on the forehead before making a very rapid exit.

As Sarah dashed out through the double-doors, Andrew came sauntering back in. He sat down on his bed, next to mine, facing me.

'Sarah not looking after you anymore, then?' he said.

'No,' I answered. 'It's Jeff now.'

'Bad luck!' he remarked. 'You'll be all right, though, Daniel. You've been here about four weeks now, so you probably won't be watched quite so closely for much longer.'

'Who is your key worker?' I asked.

'On this shift it's Mrs Hamilton, and on Mrs Causton's shift it's Michelle Newbold,' he said. 'They're both pretty good, actually – not that they watch me all the time anymore.'

I didn't really know Mrs Hamilton especially well, but Michelle had been one of the nurses who'd helped me after Nigel had beaten me up.

Further conversation was prevented as Mr Taylor came in and reminded us we only had five minutes before the morning meeting.

Andrew and I joined Michael and a couple of other boys as we straggled over to the TV room and found ourselves places to sit – Jeff calling out to me that I must sit next to him.

'Never mind, eh?' laughed Andrew, slapping me on the back as I went over to Jeff.

'What was that all about, Daniel?' Jeff asked me as I seated myself next to him.

'Nothing,' I replied dismissively.

Although, in truth, 'nothing' was a fairly reasonable comment, Jeff didn't look especially satisfied with my answer. Fortunately I was saved from having to provide further explanation by the arrival of Miss Bishop and the start of the meeting.

The meeting itself was rather disrupted by an incident arising from the behaviour of the ten-year-old Jonathan Hunter. Seated next to Miss Bishop, he had been generally fidgeting and kicking his legs in an irritating way. After a while, Miss Bishop responded. Slowly, and with exaggerated calmness, she took hold of Jonathan's arm and pulled him forcefully to the floor in front of her. This single, smooth action stunned him into silent inactivity. But Miss Bishop placed her fingers behind his ears and began applying pressure. His face contorted with discomfort and he began writhing and trying to resist.

'*You will learn to behave,*' Miss Bishop hissed at him as she seemingly applied even more pressure behind his ears.

I was shocked by what I saw, and I found myself swallowing hard. I also began to feel compelled to voice some objection, but I had no desire to draw attention to myself. Eventually, I couldn't stand it any longer, and I jumped to my feet, shaking.

'Stop it!' I yelled. 'You're *torturing* him!'

'Sit down and be quiet, Daniel,' Jeff said firmly.

'No, no,' Miss Bishop contradicted. 'Let Daniel speak.'

I hadn't expected this, but seeing that Miss Bishop was still causing Jonathan significant suffering, I accepted the implied invitation.

'This is wrong,' I said. I struggled to find the right word. 'It's *immoral.*'

I noticed that a number of the children in the meeting where obviously unconcerned about what was happening; they must have seen it all before. Perhaps even more worrying was the fact that many of them – following the lead of Sharon Gillan – groaned with impatience at my intervention.

By now, Jonathan has stopped trying to resist, and Miss Bishop had relieved some of the pressure from behind his ears.

'Well, then,' Miss Bishop said, 'if you've quite finished telling me how to do my job, Daniel, perhaps you would be so good as to sit down.'

With nothing more to say, I slumped back down into the foam chair.

The meeting returned to some sort of normality, Jonathan and I having completely quiesced, and once it was over, Jeff accompanied me over to school. He hardly said a word as he walked beside me among the throng of children processing out of the Unit, and he didn't even speak once we'd reached our destination, he just turned on his heal and left me there.

That school day brought to an end a second week without Mrs Nakamura. My understanding was that Mrs Sutton, as the most senior teacher, was supposed to be filling in for the head as best she could, but I somehow got the impression that Oakdale School was actually leaderless, and that the teaching staff just had to muddle by as best they could. This situation would continue for quite some time to come.

With this harrowing week now past, Mr Jones drove me and a handful of other children home in the Ford Transit, while I reflected on how frighteningly unstable and unpredictable my world had become.

'All the world's troubles are caused by adults,' Andrew was saying, as we worked together on a collage in the art room.

It was Monday afternoon, school was over for the day, and a few of us were taking the rare opportunity to use the art facilities. And with British Summer Time having started on Sunday, we were able to benefit from more daylight spilling in through the large windows.

Fridgerd Vogt was hovering nearby, as were Mike Kirby and Derek Ball – it having been decided, following the incident three weeks ago, that group art therapy required additional supervision.

Also engaged in various artistic endeavours were Jennie Saunders, Wendy Cole and a fourteen-year old boy called Ben Mitchell. They all listened intently – and sceptically – to Andrew's pontificating.

'Who is the cause of all wars?' Andrew asked rhetorically. 'Adults, of course.'

I wanted to point out that children didn't really have the means to wage war, but Andrew was ploughing on, leaving no space for interruption.

'And who causes all the pollution? It's adults, again.'

I could see Mike and Derek exchanging raised eyebrows, while Fridgerd smiled to herself.

'This world,' Andrew went on commandingly, 'would be a far better place if us kids were in charge.'

This provoked Mike and Derek to fits of laughter.

Andrew shot them an angry look. 'You think that isn't true?' he challenged as they guffawed. 'How could the world possibly be any worse?'

'But,' I said, managing to get a word in edgeways, 'we wouldn't know *how* to be in charge; we wouldn't know what to do. All the food would run out, the electricity would go off, there'd be no clean water –'

'But *they* don't know how to be in charge either,' he interrupted. 'Just look at the mess they've made of everything. And just look at how ruthless and violent they are. It was adults who bombed Hiroshima and Nagasaki – and it's adults here who are oppressing Julie by keeping her dosed-up on Largactil.'

'Hey!' Mike intervened. 'Hold on a minute. What we're doing is for Julie's own good.'

I saw my chance to ask the question that had been bothering me for some time. 'How come Julie is still all drugged up, but Nigel isn't? Julie didn't really hurt anyone when she –' I struggled to find the right words '– when she had her funny turn. But Nigel *beat me up.*'

'Daniel,' it was Derek who volunteered an explanation, 'I understand why you want to know why Julie and Nigel have been treated differently – of course I do – but it isn't really any of your business.'

'Of course it's his business.' It was Wendy who spoke up. 'He's the one who got hurt.'

'Look,' Derek continued, 'we have to take difficult decisions about these things, and there are things you won't know anything about that will *affect* our decisions. It's not just about whether anyone got hurt or not – there will be other reasons as well for what we decide.'

'*I'll* tell you why Julie and Nigel were treated differently, Daniel,' Wendy said. 'It's because Julie's a girl.'

'Oh, God, here we go,' moaned Ben.

'That's utter rubbish!' Mike declared.

'Is it?' Wendy said accusingly. 'I don't think so. If a boy behaves aggressively, you think that's pretty normal, even if you don't like it. But if a girl behaves in the same way, well, that's *unnatural* – and it has to be punished extra hard.'

'Mmm, that's probably right,' Jennie agreed.

'Julie is *not* being punished,' Mike answered back.

'No, no, of course not,' Wendy said sarcastically. 'It's just "a consequence of her actions".'

'I expect Wendy *is* right, you know,' Andrew commented to me.

Fridgerd stepped in swiftly at this point. 'Hey, everyone, you should be trying to get your feelings out in your art.'

'But this is not acceptable!' Mike complained. 'I will not stand here and have us accused of unfair discrimination.'

'Mike, perhaps *you'd* like to try expressing some of *your* feelings in artwork too,' Fridgerd suggested impishly.

Andrew and I sniggered, while Mike and Derek looked sheepish.

I continued working on the collage, which was becoming increasingly abstract with every new item we added to it. As I did so, it dawned on me that Andrew's bluster about the shortcomings of adults had a real point to it. He was only a few months older than me, and his words sounded completely ridiculous, but what he had done, I realised, had made an opening for a discussion on the disciplinary regime at Oakdale. While it was Wendy who came out with the revelation about sexual discrimination – which, for lack of a better explanation, I accepted – it was Andrew who had paved the way for it.

It was on a Wednesday, shortly after supper, that I had one of my more curious conversations with Andrew.

Someone was obviously listening to their radio in the quite room, as the sound of 'Save all Your Kisses for Me' was ringing out into the corridor. Andrew and I, keen to escape a song that was starting to become all-pervading, hurriedly made our way along the passage and through a set of doors into the hall. We seated ourselves on a couple of foam chairs near to some cupboards fixed to an end wall.

I'd had little cause to visit the hall previously; this was where they sometimes played music for the kids to dance to – usually a little later in the evening while I was in bed reading – but at the moment the hall was silent.

The cupboards were stuffed with old books and broken toys, and mounted in the wall just above one of the cupboards was a hatch – like the serving hatch in the dining room. I knew that behind the hatch was a secure room where they kept the medicine trolley, and I was to learn later that they also kept the record deck and amplifier there. Apparently, when a member of staff was available to play DJ, kids would shout their record requests through the hatch.

Andrew leant forward in his seat and poked around in one of the cupboards. With triumph he produced a scruffy-looking Bible.

'What are you doing?' I asked him. Knowing that Andrew wasn't remotely religious, I couldn't begin to guess what he was up to.

'Hold on a sec,' he answered, leafing through the tattered pages. 'Here,' he announced at last, 'look at this.'

He dragged his seat next to mine so that I could see the Bible over his shoulder.

He pointed out a passage from the Book of Ezekiel.

'What do you think all that's about?' he asked.

'I've no idea,' I answered, 'the language is so old-fashioned.'

'But what do you think the prophet is *seeing*?'

'A vision of some sort?' I wondered.

'I'll tell you what the prophet is seeing,' Andrew pronounced with great confidence. 'He's seeing extra-terrestrial creatures, and some sort of spacecraft.'

I wasn't sure whether Andrew was joking or serious, but I couldn't help but chuckle slightly.

'Don't you believe me?' Andrew said earnestly.

'Not really,' I replied. 'He's probably describing a dream or something.'

'A dream sent to him by God? Is that what you mean?'

'Maybe,' I said. 'I'm not sure.'

'What do you think is most likely?' he went on. 'Do you think some sort of all-powerful superbeing – God – would specially pick one particular man to have a strange dream? Or do you think that visitors from another planet may have landed and that Ezekiel just happened to be the man they came across?'

'When you put it like that,' I said, 'neither of those sounds very likely.'

'Well,' he said, 'I'm telling you that it was definitely extra-terrestrials that Ezekiel saw.

'A lot of serious research has been carried out on this by Erich von Däniken,' he went on. 'He's an expert on ancient writings, and he's found a lot of evidence for alien visits.'

Despite myself, I was captivated by what Andrew was saying.

'Look,' Andrew said, prodding a finger at the biblical text. 'He talks about the "appearance of the wheels" and "a wheel in the middle of a wheel". He describes it with incredible engineering detail. That *has* to be a spacecraft; it couldn't be anything else.'

'You're talking blasphemy!' came an irate voice from behind us.

While we had been talking, Robert King had walked in.

'What you have there,' Robert stated, standing over us purposefully, 'is a vision of God's glory. There are no spaceships, no aliens – it's a vision sent from God.'

'You're wrong,' Andrew contradicted him. 'Von Däniken has *proved* that Ezekiel saw visitors from outer space.'

'Von Däniken is a false prophet and a blasphemer,' Robert insisted.

'You're just ignorant,' Andrew said scornfully.

'No,' Robert defended himself, 'I just happen to be God-fearing – as *you* should be. Now, where did you find that Bible?'

'It was in the cupboard,' I replied.

'If you're not going to use it with proper respect, put it back,' he demanded. 'And I don't want to hear any more of this sacrilege – from *either* of you.'

Robert stormed out.

'Ignore him, Daniel,' Andrew said, 'he's an idiot.'

While I wasn't in the slightest bit convinced by Andrew's claim that alien visitation had been proven, I realised, once again, that he was probably trying to draw my attention to something quite serious – though I wasn't quite able to work out what it was. Whatever the case, there was certainly one thing he had said that would definitely have been very useful had I properly taken it in: he told me that I should ignore Robert. It would be some time before I finally recognised that Andrew had been absolutely right about this.

When the day of my case conference arrived, most members of staff were talking about James Callaghan, who following a ballot the previous day had become the new Prime Minister. As we all wandered into the TV room for the morning meeting, adult conversation seemed to be about nothing else.

'It could have been worse,' I heard Mrs Causton saying to Ted Trowbridge. 'It could have been Michael Foot.'

'It was very close, though, wasn't it?' Ted answered.

I also overheard Mr Jones saying to Michelle Newbold, 'If they had any decency, they'd let us have an election, then we could kick out those socialist fools.'

As I sat down next to John Webber, he turned to me and asked me if I was nervous about the case conference.

I said I was.

'Try not to let it worry you too much,' he said. 'I'll be there, speaking up for you when I can. And don't forget, we all want what's best for you.'

I thought to myself how much I wished Mrs Nakamura were still alive – if anyone could have been trusted to truly speak up for me, it would have been her.

'In any case,' John continued, 'things have definitely been improving lately, so hopefully we should be able to make a decision about when you can go home – but try not to get your hopes up though, just in case.'

'Why can't I be there?' I grumbled. 'It's not fair, all of you talking about me behind my back.'

'Unfortunately,' he said, 'you're too young to attend a case conference, but your mum and dad will be there for you. Look, you really mustn't worry about this; I'm sure everything will work out for the best.'

'But what about –' I didn't get to say any more as Miss Bishop had begun the meeting.

The meeting was followed by a very frustrating morning at school. I was completely unable to concentrate, as I was so absorbed by thoughts of the case conference now in progress. And when we all went back over to the Unit at breaktime, it was obvious that a handful of staff – including Miss Bishop, Mrs Fox and John Webber – were absent from the dining room. And peering through a window, I could see in the middle distance the familiar sight of my parents' Morris 1100 in the car park. My mum and dad, and who knows how many other people, were ensconced in an unknown corner of Oakdale making decisions about me. I was worried sick.

My sense of anxiety was heightened still further when I returned to the dining room again at lunchtime. I could see that my parents' car was still in the car park, and several members of staff were still missing.

'They're taking a very long time this morning,' I overheard Mr Jones commenting through the door to the kitchen. 'I suppose we'd better dish up their lunches now and then warm 'em up again when they finally come in.'

It felt very odd with just Gary, Sean and I sitting at our table without a staff member – John, of course, being one of the people who would have to make do with a reheated lunch.

John's absence freed Gary and Sean to laugh, joke and talk about various subjects that wouldn't normally get discussed at the meal table. Among their topics of conversation were sexual practices, including homosexual practices – things I'd never heard of until coming to Oakdale. This made me realise how much this place had changed me; because, as well as wanting to go home, I also wanted to return to my previous state of naïvety.

We were just making a start on our dessert course – sponge and custard – when the missing members of staff came in: Miss Bishop, Mrs Fox, Dr Rajasimha, Mrs Causton and John Webber, to name about half of them.

I glanced towards the windows, and saw that my parents' car had now gone – they had left without even seeing me – and this filled me with a terrible sense of foreboding as John approached our table.

'I'll tell you all about it after lunch,' John told me.

Mr Jones brought John a plate of rather dried-out food, which he immediately began tackling.

'Why can't you tell me now?' I said fretfully.

'Because we could do with finding a quiet little spot somewhere,' he said, 'so that we can talk about it properly. I'm sorry, Daniel, but you'll just have to be patient a little longer.'

I really was starting to feel quite ill – there were pains in my stomach from where my muscles had become so knotted, and I was feeling light-headed and giddy.

With my case conference having caused several staff members to start their meals late, there was a knock-on delay to Mrs Causton and Robert King going out to collect the medicine trolley. And so there was no relief in sight to my agony, which was definitely physical as well as mental.

It was nearly a quarter past one when we were told we could leave our tables, leaving very little time before school and the end of the shift. Fortunately, John went without his usual after-lunch cigarette, and led me out to the quiet room – which he had to unlock.

Once inside, he shut the door and we both sat ourselves down on foam chairs.

'Daniel,' he began at last, 'I'm very sorry, but you will be staying with us a bit longer. We've decided that you're not yet ready to go home.'

CHAPTER SEVEN

'Daniel,' John Webber was saying, as we sat there in the quiet room, 'you will leave Oakdale eventually – just not quite yet.'

I was now crying feverishly. Although I had feared the worst – and the worst had indeed happened – hearing it spelt out so plainly was unbearable.

'Try not to upset yourself, Daniel,' John said. 'It's really not as bad as all that.'

'But,' I blubbered, 'Dr Rajasimha told me I'd only be here for six weeks. It's *been* six weeks now – I should be going home.'

'He probably said you'd be here for six weeks *initially*, or something like that.'

I shook my head as I continued to whimper.

'Look, Daniel,' John spoke calmly, 'you've been doing quite a bit better lately, and we're all very pleased with your progress. But there are a few things that need to happen, a few things we need to get sorted out, before you can leave us for good.'

'Like what?' I managed to splutter.

'Well,' he hesitated, 'I can't really say too much about it at the moment, but believe me, we are working very hard to get everything organised for you. In the meantime, all you have to do is carry on the good work: stay positive, join in with the other kids, and make sure you don't behave in a way that gets you the wrong sort of attention.'

I continued sobbing and shaking my head. 'All I want to do is to go back home and back to my friends.'

'Don't forget, Daniel,' he said, 'it's nearly the Easter holidays. We've agreed that you can spend the entire break with your family – that's *two whole weeks* you'll have away from Oakdale. Now that's got to be good news, hasn't it?'

There was a knock at the door, and then it opened to admit Jeff Knowles.

'Hello, John,' he said, before turning to me. 'Daniel, you're late for school. Come on, let's get moving.'

'Go on, Daniel,' John said calmly. 'I'll see you tomorrow.'

I stood up and followed Jeff out of the room, still weeping.

As we walked along the empty corridor towards the foyer – the other kids were already back in school – I saw Sarah Dawes coming towards us. She stopped as she drew level with us, and reached out to give my arm a gentle squeeze.

'I heard about the case conference,' she said. 'I'm very sorry, Daniel. I know how upset you must be. I wish I could –'

'Sarah, I need to get him over to school,' Jeff said firmly. 'He's late already.'

The Easter holidays went by very quickly, and as soon as they were over my mum delivered me back to Oakdale in the usual way – and, as she left me, I cried in the usual way.

During the break a very odd feeling had started to creep up on me. I had the sense that something significant was brewing, but I didn't know what it was. But I was sure that, whatever it might turn out to be, it would have a major impact on me. There was a big change on the way. But first I was to encounter some lesser changes.

The first of these changes, which occurred upon my return to Oakdale, was an alteration in my medication. This came without any warning. On my first day back, following lunch, Sarah Dawes called me up to the medicine trolley. She was assisting Mr Taylor, who informed me that my prescription had been changed. He dropped a small capsule into my hand from a 30ml medicine cup.

'What this?' I asked.

'Dr Rajasimha has prescribed dothiepin – or Prothiaden, to use the trade name,' Mr Taylor said. 'It's to be taken three times daily.'

I wondered why Dr Rajasimha would have done this without even having seen me. Indeed, I hadn't had a single meeting with him since I'd been at Oakdale.

'Come on, Daniel,' Mr Taylor said, obviously noticing my hesitation. 'Take it.'

I swallowed it down, though I did so rather grudgingly, given that my prescription had been changed without consultation.

There was also another change in my medication that occurred, though this change was only temporary and, moreover, it was definitely accidental. From my point-of-view, however, it was a very welcome change. For three weeks it was to be a feature of Monday evenings that I would completely avoid receiving one night's dose of Mogadon. Rather oddly, this came about as a by-product of something Andrew did.

Shortly before we all went into supper on our first Monday back, Andrew came in to the dorm to find me on my bed reading.

'*Star Trek*'s back on tonight,' he said.

'What time?' I asked.

'Twenty past seven.'

'Andrew, we'll only see the first ten minutes of it before we have to come back here for inspection,' I said.

'No,' he answered, 'it's all right. I've had a word with Miss Bishop, and she says we can watch it just so long as we go straight to the dorm as soon as it's over.'

I knew very well that Andrew had a very confident and persuasive manner, but I just couldn't comprehend how he had managed to convince Miss Bishop to suspend one of her pet rulings just so that he could watch a TV programme. But sure enough, at twenty past seven, Andrew Ramsey, Gary Jameson, Michael Davey and I were in the TV room as *Star Trek* commenced.

After it had been running for a few minutes, Mr Jones poked his head round the door.

'Come on, you lot,' he said, 'you need to get yourselves to the boys' dormitory.'

'It's all right, Mr Jones,' Andrew said with great self-assurance. 'Miss Bishop said we could report to the dorm after *Star Trek*.'

Mr Jones didn't look convinced. 'I will check,' he said, 'and if I find you're lying, I'll be back in just a moment to drag you all there personally. And believe me, you'll wish you'd never been born.'

As Mr Jones disappeared, I found myself anxiously awaiting his return – but he never came. And when we all finally made our way to the dorm at ten past eight, the nighttime meds had already been dispensed.

While I was sure that notes must have been left for the night staff indicating who had received medication and who hadn't, no one on duty that night – not Mr Barry, Mr Köhler, Carrie Hancock, nor anyone else – bothered to correct the omission. I was therefore quietly pleased that for the first time in about two months I was able to go to sleep without chemical aid. And, more significantly, I awoke on Tuesday morning feeling marginally more alert than on any other morning since being admitted to Oakdale.

The very slightly improved attentiveness that accompanied my more wakeful state proved to be a bit of a mixed blessing. That Tuesday morning, Mike Kirby took Andrew, Sean, Gary and myself out of school for a short while so that we could go over to the main building for a dental check-up.

The walk over to St Anselm's was actually quite pleasant, as we made our way along a broad pathway edged by greenery, with some impressive oak trees visible in the middle-distance. We passed the modestly spired hospital chapel and some well-kept flower beds before reaching the granite façade of the main entrance. Upon going in, however, the atmosphere changed. I immediately noticed the smell of ammonia, which seemed far more overpowering than the odour of disinfectant in Oakdale. But what seemed truly horrific, as we made our way through the corridors, were the distant echoes of evident distress.

'What is all that screaming about?' I asked.

'Don't worry about it,' Mike said. 'Some of the patients here are extremely disturbed; they can't help themselves.'

As we continued on towards the dental surgery, we passed a number of vacant-looking adult patients who seemed to be aimlessly wandering the corridors, many still in their night clothes.

'This place is awful,' I murmured.

'It's best not to take any notice,' Andrew commented. 'We've just got to get to the dentist's, and then get out again.'

Indeed, once the check-up was done, it was an enormous relief to get back out into the fresh air.

On the return journey to the Unit, I noted how incongruous it was that the striking nineteenth century architecture of St Anselm's, surrounded by its pleasant flora, could seemingly house a concealed world of torment.

Another change that came with my return following Easter was the withdrawal of special oversight from my key workers. Apart from the fact that I was now free of that occasional sense of being watched very closely, the most obvious difference was that, at meal times, there was a succession of staff members joining Gary Jameson, Sean Townsend and myself at our table.

This coincided with me losing my humble status as Oakdale's newest admission. There was a new arrival, a 13-year old boy called Jeremy Newton. He appeared as soon as a space became available at the Unit as a result of Ben Mitchell being discharged.

I envied Ben, of course, now that he had been returned back to his home and school, but I was also fascinated to see, from an observer's perspective, how a new child was treated. I witnessed how Jeremy was carefully supervised by his key workers, and how this supervision was going on even when he probably wasn't aware of it. And so I realised that when *I* first arrived at the Unit, John Webber and Sarah Dawes must have been constantly following me, carefully monitoring every single thing I said and did. Even though I was sure I could trust Sarah absolutely – and John didn't seem too bad either – this realisation was a little disconcerting.

It was at teatime one afternoon, after the school day had ended, that

Andrew, Gary and I sat and chatted with Jeremy in the dining room. Remembering what my experience was like as a new kid in Oakdale, I was more than willing to be sympathetic towards Jeremy.

'So, where do you live?' Andrew asked him.

'Charminster, in Dorset,' he answered, puffing on a cigarette.

'That must be *miles* away!' I exclaimed. 'Why have they sent you *here*?'

'There aren't many units around like this,' he answered. 'I was supposed to be going to one in Somerset, but it was full up.'

'Yes, that's right,' Andrew commented. 'My dad says there are only about four or five units like this in the whole country. There's that one in Somerset, and another one in Lancaster, and I don't know where the others are.'

'What are you in for?' Gary asked, probably a bit more directly than either Andrew or I would have.

'I hate school,' Jeremy answered matter-of-factly. 'I keep bunking off. They reckon I've got "school phobia" or something. But I don't care. They're all bastards. They can think what they like.'

'That's exactly the right attitude,' Andrew said. 'I told Daniel when he first came here that if anyone gave him any trouble, he should just verbally kick 'em in the teeth. I can see I don't need to tell *you* that.'

'No, you bloody well don't,' Jeremy said hotly. 'If anyone gives *me* any trouble, I'll do more than *verbally* kick 'em in the teeth – I'll smash their fucking heads in!'

I realised, not so much from what Jeremy said, but from the force with which he had said it, that he didn't really need my sympathy, and that like Nigel he was probably best avoided.

And there were yet other things that were changing too. As April drew to a close and we moved into May, temperatures began to rise quite noticeably. This was an early start to what would turn out to be an unusually long, hot summer. With 'Save all Your Kisses for Me' and 'Fernando' constantly wafting through the balmy air, Oakdale took on a rather different character to that of the late winter when I had arrived.   My first two weekends at home following Easter also took on a rather different character – though this seemed to have less to do with the weather, and more to do plans starting to be enacted.

Under the pretext of getting the house organised now that it was spring, I had been asked by my parents to go through every item in my bedroom and decide what could be discarded. My mum and dad were also helping Mark do the same in his room, as well as clearing out many of their own, now unwanted, possessions.

'I have no idea what's going on,' I told Andrew one afternoon as we sat outside in the asphalted play area.

A few kids – Jonathan Hunter and Lisa Clayton, as well as Gary and a few others – were running about with rackets and playing some approximation of tennis. Andrew, myself and Mrs Hamilton, meanwhile, sat on the ground propped up against a wall.

'It's probably just a spring clean,' Andrew said.

'Well, we've never done one before,' I replied. 'At least, we haven't done one like this.'

'Daniel, it's good to have a clear out every so often,' Mrs Hamilton said, 'especially if yours is one of those families that tends to hoard loads of junk.'

'But I don't think we *do* hoard loads of junk,' I reasoned. 'My mum always keeps the house very tidy. I just don't understand why we're getting rid of all this stuff.'

'You worry far too much, Daniel,' Mrs Hamilton smiled.

'Yeah,' agreed Andrew. 'It's probably nothing. Adults do some pretty odd things sometimes – it's best not to let it bother you.'

Mrs Hamilton laughed. 'Andrew, just you wait till you have kids – they'll probably think everything *you* do is odd too!'

I didn't have very long to wait until I found out what was really going on. It was a Friday afternoon after school, and I was expecting to board the minibus to be driven home by Mr Jones. But as I stood in the car park, waiting in line to step onto the Ford Transit, Mrs Fox, the social worker, suddenly came rushing over.

'Daniel,' she called as she drew nearer, 'I'll be taking you home this week. Come with me.'

She turned around and led me away from the minibus queue towards her Renault 16.

Some minutes after we had left the Unit, I was puzzled to see that she wasn't taking the normal route to Loxton. Instead of continuing on the A281 after Horsham, she left the main road and drove through the town using a number of local roads. Soon we drew into a council housing estate, and she pulled up outside a small semi-detached house in Granary Way.

'Welcome to your new home,' she said as she shut the engine off.

I sat there in the passenger seat feeling thoroughly shocked. What had happened? I couldn't believe that my parents would have moved home without telling me, but that would certainly explain the 'spring cleaning' of recent weeks. The only other explanation I could think of was that the powers-that-be at Oakdale had decided to have me fostered by another family.

100

But if that was the case, it was still incredible that no one had thought to tell me about it. But neither of these possibilities seemed likely, let alone satisfactory. So faced with the unknown, I found my heart racing and my hands trembling as the tears started to flow.

'Daniel,' Mrs Fox said sternly, 'I hope you're not going to give your mum and dad any trouble. They've had a very hard week getting things ready for you. This is supposed to be a nice surprise, so when we go in, I want you to be properly grateful.'

I returned to Oakdale on Monday morning feeling numb. I was so dismayed after the weekend that I even started to question if what I had experienced was real. Had I really moved home without any warning, or had it just been a dream?

That same day, after school, Mrs Fox called me into her office once again. Unfortunately, this meant I had to miss a group art therapy session with Fridgerd Vogt, but with more pressing issues to be discussed, I passed on the session willingly.

We both adopted our customary positions: Mrs Fox seated to the side of her desk, and me facing her from across the room.

'Do you like your new home, Daniel?' she asked.

'I don't know why we've moved,' I said. 'I want to go back to Loxton.'

Mrs Fox sighed in apparent irritation. 'Daniel, we've all worked very hard to do the best for you,' she said. 'We explained to your mum and dad that it would be best for everyone if you all had a new start. And so we helped get you on the waiting list for a council house in Horsham, and we managed to pull a few strings to get you to the top of the list.'

I stared, lost for words.

'Everything will be so much better now,' she continued. 'Your dad won't have such a long journey to work, and the rent will be cheaper, so your mum and dad will have more money to spare. And after you leave Oakdale you'll be able to make a fresh start in a new school; you'll be able to leave all the problems you had Worthing Road behind you.'

'But I don't *want* to go to a new school,' I complained. 'I want to go back to Worthing Road and all my friends.'

'You'll be able to make *new* friends,' Mrs Fox said.

'My old friends and my teachers are expecting me back,' I argued.

'No, they're not,' she countered. 'We don't even know that Worthing Road would have been *willing* to have you back.'

My mouth hung open as I tried to take in the meaning of her words. Was she suggesting that I was such a problem that Worthing Road didn't want me?

'You are not going back,' she stressed. 'Besides, would you *really* want to go back there knowing everyone will tease you because you've been to Oakdale? They'll say you're mental, call you a nutter, and things like that. Wouldn't it be far better to start anew somewhere different where no one knows about the problems you've had?'

'Other kids go back to their old schools,' I remarked, 'just like Ben did.'

'Other kids aren't as lucky as you,' she replied.

I was shaking my head in a mixture of incredulity and resentment. Not only hadn't I had any say in the matter of moving, I hadn't even been allowed to know anything about it until it was too late.

'Daniel,' Mrs Fox said, 'you really *must* cheer up. This is a *good* thing. It means we're well on the way to sorting things out so that you can go home.'

'But I *can't* go home,' I said bitterly, as tears welled up in my eyes. 'You've made my parents move *away* from home. I can't *ever* go back home now.'

'Stop being so silly!' she said crossly. 'Your home is in Horsham now; it's a *nice* home, and we're going to get you into a nice school.'

The following Monday afternoon I was back in the art room. But things were rather different from all my previous visits here: there was an unusually large number of kids in the room, and apart from Jennie Saunders and Sharon Gillan, they were all boys; there was also a greater staff presence, a presence consisting entirely of younger male nurses.

The reason for this was a student art therapist on placement at Oakdale. Fridgerd Vogt introduced her to us as Judith Harrison, and told us that Judith would be with us for a few weeks, and that as well as being in the art room for group therapy on Monday afternoons, she would also be working with Bridget Fitzpatrick, the occupational therapist, in the hideout. I'd never actually been in the hideout, but I understood that this was somewhere a number of kids would visit in the afternoons after school, presumably to undergo occupational therapy (whatever that was).

Judith was an obviously attractive young woman – aged only nineteen, as I later discovered – who presented herself in a way that very much emphasised her already conspicuous features. Her voluminous blonde hair fell blithely about her carefully made-up face, gently resting on the shoulders of her tight-fitting pink t-shirt. Her t-shirt itself was tucked into an equally tight-fitting pair of dark blue jeans, flared at the bottom to reveal black leather high-heeled boots. She might possibly have been described as slightly plump, but this characteristic was smoothly constrained by the tension in her clothing. And if all this wasn't enough, she was wearing an extremely aromatic perfume which seemed to scatter in the air with her every movement.

She held all but the youngest of the boys absolutely spellbound. The same was true of the male staff: John Webber, Colin Goodman, Sam Laine and Julian Perry – all of them were regarding her with enthralled interest. Fridgerd, however, appeared to be eying her with suspicion – and not without good reason, for Judith was passing among us, ostensibly examining our artwork, in a bizarrely provocative way.

I was sitting with Jennie, and we were both making an attempt at modelling in clay. Judith came over to us, knelt down and placed an arm around my shoulders. I couldn't help but inhale her heady aroma as she complimented me on my rather dubious artistic endeavour.

'That's fantastic, Daniel!' she gushed, after asking my name. 'You must have really strong and sensitive hands – ooh, I see that you have.'

I couldn't think of any comment to make in return, as I was so staggered by the way she was treating me.

She unhurriedly withdrew her arm from my shoulders, faintly brushing her fingers across the back of my neck, before moving on to look at what Clester Henry was doing.

'Ooh,' Jennie mimicked in a soft voice, too quiet for Judith to hear, 'what strong and sensitive hands you have!'

Jennie's disapproving humour snapped me out of my trance and made me giggle.

'She completely ignored me,' Jennie grumbled. 'I hope you noticed that.'

'Yes,' I said, still giggling slightly,

Judith continued to move from one boy to another, bypassing the small number of girls. She raved about each of the boys' work and made flirtatious comments about their personal qualities, whether those qualities were real or invented by her. All the boys responded with looks of lustful adoration, often mixed with bafflement, and it seemed to me that she was thriving on the attention she was getting.

At one point Mr Jones entered the art room. I thought for a moment that he was going to join the ranks of Judith's awestruck admirers, but instead he cast his eyes around the room, observing the way Judith was conducting herself and the general male reaction to it. He then muttered irritably under his breath and stalked out again.

By now, Judith was giving her attention to Nigel Green, and as she dallied with him I noticed an expression on his face that sent a chill through me. While his face betrayed a look that was lustful, as with the other boys, it wasn't *adoring* like the others. I was too young and inexperienced to guess what this look might mean, but it frightened me.

*   *   *

That evening, Andrew, Gary, Jennie and I – among others – sat in front of *Star Trek*, enjoying the weekly relaxation of the usual nighttime inspection rule. Indeed, *Star Trek* had grown dramatically in popularity since Andrew had first negotiated an easing of Miss Bishop's decree. As there were so many kids now in the TV room it would obviously have been foolish to leave us unattended, and tonight it was Robert King who had the job of sitting with us until the night shift came on duty.

It amused me that there were now so many kids who, on Monday nights, were managing to avoid the inspection routine. Unfortunately, none of us were able to avoid our Monday night doses of Mogadon anymore – with so many of us not returning to the dormitories until ten past eight, the night staff had decided that they would dispense our meds then.

Some of the boys were more interested in discussing Judith Harrison than in watching the television, and Andrew and myself – though just as interested in Judith as anyone else – repeatedly demanded that they shut up so that we could hear the TV. Once Robert had told them to be quiet, they continued their chatter in whispers, but still occasional comments about Judith's various attributes would reach my ears.

After *Star Trek* had finished, Mr Köhler – who had relieved Robert shortly before eight o'clock – supervised us as we made our way to the dormitories. While *en route* Jennie made a few scathing comments to me about Judith and the male response she was generating.

'You boys are pathetic,' she said. 'She's not really interested in you at all. Can't you see that she's getting off on all the attention?'

'Yes, of course,' I agreed.

'So what if she's getting off on the attention?' Andrew chipped in. 'We enjoy giving it to her – the attention, I mean.'

Andrew and I gave in to a fit of immature laughter, and Jennie tetchily quickened her pace, leaving us behind.

Judith continued to be the topic of discussion the following day at the morning meeting.

As always, we were all seated in a large circle in the TV room as Miss Bishop directed the proceedings.

'Judith Harrison, the student art therapist, began a two-week placement with us yesterday,' Miss Bishop said. 'How many of you were with her in the art room on Monday afternoon?'

A sprinkling of girls and nearly all the boys raised their hands.

'Gosh,' Miss Bishop remarked, 'that's quite a lot of you then. How did you get on with her?'

A number of the boys smirked at each other, but it was Wendy Cole, the eldest of the kids, who spoke up.

'She's hopeless,' Wendy complained. 'She's no use at all. All she does is flirt with the boys – she just wants to be the centre of attention. If any of us behaved like that you'd put us in the punishment room.'

'That's not true,' Clester objected. 'She's really good. She really encouraged me with my painting.'

There was some chuckling and several murmurs of agreement from a number of the boys.

'Wendy's right,' Jennie said. 'Judith's nothing but a tart. She's just –'

'Jennie!' Miss Bishop interrupted heatedly. 'Judith is a member of staff, even if only temporarily, and you will treat her with respect.'

'Judith's certainly made an impact,' Sarah Dawes said. 'I can't wait to meet her.'

There were a few more giggles from around the room, and from nearby I heard Michael comment under his breath that Sarah must be on the lookout for a new girlfriend. Although I had had my eyes opened to many things since coming to the Unit, I was still too unworldly to know what he was talking about, and so I didn't join in with the roars of laughter from the other kids near him.

Sarah looked embarrassed, but attention was drawn away from her as Miss Bishop quickly regained control of the meeting.

'That's enough!' she declared.

Order was restored – albeit only for a brief moment – and so Miss Bishop continued.

'Now,' she said, 'I'm sure you'll all be interested to know that Judith will be with us again this afternoon, all day tomorrow and on Friday morning. Bridget can probably give us a few more details.'

'Yes,' Bridget Fitzpatrick confirmed. 'Judith will be conducting some individual art therapy sessions in the hideout and over in the school. And for anyone who's here at the weekend, she'll also be coming in on Saturday, as well as being in for some more sessions the following week. There will be a list going round at breaktime this morning, so if you're interested, put your name down.'

This information was greeted with a growing clamour of palpable excitement from many of the boys, accompanied by numerous enthusiastic – and some lewd – comments.

'All right, all right!' Miss Bishop hollered. 'Be quiet!'

The hubbub subsided and, as it was almost half-past nine, we were sent on our way to school.

*   *   *

For the remainder of the week it seemed that no one wanted to talk about anything other than Judith Harrison. And although I was starting to get used to hearing fairly colourful descriptions of imagined activities involving her, I was horrified and sickened at what Nigel had to say.

It was Thursday evening and we had all undergone the regular nighttime inspection. Mr Barry had come in and given us permission to leave the dorm if we wanted to, but as usual, I had chosen to lie on my bed and read. Andrew, Michael, Clester and Nigel remained in the dorm for a few minutes after Mr Barry had left. That was when Nigel started crowing about what he intended to do with Judith.

It was no good trying to focus on my book, so I put it back in my locker and just lay there listening.

'She's here at the weekend,' Nigel said, 'and I'll get her on her own, 'cause there won't be enough of those bastards around to stop me.'

He carried on with a very graphic account of his notional plans.

Clester, Michael and Andrew all laughed at Nigel.

'I mean it,' Nigel insisted. 'I'm fucking well gonna do it.'

'There's no way she'll let you,' Clester said. 'She might be a trollop, but she's still a member of staff.'

'I don't care if she fucking lets me or not,' Nigel bridled. 'I'm gonna do it to her anyway.'

The others' laughter now sounded nervous, but obviously angered by this laughter, Nigel stormed out of the dorm.

It wasn't long before Clester and Michael also left, and once they were gone I asked Andrew if there was any chance that Nigel really would do what he said.

'Nah,' Andrew said, 'he won't get a chance. Whoever's on duty will keep an eye on him – they all know what he's like.'

'Maybe,' I said uncertainly, 'but when I was here for a weekend and he beat me up, it was ages before Mr Jones and Robert came to get him off me. He's really vicious – he might have *killed* me if they hadn't got to me in time.'

'Stop worrying,' Andrew said. 'It'll be all right. Some of the staff here may be complete gits, but they're not stupid – well, not *all* of them, anyway. Judith'll be all right.'

Andrew then meandered out of the dorm, leaving me to return to my book, an Arthur C Clarke novel that he'd recommended to me. But as always in the Unit, I was unable to concentrate.

I was still desperately worried on Friday morning. So much so that, after breakfast, I tracked down Mr Taylor and attempted to share my concerns with him.

I cornered him in the corridor near the playroom.

'Mr Taylor, I need to talk to you,' I said.

'What is it, Daniel?' he answered with irritation.

'It's about Judith Harrison and –'

'Not you as well,' he sighed. 'You're far too young for her, so just leave her alone.'

'That's not what I mean,' I said in frustration. 'It's Nigel –'

Mr Taylor started walking away from me. 'I'm not interested, Daniel,' he said. 'I've got more important things to do.'

Having failed with Mr Taylor, I reasoned that if anyone was going to listen to me, it would be Sarah Dawes, but by the time I found her, the morning meeting was about to start, so I didn't get a chance to say anything to her either.

As I entered the dining room at breaktime, I caught sight of Judith herself, sitting at one of the tables smoking and drinking coffee while surrounded by small group of rather animated boys.

I went over determined to grab her attention.

'Judith,' I said as assertively as I could, 'can I talk to you for a minute?'

'Of course, Daryl,' she smiled. 'Why don't you pull up a chair and join us?'

'No, I'd like to talk to you on your own,' I said, ignoring her mistake with my name.

The other boys groaned.

'I only want to talk to you for a minute,' I added.

'Okay,' she said, getting to her feet, leaving her coffee cup behind on the table.

She stood with me in the centre of the dining room, with the bustle of kids and staff all around us.

'Judith,' I began, 'you're coming in at the weekend, aren't you?'

'Yes. Will you be here?'

'No – I go home at weekends. But Nigel's going to be here.'

'Which one is Nigel?' she asked.

I looked around, but I couldn't see him. 'The thing is,' I went on, 'he's been saying things about you.'

'Really?' she laughed. 'How exciting!'

'No,' I responded, becoming annoyed with her. 'He's *dangerous*. You need to make sure you're never on your own with him.'

'Are you worrying about *me*?' she beamed. 'How sweet!'

She put her arm around me and drew me close, her cigarette smouldering by my right shoulder.

'I'm serious,' I coughed as I accidentally inhaled some of her smoke. 'He's said some awful things.'

'Don't you worry about me,' she cooed in my ear. 'I know how to handle boys.'

She withdrew, gave me a wink, and returned to her seat.

I was left standing there, furious that no one – not even Judith herself – would listen to me. I wondered if I ought to talk to someone else – maybe I should try Sarah again – but I felt so angry, demoralised and miserable that I just wanted to be free of it all. In any case, it wasn't as if I hadn't tried, was it? And so I resolved that I would do my best to put it out of my mind, that I would spend the weekend at home not giving Oakdale another thought until Monday morning.

CHAPTER EIGHT

I was sitting in Mr Baker's class on Monday morning, having just opened up my SMP maths book at the point where I had left it on Friday. I was reluctantly preparing my mind for numerical problems when Mrs Burrows, the school secretary, came in.

'Mr Baker,' she said from just inside the doorway, 'Judith is ready for Daniel now.'

I had forgotten that on the previous Tuesday I had put my name down on the list for an individual art therapy session.

'Okay, Daniel,' Mr Baker said, 'leave your things and go with Mrs Burrows.'

I followed the secretary out of the classroom and along the short passageway to an open door at the end; this led into a modest-sized room where Judith Harrison was waiting.

'I'll leave you to it,' Mrs Burrows said, before making her way back down the passage.

'Come in, Daniel, and sit down,' said Judith.

She was sitting at a table with various art materials laid out on it. Next to her was an empty chair, which was where she indicated I should sit.

Judith appeared quite different from how I had seen her in the previous week. The tight-fitting clothes were gone, replaced by a more mundane top and skirt, and her makeup was more restrained and her abundant blonde hair tied back. As I sat next to her, I also noted that she was no longer wearing the pungent perfume of last week.

'You were right about Nigel,' Judith said. 'I should have taken you more seriously.'

'Are you all right?' I asked. 'He didn't do anything, did he?'

'No, he just gave me a bit of a fright. Luckily, Bill Jones and Ted Trowbridge were around – they came to my rescue.'

'What happened to Nigel?' I asked. 'I haven't seen him this morning. He isn't still in the punishment room, is he?'

Judith looked down at the table. 'No,' she said, a little awkwardly. 'They put him in the time-out room for a bit – after sedating him – but they got the doctor in to see him, and the doctor had him transferred over to the main building.'

'He's gone to St Anselm's?' I was astounded. 'But he's only fifteen!'

'I know,' she said uneasily. 'Apparently, the doctor said he was too violent for Oakdale, and that it would be easier to control him in the main building.' She paused, and then looked at me. 'It's all my fault. If I hadn't led him on in the first place – or led *any* of you on – then this wouldn't have happened. Or even if I'd just listened to you and been more careful.'

I exhaled heavily. 'But it wasn't *you* who decided he should go to St Anselm's,' I said.

'I suppose so,' she agreed.

'I heard that he got done for GBH,' I said, 'but they sent him here because he was unbalanced, or something.'

'I'm afraid I wouldn't know,' Judith said.

'They're probably saying he's gone to St Anselm's as a "consequence of his actions",' I remarked. 'That's what they always say – but it would have been much better if they'd punished him properly in the first place, rather than sending him here. I suppose they've got him drugged-up to the eyeballs, and they're just going to keep him completely out of it.' I paused for breath. 'It's not right.'

'Daniel, how old are you?' she asked.

'I'm twelve.'

'Well, I don't know if everything you say is true,' she said, 'but you sound pretty mature for twelve.'

'Yeah,' I found myself quietly giggling, 'and I've got strong and sensitive hands too.'

Her face cracked a smile and she burst out laughing. And then, once she had recovered her composure, she said, 'Okay, let's do some drawing.'

I was back in Judith Harrison's company again in the afternoon. The core group of Andrew Ramsey, Jennie Saunders and myself – plus Gary Jameson and Wendy Cole – were in the art room for the usual Monday after-school group therapy session. Fridgerd Vogt was hovering around with Judith, the two of them observing and making comments on what we were doing, while Derek Ball and Sarah Dawes kept an eye on things.

Mercifully, the art room was not nearly as crowded as it had been the previous Monday, and I found the less busy atmosphere far more conducive as I had another go at painting a seascape.

'Thank God they've got rid of Nigel,' Andrew was saying.

'But I don't think it's right what they've done, Andrew,' I quietly objected, not overly pleased at having my attention drawn away from my painting.

'You're kidding!' Jennie said with surprise. 'I thought you'd be pleased he was gone after what he did to you.'

'Well,' I said, a bit indecisively, 'I'm glad he's gone. But I don't think it's right what they've done to him. He should have had a *fair* punishment, not be shoved out of sight in St Anselm's.'

'Daniel,' Derek said, walking over towards me, 'I'm sure what we've done is for the best – not that it's really anything to do with you.' He paused for a moment, and then spoke again. 'Now, I think we should change the subject.'

'Well, I think Nigel's got what he deserves at last,' Wendy said, and looking pointedly at Derek, she added, 'You lot let him get away with so much for so long. Julie wasn't nearly so bad, but she didn't get away with *anything* – she's still out of her head on Largactil.'

'Wendy, that's enough!' Derek rebuked her. '*Change the subject.* Just forget Nigel – it's not fair on Judith.'

'Oh, I don't mind,' Judith commented, before noticing the look on Derek's face. 'Well,' she changed her tone slightly, 'perhaps it *would* be better if we talked about something else.'

I happened to catch Sarah's eye at this point, and I noticed her suppress a smile. I glanced over to Fridgerd and saw that she too was stifling her amusement. Although I also found the interaction between Derek and Judith marginally entertaining, the actual issue was not funny, and I was irritated that a ban had been placed on its discussion.

While Derek ambled back to stand with Sarah, Fridgerd seemed to notice my discomfort. She came over and encouraged me to concentrate on my painting, and – as she typically did – to put my feelings into my art.

All was quiet in the art room, and I started to wonder if Andrew was going to fill the silence with some more of his pearls of wisdom. Naturally, he didn't disappoint.

'"Look before you leap",' he suddenly announced. 'Don't you think that's a stupid saying?'

Wendy, never the most positive among us, gave him an unenthusiastic withering look.

'It's very unhelpful,' he ventured on. 'It advises you against taking risks – but we *need* to take risks.'

'Maybe,' Sarah said, having been sucked in by him, 'but it makes sense to avoid *unnecessary* risks.'

'But there *aren't* any unnecessary risks,' he argued. '*All* risks are necessary, otherwise we just play safe and never *do* anything.'

I wasn't sure this was going to turn out to be one of Andrew's more illuminating 'lectures', but I listened carefully anyway, even though I wasn't going to bother participating.

Andrew did the rounds of various examples to illustrate his argument – including seat belts and umbrellas! – all of which were rather unconvincing. And yet, as always, he managed to press something of his point home despite all his hot air and exaggeration.

I ended up thinking of my own situation. I thought about my move from Loxton to Horsham, and how I hadn't been at all prepared for it. But it now seemed that maybe this was all about risk: I couldn't go back to the way things were before I came to Oakdale, and so I had to risk going forward to something new. But I didn't find this way of thinking especially motivational, because *I* hadn't been the one to *choose* the risk – others had made the choice for me. Taking risks was all very well, but I was angry at the thought of others taking risks on my behalf without my agreement. But I was still a child, of course, and perhaps this was always how it was for children.

Lost in my thoughts, I hadn't been aware that Sarah was now standing beside me. She gave me a soft nudge with her arm.

'Are you all right, Daniel?' she asked. 'You look very deep in thought.'

'Yes,' I said, giving her a tiny smile. 'I was just thinking that maybe we should only take our *own* risks; not take risks for anyone else.'

She gently ruffled my hair, and I felt very grateful that she seemed to understand.

It was breaktime on Tuesday morning, and after having had a squash, I was filling the remaining ten minutes before returning to school simply by wandering around the Unit.

I passed Robert King in the corridor near the entrance to the hall.

'Daniel,' he stopped me, 'you're just the man I wanted to see. Come and sit down for a minute.'

He took me into the empty hall, and we sat down in a couple of foam chairs resting against one of the longer walls.

'So, how do you like living in Horsham?' he asked.

I was surprised, and a little suspicious, that he seemed to be taking such a friendly interest in me. Previously I had found him rather stern and critical – judgemental, even – and while I couldn't describe his current manner as easy-going, he was certainly being rather more amiable than usual.

'I'd rather be back in Loxton,' I said honestly. 'And it's a bit noisy where we live – I can hear the trains going by at night.'

'Well, it sometimes takes a while to get used to change,' he said. 'One thing that might help would be if you and your family got involved in something in the local community. Maybe there's a church you could go to.'

I eyed him guardedly. 'We don't really go to church very often,' I said. 'I'm sure we'll find one to go to at Christmas, though.'

'Well, that's good, of course,' he said. 'But you'd all find it easier to really become a part of your community if you found one now, and started going there regularly.'

With the exception of Christmas carol services, all the occasions when I'd been to church with my family in Loxton – which weren't many – had been extremely dull, and so I didn't welcome Robert's suggestion with much enthusiasm.

'I live near Horsham myself,' he said, 'and I know a good, lively independent evangelical church near you where I'm sure you'd be very welcome.'

I didn't know what an independent evangelical church was, but I got the feeling that Robert was trying to manipulate me for some reason, and so I told him my family was Church of England – which was true, nominally.

'That's fine,' he said. 'I just think that this particular church, The Living Springs of Zion Church, would be very good for you. I know you're caring, and that you've got strong ideas about what you think is right and wrong; well, at Zion, they'd be able to bring the best out of you, *and* they'd protect you from being led astray by unhelpful, ungodly ideas.'

This conversation with Robert felt very uncomfortable, and I sat there longing for breaktime to be over.

'The things is,' Robert continued, 'you'll be starting at a new school soon, and you'll need a good solid base to support you. *All* of your family could do with a good solid base. So, just think about it, will you?'

Keen to escape this exchange, I readily agreed, only to find that the morning break had now come to an end anyway. And so I left the hall and hurried down the corridor to the foyer, eager to put some distance between Robert and myself.

That afternoon, after school, I talked to Andrew and Jennie about my curious encounter with Robert King.

We were sitting together in a corner in the TV room, away from the small group of kids watching *Animal Magic* under the supervision of Mrs Hamilton.

'I told you before,' Andrew said, 'Robert King is an idiot; just ignore him.'

'Yeah, maybe,' Jennie said. 'But he's probably right about Daniel and his family needing to become part of their community. I don't know what my family would do if *we* ever moved house; it wouldn't be easy leaving everyone we know behind. I suppose you *do* need to join some sort of group, or something, so that you can get to know people.'

'I suppose so,' Andrew said, 'but you don't want to get in with a load of superstitious Jesus-freaks who'll try and control every part of your life.'

'Every part of my life is *already* controlled by someone,' I said.

'Yes,' he accepted, 'but you're going to be leaving the Unit soon. You don't want to end up in the clutches of total morons as soon you've got away from these bastards here.'

'Yeah, but maybe it wouldn't do any harm to learn a bit more about God,' I reflected.

'There isn't any God,' Andrew said firmly.

'*I* think there is,' Jennie disagreed.

'There's no evidence at all that God exists,' Andrew insisted.

'Yes, there is,' Jennie said. '*Jesus* is evidence.'

'Oh, God!' Andrew said, the irony apparently being unintentional. '*You* don't go to church, do you, Jennie?'

'No,' she answered, 'but I still believe in God because of everything Jesus said.'

'But there's no evidence for him either,' Andrew stated.

'No, you're wrong about that, Andrew,' Jennie said. 'It's an historical fact that Jesus existed.'

'No, it isn't,' Andrew said dismissively. 'It's all rumour.'

'Well,' Jennie said, 'you can't prove that God *doesn't* exist.'

'Of course not,' Andrew laughed. 'You can never prove a negative. But,' he continued after drawing breath, 'I suppose it's possible that there might be some form of cosmic intelligence out there,' he speculated. 'Yes, *that's* an interesting possibility.'

It wasn't difficult to see that Andrew was warming to the subject and was about to start holding forth with colourful notions and confidently-voiced opinions.

'Now, what form would a cosmic intelligence take?' he asked rhetorically.

'I don't know and I don't care,' Jennie sighed, getting up and walking out.

Although I would have been happy to hear Andrew's musings on this topic on another occasion, I really didn't feel like it at the moment, and so, seeing that *Animal Magic* was drawing to a close, I said, 'I'm going to go and watch *Rentaghost*.'

It was a weak excuse, as I didn't particularly like the programme, and I knew full well that in a few moments several staff members would be coming in to watch *Crossroads* on the other channel. Despite this, however, it enabled me to successfully extract myself from Andrew's theorising and sit in front of the television with my own thoughts.

*   *   *

The half-term break was looming, and this seemed to be what was concentrating the mind of Mrs Fox, the social worker, when she took me into her office on the Thursday afternoon. Fortunately, this would turn out to be a very brief dialogue, and it hardly seemed necessary for us to settle ourselves in our standard positions.

'You'll be going home for half-term tomorrow,' she said, 'which means you'll have a whole week in your new home, a whole week to get a bit more used to things.'

I murmured acknowledgement.

'We had hoped that you'd be able to start at your new school immediately after the half-term break,' she explained, 'but it's taking a bit longer than we expected to get things organised.'

'I don't even know what school I'll be going to,' I said.

'Well, the thing is,' she replied, 'they're reorganising the schools in Horsham this year, going comprehensive, so in some ways that makes things a bit easier. After all, you never took the 11-Plus, did you? And your mum and dad don't think you would have passed it anyway, so you'll be a lot better off in another comprehensive school, like Worthing Road was.

'Anyway,' she carried on, 'your parents and I have already narrowed down our options to Forest Boys' School and Shelley School. We've managed to visit both of them, but we haven't yet decided which will be best for you, or discovered which would be most willing to have you.'

'Don't I get any say in this?' I complained. 'Why can't *I* go and visit them?'

'Leave it to us, Daniel,' Mrs Fox said. 'You don't need to worry about this – we will do what's best for you.'

I opened my mouth to further voice my dissatisfaction, but Mrs Fox cut me off and sent me on my way.

The half-term break in my new home seemed very strange. I still hadn't got used to it *being* my new home; apart from the fact that all our furniture and belongings were there, it felt to me as though I was in holiday accommodation. There was still some part of me that expected to return to Loxton – it wasn't just that I *wanted* to return to Loxton; at some level I was still *expecting* it. But by the end of the week I was at least considering what it might be like *if* this was to be my home from now on. This was still a long way from accepting the situation, but it was probably a small step towards it.

By the time I returned to Oakdale on the following Monday, things had been set in motion. It almost felt as if the Unit was starting to squeeze me out.

There were three kids who hadn't returned following the break – some new kids having now taken their place – and, of course, Judith Harrison was gone as well. It felt as though I was being washed out by the same current that had taken them.

At morning breaktime, John Webber and Mrs Causton took me to the dormitory, asked the two other boys already in the dorm to leave, and told me I needed to drop my trousers for an injection.

'What injection?' I asked. 'And why can't I have it in my arm?'

'It's your new meds,' Mrs Causton said. 'Dr Rajasimha has changed your prescription ready for when you start at your new school in a couple of weeks. And no, you can't have it in your arm, it needs to go into a muscle in your backside.'

I wanted to know why my medication had been changed again, and I also wanted to know about my new school – this being the first definite news I'd had about it. I had so many questions.

'Go on,' John urged. 'Drop your trousers and underpants and lie face down on your bed.'

Unhappily, I did as I was told.

'What is this stuff you're giving me?' I asked, as Mrs Causton pierced the skin of my left buttock with the syringe.

'It's called fluphenazine – or Modecate,' John answered. 'And the good news is, you won't need to have another injection for three weeks.'

'You'll get your next dose at your GP's surgery,' Mrs Causton explained, withdrawing the needle from my posterior.

Having appropriately restored my clothing, I sat up on the bed and asked if it was another antidepressant.

'Not really,' John replied.

'Basically, yes,' Mrs Causton contradicted him.

I would, of course, have been horrified if they'd told me what it really was, and – not that I could have expected an explanation – I would certainly have demanded to know why Dr Rajasimha had decided to prescribe an antipsychotic often used in the treatment of schizophrenia.

Not having been given any satisfactory information about my new medication, I decided to ask about my new school.

'I can't remember what school Mrs Fox said you'd be going to,' Mrs Causton said, 'but you'll be starting there in two weeks time, on the Monday after next.'

'You'll have a nice easy start,' John commented, 'as you won't be there very long before the start of the long summer holiday.'

'I'm sure Mrs Fox will tell you all about it later,' Mrs Causton said.

Infuriatingly for me, Mrs Fox didn't have time to see me that afternoon, and so I remained in the dark about the school I would soon be attending.

It absolutely astonished me that no one thought it important to keep me informed about things of such enormous personal significance to me. It was as though I was some extraneous piece in a game being played by adults, and it simply didn't matter to them whether I knew what was happening to me or not, just so long as I willingly let it happen and didn't interfere with their plans.

Having been relatively untroubled by unwanted side effects from the Prothiaden – apart from the ongoing mild grogginess that I was well used to – I was to find the Modecate rather more problematic. As the week continued I became increasingly woozy and started to experience mild tremors as well. This was all very troubling, especially as I needed to be alert and in control when I started at my new school. Furthermore, the situation wasn't helped by rising temperatures as we moved towards the beginning of an extended heat wave. With 'You to Me are Everything' and 'Silly Loves Songs' bouncing through the airwaves – and continuing to play incessantly in my brain even when there was no radio in earshot – I was continually trying to clear my head of this repetitive clutter and mentally claw myself to full wakefulness.

It was on Wednesday that Mrs Fox finally deigned to inform me that I had been enrolled at Shelley School. I was somewhat bothered that, of the two schools that had been under consideration, this was the furthest from my home – and there was no convenient bus route. And so I would find myself with a good half-hour's walk to school from now on. While this was, no doubt, very healthy, it felt to me like an added burden. I was growing more and more anxious about what was coming, and it seemed to me as though obstacles were being placed in my way to make things even more challenging. The worst of these obstacles, though, was the medication. With it being slowly released in my body over a three-week period there was no option to quickly withdraw from it.

I discovered on Thursday morning just how disabling the Modecate was. As usual, several of us piled into the minibus for our weekly school trip to the swimming baths in Haywards Heath. I was already feeling rather sleepy as we set off, but by the time Mr Jones had turned onto the A272, the Transit's motion, coupled with the heat, was causing me to nod off. Although Ted Trowbridge woke me when we arrived at the pool, I was so lethargic that I was only allowed in the shallow end. Just like Julie Wilson, I was a hostage to my meds, and the indignity of it was deeply disturbing. As I struggled out of the pool at the end of the session, I almost began to wonder if the decision to give me Modecate was a deliberate attempt to sabotage me as I was about to be discharged from Oakdale.

'No, of course it isn't,' John Webber told me when I expressed this thought to him back at the Unit.

We were standing outside in the play area by the TV room. Lunch was over with, and there was just a short while remaining before staff from the afternoon shift would direct us over to school. The glare of the sun was dazzling my heavy eyes as I watched Jonathan Hunter and Donna Bennett chasing about on the scorched asphalt.

'Then why have you drugged me like this?' I asked.

'Daniel,' he answered, 'it's normal to feel a bit drowsy to start with. Mind you,' he went on, 'you do seem to have had a rather extreme reaction. It'll get better though. The reason we started you on the Modecate now, before you leave us, is so that you'll be used to it by the time you start at your new school.'

'I'm never going to get used to it in the time that's left,' I said.

'Oh, I'm sure you will,' John disagreed. 'Dr Rajasimha wouldn't have given it to you if it wasn't going to be all right.'

It was my final Monday in Oakdale, the start of my final week. In just a few more days I was due to go home for good and become a pupil at Shelley School.

As I sat in the Oakdale School assembly, I was struck by the thought that, in the time I'd been here, the school had been without a headteacher for all but my first two weeks. It seemed such a long time ago that Mrs Nakamura had been here, leading assemblies and helping me with my French. It was almost as though I had dreamt her up myself, now that the terrible shock of her death had merged with the anguish of so many other events and experiences.

From the front of Mr Baker's classroom, Mrs Sutton directed us to turn to Number 19 in the hymnbooks, and with Mrs Conway at the piano, we began our feeble attempt at singing 'God is love: let heav'n adore him'.

As we sang, I pondered over how much had changed since February, and – as I had always done – I regretted ever having been brought to Oakdale. I mourned the loss of the life I had known in Loxton and at Worthing Road Comprehensive School, however unsatisfactory it may have been, realising that it was every bit as dead as Mrs Nakamura.

I glanced round the room, and remembered the faces I'd become used to during my time at Oakdale and which were now gone. Ben Mitchell and Nigel Green had gone, of course. Sharon Gillan had gone too, and so had Michael Davey. In their places were other kids, kids I would never really get to know. And soon I would be gone too, and someone else would take my place. As I pondered this, I thought of Wendy Cole who had also left, having turned eighteen. Rumour had it that almost as soon as she had been discharged, she had thrown herself under a train and died instantly. I was disturbed that I felt no real sense of shock about this, I just felt numb at the realisation that, once the faces were gone, there was no way of knowing what had really become of them. And, of course, I wondered what was to become of me.

The unwanted side effects of the Modecate were lessening slightly, but I still felt as though I was walking around in a fog, and I was not beyond occasionally dozing off. I would have liked to have been more alert for my last few days in Oakdale, as I realised there were a couple of people I would miss, and whose company I should make the best of while I could.

Mr Taylor's shift was covering the mornings during my final week. This rather limited my opportunities for spending any time with Sarah Dawes, and at present her duties meant that much of her time was taken up with the younger children.

I found her, towards the end of morning breaktime on Tuesday, in the playroom working with Tracy Grafton. They were keeping an eye on a few of the smaller kids as they played energetically with assorted noisy toys.

'What brings you in here?' Sarah asked me.

'I'm not going to be around much longer,' I said, 'and I, er, just –'

I would have felt really stupid saying, 'I just wanted to see you,' and so I let the sentence die.

She smiled. 'I know, I'll miss you, Daniel, you're a good kid.'

'I hope everything works out well for you,' Tracy added.

'It's going to be really weird leaving here at last,' I said, raising my voice above the din of the kids.

'Hopefully not as weird as actually being here,' Sarah remarked.

I smiled thinly.

'Oh, come here,' she said, drawing me towards her in a vigorous hug. 'I'm sure I'll see you a few times more before you finally go, but I'll give you a big hug now in case I don't get another chance.'

I hugged her back, and mumbled some rather incoherent words of thanks to her. Sarah had been the only thoroughly reliable adult I had known in Oakdale, and I wanted to thank her properly, but I had no idea how to go about it.

Clearly I'd been holding on to Sarah for rather too long. Tracy intervened, saying, 'Daniel, I think you should let Sarah go.'

'It's all right, Tracy,' Sarah said, still embracing me. 'Daniel and I old friends now – and, besides, *I* need a good hug even if he doesn't.'

*   *   *

The other person I wanted to spend a bit of time with was Andrew, and this was far more easily achievable than contriving to be in Sarah's company.

'Well, I'm not going to be here for much longer either,' he told me.

It was Wednesday afternoon, and most of the kids and staff had disappeared from the dining room following their after-school cups of tea, but Andrew and I remained, sitting at one of the tables.

'Are you going back to your old school, Andrew?' I asked him.

'No, no,' he said. 'After the summer holidays I'm going to Appledorn College. It's a private school somewhere over in Kent.'

'What? A boarding school?'

He nodded his head.

'How can your parents afford that?' I asked, amazed.

'They can't,' he grinned. 'The Local Authority is paying for it.'

'So,' I said, with a sense of finality, 'that's it. We're both going. It's all over.'

'Yeah, and not a minute too soon,' he said flatly. 'I'll tell you one thing: I won't miss Oakdale one bit. Those bastards made a mistake sending me here in the first place, but they won't be able to touch me where I'm going. Just you make sure that *you* stay out of their reach from now on as well.'

I agreed that I would.

'And remember,' he added, 'wherever you go, whatever happens, if anyone gives you any trouble, just verbally kick 'em in the teeth.'

Friday afternoon arrived. But this time I was not being taken home in the minibus, nor was Mrs Fox taking me in her Renault. Instead, my mum and dad, together with my brother Mark, came to collect me.

I had a very peculiar and unpleasant feeling as we left Oakdale in our Morris 1100. Although there seemed to be a definite current washing me away from the Unit, I just couldn't rid myself of the thought that maybe I wasn't completely free of Oakdale. There was another current reaching out and tugging at me, trying to wash me back in again. If only my head had been clearer then it would have taken less effort to resist its pull. But all the same, I *was* resisting it, and resisting it very well – but how long could I keep it up?

CHAPTER NINE

Ten months after having left Oakdale I was dragged back there, kicking and screaming.

The time I had spent back at home and as a pupil at Shelley School hadn't been easy. In many ways, it was some of the smallest things that had proved the most difficult.

One of these small things arose from the fact it had been impressed upon me, both by Mrs Fox, the social worker, and by my parents, that I mustn't say anything to anyone at Shelley about my time in Oakdale. My 'official' story was that my family had moved from Loxton to Horsham, and that I had come straight from Worthing Road Comprehensive to Shelley; I was not to admit to the intervening period of time. No doubt I had been told this for my own good, to avoid getting teased for having been a 'mental patient'. But without having worked out every single possible aspect of this story, I got tangled up in knots. No more so than during my first week at the new school.

I was standing by the desk of my history teacher, Mr Owen, as he supplied me with a couple of books. While he did this, he asked me – *in the hearing of the whole class* – when I had moved house. Despite feeling a little uncomfortable, I told him the truth: I'd moved in May. He then asked me if, until now, I'd been having to travel in order to continue attending my old school. Despite now feeling quite awkward, I told him the truth: I hadn't. He then wanted to know *exactly* when I'd left my old school. Despite now feeling extremely uneasy, I told him the truth: I'd left in February. Not surprisingly, he then asked me what had happened between leaving my old school and arriving at Shelley. Despite now feeling quite frantic, I *still* told him the truth: *I wasn't allowed to talk about it.*

He was interrupted at this point as another pupil came up to him to with an urgent query, and so he didn't get to question me any further. But, for me, the damage was already done. There, in front of the whole history class, I had effectively admitted to having some sort of secret; I had admitted that there was something about the most recent four months of my life that was hidden.

Inevitably, a handful of my classmates questioned me about my secret when they got the chance a little later. In reply I tried being vague, I tried being evasive and I tried being completely unresponsive. None of these approaches was satisfactory, and they all made a less than ideal first impression on my new peers.

Another difficulty I had was the ongoing unwanted side effects of my medication. Fortunately, my nightly dose of Mogadon was discontinued soon after my return home, thus somewhat reducing my morning grogginess; but the three-weekly Modecate injections continued, with the result that I often felt sleepy – though not as much as I had done to start with – and I continued to be troubled by intermittent tremors. My headmaster, year head and form tutor, of course, all knew of my situation, but many of the other teachers who had me for various lessons did not, and they were often impatient with me on those occasions when I was drowsy in class.

It must have been the cumulative effect of a number of difficulties that sent me sliding back into depression, but now seeing Dr Rajasimha again on a regular basis, he seemed to determine that my main problem was anxiety. Shortly after my thirteenth birthday in November, he decided to put an end to the Modecate injections, for which I was grateful, and prescribed Valium in its place – presumably thinking that anxiety was now more of an issue than any other supposed condition. Given that he prescribed a relatively high dosage, this, if anything, made me even more dozy, and for the remainder of my time at Shelley, I felt as though I was fighting to maintain awareness of what was going on around me. I became more and more frustrated – negating the supposedly tranquilising effect of the Valium – and this, coupled with my battle to stay alert, made me very short tempered. If this wasn't enough, my coordination was suffering, and I found myself becoming quite clumsy. And so the struggle was getting harder, the descent into depression was continuing, and my once regular attendance at Shelley was becoming sporadic.

With Mrs Fox having started to make regular visits to my home from mid-February onwards, she began to talk about the possibility of a brief readmission to Oakdale. I was resistant, and so too were my parents – to start with.

Matters came to a head late one Sunday afternoon in April. I was feeling sleepy, frustrated and exceptionally tetchy – all at the same time – as I began to dread the following day at school. Something inside of me must have snapped, and for the first time since early childhood, I exploded into a major screaming fit. I lashed out uncontrollably at everything and everyone around me. My brother Mark, now five, was sent to his room to escape the onslaught, while my dad attempted to wrestle me to the floor – though not before I had managed to send the coffee table flying.

I assumed that my mum, retreating momentarily, must have telephoned Mrs Fox, as it wasn't very long before the social worker arrived on the scene.

Mrs Fox was shown into the living room by my mum, and found me lying on the carpet with my dad watching over me. I was now utterly drained of energy, exhausted from my outburst.

Although I lay there dazed, I heard most of what they were saying about me. While my parents both maintained, with distressed bewilderment, that they'd never seen me like this before, Mrs Fox was insistent that I was seriously ill and that I had to be returned to Oakdale immediately.

I wanted to protest, I wanted to say I was sorry, and that I'd never behave like that again, but I had no strength, and no words escaped my lips. And so I was bundled into Mrs Fox's Renault 16, accompanied by a hastily-packed suitcase, and taken back to Oakdale.

During the short journey I must have regained some energy, as I became angrily defiant when I saw Mr Jones, Colin Goodman and Julian Perry coming out to meet me as Mrs Fox drew into the Oakdale car park.

They pulled me vigorously from the car, forcing me to the tarmacked ground to restrain me. They then dragged me insistently along the ground as I tried desperately to free myself from their grip. But I was helpless against their combined strength, and they soon had me in the building, forcing me along the corridor to the boys' dormitory. Once there, I was thrown onto a bed – on the other side of the dorm from where I had previously slept – and held firmly in place. At this point, Mrs Causton entered the dorm with a syringe in hand, and injected the substance into one of my buttocks.

'That should be enough to put him out for a while,' she said.

Assuming both drug and dose to be similar to what I had been given on an earlier occasion, I knew that very soon my consciousness would be met by oblivion.

I awoke mid-morning on Monday to the sound of 'Chanson D'Amour' coming from the radio in the nurses' station. Sitting by my new bed on a standard Oakdale foam chair was Derek Ball.

'Welcome back to the land of the living, Daniel,' he remarked.

I was desperate to relieve my bladder, and so I forced my reluctant legs from under the sheet and quilt so as to haul myself to my feet. Fortunately, I had not been completely stripped of my clothes – which is what I'd expected based on previous experience. Instead, I found my underpants had been left on, which, though hardly dignified, was a considerable improvement on being naked.

'And just where do you think you're off to?' Derek asked.

'I need the toilet,' I explained weakly.

'All right, then,' he said.

I shuffled one foot in front of the other as I made my way unsteadily through the wedged-open double-doors to one of the toilet cubicles just outside the dorm.

With that urgent call of nature answered, I became aware of how deeply hopeless and miserable I felt, and hot tears formed in my eyes as I returned to the dorm and collapsed back on the bed.

Derek helped me to get comfortable by straightening out my sheet and quilt. His willing aid surprised me a little, as I was expecting disapproval following the events that had brought me back here.

'I'm not being unkind or anything,' he said, 'but I hoped I'd never see you again.'

My eyes stung from my weeping, as I lay there knowing that because of my foolish tantrum yesterday, I had thrown everything away. I gazed at the ceiling, realising that in all probability, many, many months of incarceration lay ahead of me in Oakdale. This time there was no light at the end of the tunnel, no promise of discharge in the foreseeable future. I felt truly condemned.

Looking around me, I noticed that the walls and carpet were now rather more scuffed than they had been when I was last here. The Oakdale building had suffered ten months of use and abuse since I had left last June. Both the Unit and myself were older by ten months – and more dismal by ten months.

'Try not to upset yourself, Daniel,' Derek said. 'You'll probably be able to get up and dressed this afternoon, and once you've settled back down here and made a few new friends things will look a bit brighter.'

'Aren't any of my old friends still here?' I whimpered.

'You've been gone quite a while,' Derek answered. 'Lots of kids have come and gone in that time – there won't be many left that you knew.'

This made me sob all the more.

'Come on, Daniel,' he encouraged, 'you've just got to adjust to us again, get used to things.'

At that moment a group of five boys came running through the open dormitory doors – it was morning break.

'Hey,' said one of them, a twelve-year-old called Greg Peterson. 'The new kid's awake.'

'He's not new,' came a distinctive West Indian accent that I immediately recognised – it belonged to Clester Henry. '*He* was here before *you* were.'

While the other kids either flopped down on their beds or rummaged in their lockers, Clester came over to me.

'Hello, Daniel,' he said. 'Do you remember me? It's Clester.'

I guessed that Clester must now be fifteen, and as he was still here I imagined he must be in Oakdale long term. Although I never really knew Clester all that well – and had no idea what sort of disorder had brought him to the Unit in the first place – it was good to see at least one recognisable face.

'Yes, I remember,' I answered quietly.

'Bad luck – getting sent back, that is,' Clester said, before walking off to his locker.

It wasn't very long before Sarah Dawes entered the dorm to announce that breaktime was over.

'Come on, back to school, you lot!' she called.

Then she spotted me, lying in my bed, and gave a little smile. 'I'll come over and see you in a few minutes, Daniel,' she said.

Sarah led the five boys away in the direction of school.

'There, Daniel,' Derek said positively. 'Clester remembers you – and so does Sarah, of course. And once you make a few more friends, things will seem much better.'

Sarah returned after about fifteen minutes, and she came over and sat on my bed.

'Everything okay, Sarah?' Derek asked.

'Yeah, no problems,' she answered.

'If you've got a few minutes,' he began, 'perhaps you could mind Daniel while I make a start on writing-up the Cardex.'

'Sure,' she nodded, taking Derek's place in the foam chair as he got up and left.

'Oh, Daniel,' Sarah said, a little sadly. 'What are we going to do with you? I was sure you were going to be fine once you got home and started at your new school. What went wrong?'

I told her as best I could.

'No wonder your mum and dad called Mrs Fox,' Sarah said, after I told her what I'd done yesterday afternoon. 'That's not like you at all. They must have been absolutely shocked.'

'I know,' I said tearfully, feeling thoroughly ashamed.

'Never mind, though,' she smiled, reaching out to clasp my shoulder warmly. 'I'm sure it'll all be forgotten in time.'

'But I'm stuck back here because of it,' I moaned.

She looked at me with an understanding smile, and for a moment her empathy with me seemed so great that I thought she was going to comment that Mrs Fox had overreacted. But instead she said, 'Just concentrate on getting yourself back together; it sounds like you've had a bit of a rough time, and you've kept on going despite everything, and now you just need to recharge your batteries.'

'I suppose so,' I agreed.

'I hear that you should be able to get up this afternoon,' Sarah remarked. 'But I bet you're still a bit woozy, so if I were you I'd try and get a few minutes sleep before lunch, and then we'll see how you're doing.'

She shifted herself closer to me and started stroking my hair. I was comforted by her tenderness, and despite the restraining effects of the medication, I was also slightly aroused. Since I was last at Oakdale, adolescence had gained a more determined hold on me.

Though up and dressed in time for lunch, I was still unsteady on my feet, my balance impaired and my head muzzy. It was a relief being able to sit down once Derek Ball had led me to my new place in the dining room. Derek seated himself next to me, and it became obvious that he was now my key worker on this shift. Then, suddenly, a herd of kids came charging into the room.

One of the two boys who joined us at the table was Greg, whom I had seen briefly in the dormitory at breaktime; the other was a fourteen-year-old called Roger Hampton.

Derek began the introductions, explaining to Greg and Roger that I had been at Oakdale before, but that the friends I knew at that time were gone now, and so it would be appreciated if they could help me settle back in.

'Do you know whose class you'll be in at school?' Greg asked me.

'I used to be in Mr Baker's class,' I said.

'*I'm* in Mr Baker's class,' he said. 'Roger's in Mrs Sutton's.'

'Is there a new headteacher now?' I asked.

'No,' Roger replied, 'but I think there's supposed to be one coming. The last one died.'

'I know,' I answered.

'You knew Mrs N., didn't you, Daniel?' Derek said.

'Yes,' I answered. 'She was really good to me – although I was only here for two weeks before she died.'

'Well, I think they've managed to *recruit* a new head,' Derek told me, 'but I heard it'll be a little while yet before he's ready to start.'

Barbara Heaton, one of the auxiliaries, was making her way along the tables and directing kids and staff to join the queue for the soup course. Once she moved on from our table, I got myself in line behind Greg and Roger.

After collecting my soup – chicken and mushroom, supposedly – from Tracy Grafton at the serving hatch, I was momentarily confused and started towards the place where I used to sit. But I realised my mistake as I soon noticed three girls, supervised by Mrs Hamilton, now occupying that table. I was walking a little erratically anyway, and so I probably altered course before anyone saw, thus returning to my new place without too much embarrassment.

As I slurped my soup, I looked around the room to see how many faces I recognised. All but two of the staff members were familiar to me, but there were very few kids I remembered. Apart from Clester, I recognised Jeremy Newton – who I remembered being admitted – and I spotted Jane Sparrow, who was as thin as ever. Julie Wilson was still here too, and though she didn't appear quite as heavily sedated as before, it was obvious that they were continuing to keep her under control with drugs. One of the younger kids was also familiar to me – Sally Abiola – though she had grown quite a bit since I last saw her.

'Checking to see who you recognise?' Derek asked me.

'Yes,' I answered.

'It not just the kids who will have changed while you've been away,' Derek said. 'A few of the staff have changed as well. Jeff Knowles has gone to work up in Derby, and Ted Trowbridge has retired. Oh, and do you remember the art therapist – Fridgerd? Well, she's gone back home to Norway.'

'So who does the art therapy now?' I asked, remembering it to be one of the few activities I enjoyed at Oakdale.

'No one at the moment,' Derek replied.

'So the art room won't be open after school today?'

'No, unfortunately not,' Derek said.

'But you can do drawing and stuff with Bridget,' Roger said helpfully.

'Yes, that true,' Derek confirmed. 'You remember our occupational therapist, Bridget Fitzpatrick, don't you?'

'Yes,' I said. 'Though I never really saw very much of her when I was here before.'

'Well, I expect she'll be in the hideout after school,' Derek said. 'If you go and see her then I'm sure she'll sort you out with some art stuff.'

Although I knew where the hideout was, I'd never actually been in there – I guessed that the reason for this was that no one had directed me towards occupational therapy before. Anyway, I concluded that I would give it a try.

Lunch continued with the main course followed by dessert. Then Barbara Heaton came by with a metal jug full of tea, and remembering that the tea would already be mixed-up with sugar, I declined.

'Tea without sugar is coming in a minute,' she said.

Derek must have noticed my surprise at this; as Barbara continued on to the next table, he began telling me that they had started making unsugared tea available because there had been a couple of kids at the Unit who suffered with diabetes – and besides, a few members of staff had been lobbying for unsweetened tea anyway.

A few minutes later, Barbara returned with another metal jug, and this time I accepted the offer of tea.

And then I was reintroduced to the ritual of the medicine trolley.

Mr Taylor and Mike Kirby wheeled the oak-laminated cabinet into the dining room. Mr Taylor then unlocked it while Mike began calling kids up to receive their meds.

'Daniel Kinsley,' Mike called.

I dutifully responded, making my way a little unsteadily towards the trolley.

'Well, here's a face I didn't expect to see again,' Mr Taylor remarked. 'I see you're on diazepam now – a pretty high dose too: three times a day. Well, that'll keep you quiet.'

He dropped the Valium tablet into my hand from the standard 30ml plastic medicine cup, and I swallowed it down

After all the meds had been dispensed, the cigarettes were handed out, and I gained some small satisfaction from discovering ours was a non-smoking table.

Soon after the change of shifts, it was time to go over to school.

I was a little worried to discover that Robert King was my key worker on Mrs Causton's shift, as I remembered well his intensity in connection with religion. This was not a concern at the moment, however, as all he did was accompany me with the other kids as we left the Unit and crossed the grassy play area to the school building.

'I'll take you to see Mrs Sutton,' Robert said as we entered the school, 'and she'll tell you what class you're going to be in.'

He led me down the passageway into Mrs Sutton's class.

We entered a classroom that was almost exactly like Mr Baker's, albeit in mirror image. As we passed beyond the threshold I saw that a handful of kids were rifling through their drawers or settling themselves in their places. Mrs Sutton, meanwhile, was standing over her desk. A stray lock escaped from her tied-up grey hair as she shuffled some books and papers into order. As we advanced further, she looked up.

'Ah, Daniel,' she said, coming over to meet us. 'You're going to be in *my* class now. Come and sit down and we'll have a bit of chat.'

'I'll see you at teatime, Daniel,' said Robert as he left.

Mrs Sutton directed me to a chair at an empty table. 'I'll be with you in just a minute,' she said, as she went to attend to a couple of the other kids.

There were seven other pupils in my class, all of whom were older than me. I was slightly surprised to discover I was already acquainted with more than half of them: Clester, Jeremy, Roger, Jane and Julie. The other two, Susan Jarman and Claire Knight, appeared to be around fifteen and sixteen respectively, and it looked as though they were eying me with a kind of condescending curiosity.

After having made sure that all the other kids were engaged in approved tasks, Mrs Sutton grabbed a vacant chair from another table and set it down opposite me. She seated herself in it and began talking.

'Well, Daniel,' she said, 'it's a shame to see you back here, but I'm sure we'll get along fine. I remember you very well from when you were here before.'

I was slightly surprised by this, as I didn't recall having a great amount of contact with Mrs Sutton.

'You weren't really much more than a small boy when we first met, were you?' she continued.

Given that it was little more than a year ago when we would have met, I wondered if perhaps she was confusing me with someone else.

'So, how old are you now, Daniel?' she asked.

'Thirteen.'

'Ah, thirteen, eh? You're becoming a young man.' She paused for a moment. 'Of course, it's all very different now from when my late husband was a young man. It was between the wars when he was your age, and little did he know that he was going to have to fight for his country before very long.'

I stared at her, unsure of the direction the conversation was taking.

'Hopefully there won't be another war now,' she went on, 'so you won't have to worry about anything like that. Mind you, joining the forces is a very noble thing for a young man to aspire to. Mr Sutton was Army: Royal Signals. Despite everything, it did him the world of good.'

'I don't want to join the Army,' I said timidly.

'Well,' Mrs Sutton said, 'you're only on the cusp of becoming an adult, you don't have to make any decisions yet – but you will do before too long.'

The implication that I might soon have to make major decisions seemed very worrying, especially as I was back in such a powerless position, having failed to survive for long at Shelley School. But before I could become too morose, Mrs Sutton resumed talking.

'The thing is, Daniel,' she said, adopting a confidential tone, 'this country's going to need young men like you. You're a bright boy, and you know right from wrong. You're not like some of the filthy beggars we've got here.' She looked around at the other kids in the room. 'In fact, I'm tempted to call them something a bit stronger than "beggars".'

I wasn't sure who, in particular, she was so disapproving of, and I was still puzzled over why she thought she knew me so well.

'Sometimes I don't know why I bother with this job,' she said. 'Most of the brats I have to teach are idiots, delinquents or foreigners. That's why I'm so pleased to have you in my class. And Jane, too – she's a good girl. It's just a shame that she insists on starving herself. But if it wasn't for people like you two I'd hand my resignation in tomorrow.'

Mrs Sutton went on talking for quite some considerable time while I struggled to stay awake. Despite my sluggishness I was aware that much of what she was saying was obviously questionable, but she was also very charismatic, and so I forced my heavy eyelids to stay open while I listened as intently as I could.

But after a while I started to ask myself whether she was ever going to get round to giving me some work to do.

She must have been talking almost non-stop for an hour before she finally announced that she needed to sort out some English and maths textbooks for me.

'It won't be like it was when you were here before,' she said. 'I don't think your old school will be sending anything for you to be carrying on with, so we'll need to organise your lessons ourselves.'

With that, she went over to her desk and picked up two large soft-cover volumes together with a couple of exercise books.

'Here,' she said, returning with them and sitting down again.

She thrust in front of me a volume entitled *Ahead in English* and a *Beta Mathematics* book.

'These should keep you going for a while,' she said. 'Just work your way through them at your own pace, and come to me if you have any problems.'

'What about my other subjects?' I asked.

'Just you concentrate on your English and maths for now, Daniel,' she replied. 'That's all that matters, really. Employers want people who can read and write and add up – the rest isn't all that important. You'll get training for anything else you need to know once you've left school.'

I was extremely dubious about Mrs Sutton's claims, and for the first time it occurred to me that my education was going to suffer considerably if I remained in Oakdale for any length of time. But what choice did I have?

At half-past three I joined the throng of children leaving the school and returning to the Unit. We streamed noisily through the corridors, passing the time-out room, the playroom, the TV room and the quiet room, before arriving in the dining room to join the queue for tea or squash.

Rose Boyd, the auxiliary, was serving the drinks from her trolley, and I was pleased to see that, once again, there were two jugs of ready-mixed tea, one with sugar and one without. I took a cup of unsweetened tea and then looked for somewhere to sit. I saw Jane sitting on her own at one of the tables, and as she was one of the kids I remembered from before, I went over and joined her.

Jane had barely changed in the last ten months. As she was now fourteen

I expected her to at least look a little different. But she remained horribly emaciated, with dry and pallid skin, sunken eyes and lank hair – and she didn't appear to have grown at all. It was a depressing sight, and for my own good I probably shouldn't have chosen to sit with her. But I was here now, and so I felt I had to try and be friendly.

'How are you these days?' I asked stiltedly.

'The same,' she answered. 'Nothing's changed. They still keep forcing me to eat – but *look* at me: I'm *obese*!'

For a moment I thought she was joking, and I wondered if I was meant to smile in response; but her bony face was intensely earnest, so I realised that this was not an attempt at black humour.

'You can't mean that,' I said. 'I've never seen anyone as thin as you.'

She smiled a small but frighteningly skeletal smile. 'You're trying to be nice,' she said, 'but I know what I look like.'

I now seemed to recall that she couldn't be reasoned with on the subject of her weight, and so I gave up the attempt and tried another topic instead.

'I used to be in Mr Baker's class,' I said, 'but they've put me with Mrs Sutton now.'

'I know.'

'What's Mrs Sutton like as a teacher?'

'Utter crap!' Jane said.

'She says *you're* one of her best pupils,' I responded.

'That's because I get on with my work without bothering her. She doesn't really do any teaching at all. If you're reasonably bright, she just gives you textbooks and leaves you to get on with it – you don't get any attention from her at all. But if you're *not* very bright, then you get *loads* of attention, because she concentrates on keeping you under control.'

'But she gave *me* plenty of attention this afternoon,' I said.

'Yeah, but only so she could waste your time with her stupid stories,' Jane commented bitterly. 'Sometimes it's better when the other kids give her trouble, because then you don't have to listen to her endlessly going on about what her husband did in the war.'

I had to agree that Mrs Sutton probably *was* wasting my time this afternoon, even if she was very entertaining.

'And she's a total bigot,' Jane added. 'Just look at Clester. He's not stupid, but Mrs Sutton treats him like he is because she's so prejudiced.'

I wasn't sure about this, as it seemed very unlikely that Mrs Sutton would be allowed to get away with that kind of unprofessional behaviour; but then, it also seemed unlikely that we'd only get to study two subjects.

'Is it right that we only do English and maths with Mrs Sutton?' I asked.

'Pretty much, yes,' Jane confirmed. 'She can't be bothered with anything else; it's usually English in the morning and maths in the afternoon. Apart from going swimming with Mrs Conway on Thursday, that's it – there's nothing else.'

Robert King joined us at this point.

'How was your first afternoon back at our school?' he asked me.

'That's what we were just talking about,' I said, avoiding a direct answer.

'I was just telling Daniel what Mrs Sutton's like,' Jane said. 'He was in Mr Baker's class before, so he doesn't really know yet how incompetent she is.'

'Jane!' Robert exclaimed. 'That's no way to talk about your teacher.'

'But she *is* incompetent,' Jane stood firm.

'I'm sure that's not true,' Robert responded.

'No, *no-one* believes it's true,' Jane said. 'That's why she gets away with it.'

'Perhaps we'd better talk about something else, then,' Robert suggested. Turning to me, he asked, 'What are you planning to do with the rest of the afternoon?'

'At lunchtime, Derek said it might be a good idea to go and see Bridget in the hideout.'

Robert quickly cast his eyes around the dining room.

'I see that Bridget is still drinking her tea,' he said, 'but I'll take you over to the hideout myself when we're all finished here.'

The hideout was located close to the hall and consisted of two rooms, partially separated by a dividing panel. The first room was brightly lit by large windows along two of its walls; they looked out towards the school. This room housed a low table, child-sized chairs and assorted toys, broken crayons and some rather forlorn-looking dolls. Three of the younger children were busy playing on the floor with a box of plastic dinosaurs.

The first room in the hideout led into a second, which was less well illuminated, having only one small frosted window above a kitchen-style sink and draining board. There were four of the foam seats lined up against the back wall, with the floor space being taken up by a couple of smaller plastic chairs. Cupboards dominated the other wall, while children's drawings were pinned to the dividing panel.

Bridget Fitzpatrick was seated in one of the foam seats, and either side of her was a teenage girl, neither of whom I really knew. The girl on her right was Susan Jarman – who I'd seen give me a disdainful look in Mrs Sutton's class – and the other was a girl of about my age called Louise Bray.

'Bridget,' Robert said as he propelled me into this second room, 'you remember Daniel, don't you?'

'Yes, of course,' Bridget replied. 'Though I don't think you ever came to see me when you were here before, did you, Daniel?'

I shook my head.

'All right if I leave Daniel with you?' Robert asked her.

Bridget nodded. 'Yes, fine.'

Robert left me standing in the middle of the hideout's second room.

'Come and sit down, Daniel,' Bridget said, gesturing towards a vacant foam seat next to Louise.

I sank down into the chair.

'So what brings you to my hideout, Daniel?' Bridget asked.

I had, of course, come in because Derek Ball had told that this was now the place to do artwork; however, I could see that the hideout was not nearly as well equipped as the art room had been, and in any case, there wasn't sufficient space to do very much.

'Derek told me that since Fridgerd left, a lot of kids come in here to do art,' I explained.

'Well, yes, that's true,' Bridget verified. 'But I'm not really set up for it today. I'll tell you what: I'll have a bigger table put out there for tomorrow –' she pointed to the first room '– and you can come in and do some art then.'

'Okay, thank you,' I said, as I began to stand up.

'Don't run off, Daniel,' Bridget said. 'Stay for a while. We were just talking. We're trying to identify all the things that really annoy us.'

I sat back down.

'By the way, do you know Susan and Louise?' Bridget asked.

I told her I didn't really, and she introduced us.

Susan claimed to be in Oakdale while they worked on stabilising her epilepsy; Louise, on the other hand, believed that her parents' break-up had led to her suffering severe anxiety.

We chatted together for some time, and came up with a very extensive list of things that annoyed us – and, although she didn't say so, I suspected that I was one of the things that annoyed Susan.

'What we need to do now,' Bridget said, 'is to pick out just a few *really* annoying things, and then let's think about what we can do about them.'

Before very long it was five o'clock and time for Bridget to go home.

'Okay, I need to lock up now,' she said. 'We can continue with this another time. But you've all had some great ideas, so thanks a million for that.'

Bridget ushered all of us, including the younger kids, out of the hideout.

'And don't forget, Daniel,' she added as she closed the door, 'I'll have it all set up for you to do some artwork in here tomorrow after school.'

After saying goodbye to Bridget, I made my way to the boys' dorm, intending to lie down for a bit before supper. I wasn't meaning to sleep, just to rest, but my ongoing bleariness meant that as soon as I reclined on top of my quilt, I drifted into a stupor.

Robert King came and woke me up.

'Wake up, Daniel,' he shook me. 'If you sleep during the day, you won't sleep tonight.'

I rubbed my eyes and reluctantly got to my feet.

'Come and get something to eat,' he said, steering me out of the dorm and along the disinfectant-scented corridors I knew so well.

Greg and Roger were already seated as Robert and I entered the dining room and took our places across the table from them.

Rose Boyd soon directed us to join the queue for the serving hatch, and so we went up to collect our servings of an extremely bland shepherd's pie.

Back at the table, Roger swallowed a mouthful and remarked, 'God, this is disgusting!'

Robert reacted with the firmness I remembered him for. 'Roger,' he said, 'I don't want to hear you swearing. Is that understood?'

'What swearing?' he replied.

'You do not take the Lord's name in vain,' Robert said sternly. 'That is not acceptable. Do you understand?'

'I suppose so,' Roger grumbled.

While this was a very minor incident, it brought to mind an awareness that Robert maintained very definite boundaries between what he considered acceptable and what he did not. While I still had some reservations about him, it seemed to me that there was a certain security to be found in his ordered and dogmatic outlook. In many ways, being in Oakdale felt decidedly unsafe, so perhaps it would be no bad thing to seek refuge in Robert's decisive and certain attitude.

After supper I planted myself in the TV room, having insufficient energy to do anything else, and also having decided that it was far too early to go to bed.

I sat there in front of the television with a small number of other kids – plus John Webber – but, being half-asleep, I had very little awareness of what I was watching. However, I was just about alert enough to notice that, at half-past seven, no one had reminded us to report to our dormitories for inspection.

'How come we haven't been told to go to our dorms?' I asked Greg, who was sitting next to me.

'Uh?' Greg responded.

'We don't do that anymore,' John said. 'And as you're thirteen now, Daniel, *you* don't have to report to the dorm till ten o'clock.'

There was no way I was going to manage to stay awake until then, but I remained vacantly gazing at the screen until about half-way through *Panorama* – hardly the most engaging of programmes for kids of my age – at which point I gave up and took myself off to bed. Thus my first full day back at Oakdale came to an end.

CHAPTER TEN

It felt very odd, on Tuesday morning, to be shepherded back into my old classroom for school assembly.

Mr Baker spotted me as I came in with the others, and he immediately intercepted me.

'I wasn't expecting to see you back here,' he said, directing me to sit at a particular table.

Louise Bray came and sat next to me, as Mr Baker made his way to his own place at the front of the class, seating himself between Mrs Sutton and Mrs Burrows, the school secretary. As always, Mrs Conway was positioned over to the right at the piano.

As soon as we were all settled in our places, Mrs Sutton said, 'Good morning, everyone.'

'Good morning, Mrs Sutton,' came the group response.

'Turn to Number 89 in the green hymnbooks,' she instructed.

There was a general muted hubbub as we all thumbed our way through the pages until we found the correct hymn, and then Mrs Conway struck up with the introduction and we half-heartedly sang 'When Jesus walked by Galilee'.

If it had felt strange coming back into Mr Baker's classroom, it felt even more peculiar having to leave when assembly was over. But I merged with the group of kids heading for the other two classes, and followed Mrs Sutton's group as we peeled off upon reaching the door to our class.

'Right,' Mrs Sutton declared as we entered the room. 'Get your English books out and settle down.'

I quickly recovered what I needed from the drawer assigned to me and immersed myself in the rudimentary and unchallenging content of *Ahead in English*.

Occasionally I would look up from my work and see that the other kids – with the exception of Jane Sparrow – were expending very little effort, but that this didn't seem to concern Mrs Sutton. The only time she intervened was when Claire Knight tore a page out of her exercise book, made a paper aeroplane, and threw it at Julie Wilson – who, incidentally, showed no reaction. At this point, Mrs Sutton jumped up from behind her desk, ran over, and started ranting at Claire about what a hooligan she was, admonishing her almost as if she had committed a crime against humanity.

Eventually, Mrs Sutton eased up a little in the tone of her reprimand and made a cursory attempt at urging Claire to do her work.

Mrs Sutton then came over towards me – and as she did so, I saw Claire mouth the words 'fuck you' at her.

'I'm surrounded by half-witted reprobates,' Mrs Sutton muttered at me. 'Would you believe the barefaced insolence of that girl? She treats my classroom as though it's her personal playground!'

I looked up, not knowing at first whether I was expected to respond or not. Apparently I wasn't, as she then patted me on the shoulder and said, 'Thank goodness for you, Daniel. If it wasn't for people like you, I'd be completely wasting my time here.'

She then headed back to her desk, picked up what appeared to be a hardback novel, and began to read, paying no further attention to any of us.

By the end of my first week back I had already fallen, without protest, into a stagnant, undemanding and soul-destroying routine as one of Mrs Sutton's pupils. The only thing that seemed to offer any respite was going to the hideout after school to draw and paint, or just to talk with Bridget Fitzpatrick. But even with that small opportunity for creativity or conversation, I felt I was not being moved forward. Thus I began – unconsciously at first – to look for other things, other events, other interactions, that might offer me direction.

Perhaps surprisingly, I was allowed home for the weekend following my first week back. The social worker, Mrs Fox, took it upon herself to deliver me home on the Friday and to collect me again on the Monday morning.

By that time I was already beginning to find myself growing closer to Robert King, his responsive attitude towards me, coupled with his principled rigidity, providing an odd sense of possible forward momentum. It was on the Tuesday afternoon of my second week back – while Robert was off-duty – that a pivotal moment occurred.

I was seated in the TV room with a sprinkling of kids and three staff members. It was shortly before suppertime, and the early evening news programme was on. While a report was running about the Queen launching a new aircraft carrier, the HMS *Invincible*, I turned to Clester Henry, who was sitting beside me, and made a comment about Robert.

'Why do you keep going on and on about Robert?' he asked with irritation.

I hadn't realised that I had been.

'You sound like you fancy him, or something,' Clester said accusingly. 'You're not a bloody poof, are you?'

I was taken aback by this, and my immediate impulse was to exclaim, 'No, of course not!' But I didn't follow my impulse; I stayed silent and turned the question over in my head.

It was obvious to me that I was not attracted to men or boys – I definitely liked the opposite sex. This had been clear for quite some time, and had become even more apparent in the last few months. So, why then didn't I follow my initial intent and refute Clester's suggestion?

'You are, aren't you?' he said, responding to my silence in a raised voice. 'You're a bloody poofter, a fucking homo!'

'Clester!' It was Mike Kirby who voiced the rebuke. 'I won't put up with that kind of talk.'

'I don't care,' Clester said, getting up from his seat. 'I'm going. I'm not sitting next to no fucking queer!'

He stomped out, leaving me shaken.

'Are you all right, Daniel?' Mike asked.

'Yes,' I replied, feeling a little self-conscious. 'I'm fine.'

The thought was now planted in my head. How would it be if I *were* a homosexual? I knew, of course, that I wasn't; but what if I *tried* to be. Robert had become a great source of care and stability, and if I declared to him that I loved him, then that would definitely secure his complete attention.

And so I started to formulate a plan – an *insane* plan. I would now pretend to be a homosexual – no, I *would* be a homosexual. I would decide in my own mind how I was going to *feel* about Robert from now on, and I would *tell* him how I felt. Then I would be able to move forward in a new relationship, one that would help me amidst the misery and drudge of being an Oakdale patient.

The following morning I awoke with my peculiar plan still at the forefront of my mind, and on seeing Robert King in the dormitory, ensuring that we were all getting washed and dressed, I realised that I was feeling very nervous. So nervous, in fact, that my apprehension gained priority over my drug-induced lethargy.

I needed to carefully pick my moment, to find an opportunity to get Robert alone and say my piece. But over breakfast, as I alternated between looking at Robert – seated next to me – and casting my eyes around the dining room, it was clear that I was *not at all* attracted to him. On the other hand, a couple of the girls, Susan Jarman and Louise Bray, *did* appear fairly attractive, as did Michelle Newbold, one of the female staff members currently on duty. This *should* have led me to abandon my ridiculous plan – but it didn't.

Throughout the morning at school I rehearsed in my mind what I was going to say to Robert when the chance came, and I imagined him responding to me in various unlikely ways. If I had been able to stand back from the immediacy of my planned task, I could have drawn on what I knew about Robert to predict quite accurately what his response would be. But instead I managed to convince myself that the most implausible of all possible reactions would be the one I got.

Finally, shortly after lunch, I stopped Robert as we were leaving the dining room and asked if I could talk to him privately. He led me to the quiet room, unlocked the door, and we went in.

After he closed the door, we sat down.

My mouth was dry and I was trembling as I looked him in the eyes and awkwardly told him that I loved him.

'I love you too, Daniel,' he said. 'I love *all* God's children.'

'No, that's not what I mean,' I said, frustrated that he didn't seem to understand. 'What I mean is: *I love you.*'

The expression on his face, initially quite blank, began to slowly shift to a look of restrained rage.

'That,' he said with quiet anger, 'is the devil talking.'

'No, it isn't,' I said, deflated. 'Love isn't evil.'

'The kind of love *you're* talking about *is*,' he contradicted. 'It's wrong to desire someone of the same sex as yourself. God *hates* that.'

'But –' I tried to frame an objection.

'There's no buts,' he said. 'You need to repent. You must get on your knees and pray – pray that God will forgive you and cure you of your iniquity.'

I didn't know what the word 'iniquity' meant – was it some sort of illness? – so I wondered what difference being cured of it would make to me.

'Come on, Daniel,' he said determinedly. 'Get down on your knees.'

In the face of Robert's insistence, there was nothing I could do other than slide off the foam chair and kneel on the carpet.

'Bow your head,' he said severely, 'and pray to God in the name of Jesus Christ. Say you are sorry for these wicked desires of yours, and ask that he have mercy on you.'

I didn't quite know what I was supposed to do.

'Go on,' he urged. 'Pray – pray aloud.'

I felt extremely uncomfortable; I didn't *want* to pray aloud. If God really existed, if he was really there listening, then I wanted this to be between him and me; I didn't want Robert overhearing.

'Go *on*,' he pushed.

With timid inelegance I attempted to pray, trying to remember other prayers I had heard so that I could use them as a pattern. I tried to formulate an appropriate form of words to say I was sorry for telling Robert I loved him, and for having bad desires, and to ask for forgiveness and healing.

'Now,' Robert prompted, once I'd completed my prayer, 'say that you offer this prayer in the name of Jesus and in the power of the Holy Spirit.'

I did as he told me, and at last he let me get up off the floor.

'Now go on your way,' he said, rising from his seat, 'and make sure you put a stop to this sinning.'

He made for the door, opened it, and we emerged together into the corridor.

Clester Henry, Roger Hampton and Claire Knight were nearby, and as they saw Robert and I come out of the quiet room they began giggling.

'Haven't you three got anything better to do?' Robert challenged them abrasively.

Claire shrugged her shoulders, and they all drifted off down the corridor.

'I'm going to make some notes on you in the Cardex,' Robert said. 'I'll see you tomorrow.'

He strode off in the direction of the dormitories and nurses' station, leaving me standing there feeling stunned, insecure and perplexed.

Derek Ball, having just come on duty, must have passed Robert further along in the corridor, as he rounded the corner and approached me from that direction. Seeing me standing vacantly by the quiet room door, he asked me if I was all right.

I nodded.

'Are you sure?' he said. 'You don't *look* as if you're all right.'

'I'll be okay,' I said hoarsely.

In school that afternoon, every time I looked up from my *Beta Mathematics* book I saw either Clester, Roger, Claire, or all three of them, looking at me and smirking. I also heard loud stage whispers passing between them.

At one point, my eyes met Claire's and she hissed, 'What do you think you're looking at, bum boy?'

I quickly looked away, trying to lose myself in maths, but there was nothing I could do to insulate myself from their taunts.

For the most part, Mrs Sutton seemed oblivious to what was going on. She finally reacted to them when their noisy whispering reached a particularly rowdy peak. She shot up from behind her desk and stormed over to them, scolding them for generating such a childish racket.

'This is a classroom, not a zoo,' she barked at them, 'but if you continue behaving like imbecilic hyenas I will have you sent out.'

Mrs Sutton made no reference to the content of what they had been saying, only to the volume level and their infantile manner.

Eventually it was time to return to the Unit for tea. As I entered the dining room and got in line, it felt as if everyone was looking at me. I was so sick with embarrassment that, after I'd collected my drink, I made my way to an unoccupied table and sat alone.

I didn't remain alone for very long, as Jane came over and joined me.

'What exactly are you playing at, Daniel?' she said, looking at me with her usual gaunt expression.

'What do you mean?' I responded feebly.

'Everyone knows what you said to Robert King,' she said. 'Clester and some of the others listened at the quiet room door when you were talking to him after lunch.'

I looked down and stared fixedly at the orange surface of the table.

'If you're a queer,' she went on, 'they'll probably just give you more drugs – they'll try and control your urges; they'll try and *change* you.'

I was slightly shocked at this as I hadn't considered further medication to be a possible consequence.

'They wouldn't do that, would they?' I said, looking back up at her. 'You can't change that sort of thing with medication.'

'That won't stop them trying,' she answered. 'They've done it before.'

'Have they? When?'

Jane proceeded to tell me about a teenage boy who was at the Unit during the period I was away. Apparently he had very definite homosexual tendencies – and these, supposedly, were the reason for him being in Oakdale. According to Jane, they had him dosed up on a combination of Largactil and some other drug whose name she couldn't remember, leaving him extremely docile and thus incapable of acting on his sexual inclinations.

I couldn't tell whether Jane was making all this up, whether she'd misinterpreted a treatment regime for some other condition, or whether this was a genuine account.

'So what happened to him in the end?' I asked.

'I'm not sure,' she answered. 'I think they moved him to the main building.'

'To St Anselm's?' I said.

'I think so,' Jane replied. 'The point is,' she went on, 'this is what they'll do to you if you're not careful.'

I wondered if anything could be any worse than my present situation. I was already fairly subdued by medication and, in any case, it felt as though I was living without any hope. If they chose to, of course, they could subdue me further, and they could transfer me to another institution – but how much difference would that really make?

'Daniel,' she persisted, 'it isn't worth risking that sort of thing for Robert King. He's a pillock, an idiot!'

I remembered how my friend Andrew Ramsey, from my previous time in Oakdale, had also called Robert an idiot. But just because two kids – Jane and Andrew – were in agreement about a particular member of staff didn't make them right about him.

Perversely, it now occurred to me that the best way I could 'prove' my feelings to Robert would be to risk the kind of treatment Jane had described. If I was prepared to submit to heavy medication, and even to being locked away in an establishment potentially more callous and repressive than Oakdale, then Robert would be convinced that I was genuine. And I knew that Robert was an ethical man – so he couldn't *possibly* allow me to be abandoned to such a fate.

For the remainder of the week, and continuing into the following week, I kept trying to impress upon Robert King that my feelings for him were not only sincere, but perfectly honourable too. But he was clearly outraged and frustrated with me, and he often reminded me of how I had prayed forgiveness for my improper yearnings. If my prayer wasn't honest, he told me, then God would be very angry.

I argued with him, saying that there was nothing wrong with my 'desires'. One afternoon after school, he responded by taking me into the hall, where he found in the cupboard the same old tattered Bible that Andrew had found all those many months ago.

'I will get a more modern version of the Bible for you,' he said, 'but this will have to do for the moment.'

He got me to sit down, and placing himself next to me, he thrust the Bible in front of my face, pointing to a particular passage in the Book of Leviticus.

As it happened, I was able to offer a moderately well-reasoned response to this verse; this, ironically, was an indirect result of a conversation Robert had with me back in June of last year. At that time, he had tried to interest me in attending church as a way of becoming part of my local community in Horsham. Although I hadn't acted on his advice – apart from going with my parents to a service at Christmas – he had sufficiently sparked my interest to attempt reading various portions of the Bible, albeit it mostly at random. And so I had already come across this passage, and I knew its place in the biblical narrative.

'But surely that doesn't really count anymore,' I said, drawing upon my knowledge, such as it was.

Clearly he was incensed by my comment. 'Doesn't count anymore?' he thundered. 'It's the *Word of God* – it *always* counts.'

Despite being rather cowed by his reaction, I somehow managed to press on with my argument. 'But we already know that God wanted his people to multiply,' I said. 'They had to build-up the population. And once the people were preparing to settle in the Promised Land, they especially needed to increase their numbers so that they'd become a strong country. They couldn't do that if they were all homosexuals.'

'Well, maybe,' Robert said doubtfully.

'But none of that counts anymore,' I continued. 'The world is now *full* of people – so we don't have to worry about building-up the population anymore.'

'All right, Daniel, that's quite enough!' Robert said irritably. 'It's not your place to second-guess why God gave us particular laws. He *might* have given us that law to make sure we increased the population, or it might have been for some other reason – *it's none of our business*. What matters is that it's *God's law*, and it's up to us to obey it – or face the consequences.'

I might almost have allowed myself a sardonic smile at this if I hadn't been so unnerved by Robert's annoyance with me: whereas the possible consequence I'd been told about by Jane was increased medication and transfer to St Anselm's, the consequence described in the Bible was being put to death! Neither of these was a pleasant prospect, but I still found the contrast between them grimly amusing.

As I thought Robert had finished emphasising the unacceptability of my position, I started to rise from my seat, but he demanded that I sit back down again.

While some discussion had followed the stress he placed on the verse from Leviticus, it turned out that he intended that passage as no more than an appetiser. Moreover, he was not now going to allow any such discussion as he moved on to his concluding evidence. He flicked through the pages of the Bible until he came to the Epistle to the Romans, and then he jabbed his finger triumphantly at the passage which was to be his endgame.

'Look at this,' he said. 'The Apostle Paul tells us that the wrath of God will be shown to any man – or woman – *who goes against nature*. He talks about people having "vile affections" for each other. And *that* is what you have for me: a *vile affection*.'

With Robert now having moved on to a context in which my argument about population growth no longer applied, I had to think of another response. All I could come up with was trying to undermine the credibility of the Apostle Paul – an approach which I knew would not work with Robert – and so I had to resign myself to conceding.

During morning break on the Friday of that week, Sarah Dawes took me to one side and sat down with me in a corner of the TV room.

'Daniel,' she began, 'I've got to ask: what do you think you are up to with Robert King?'

I must have given her a look suggesting I thought the answer was self-evident.

'I just don't get it, Daniel,' she said. 'Why are you doing this? Why are you chasing after him?'

'I love him,' was my simple answer.

'No, you don't,' she challenged me. 'I *know* you don't.'

'But I do,' I contradicted her.

'Daniel,' she adopted a patient tone, 'you *are not gay*.'

I had only recently learned what the expression 'gay' meant, and in spite of my recent behaviour, I knew full well that Sarah was right and it didn't actually apply to me.

'Daniel,' Sarah continued, 'you *do not* love Robert; you *do not* fancy him; you *do not* feel *anything* like that for him.'

I looked at her for a moment, and then said, 'How do you know?'

'I just know,' she said, seemingly unwilling to provide a fuller explanation.

I looked at her and suddenly recalled the various rumours I had heard about *her* sexuality. Since I had first come to Oakdale, I had heard a good deal of explicit gossip on this subject, but it all seemed rather distant from my experience; despite hearing constant references to Sarah, I hadn't really connected any of it to the person I knew. It was as though the matter belonged to some far away country whose people I would never meet. But sitting here with Sarah, I realised that the issue was not as far removed from my world as I had supposed.

'Daniel,' she said, 'you're a sensitive boy, and so I don't want to embarrass you, but I've seen the way you look at some girls – I've even seen the way you look at *me* sometimes.'

I felt my face colouring – I *was* embarrassed.

'I *know* you are not gay,' she said, 'and *you* know it too.'

'I suppose so,' I finally admitted.

She smiled. 'That's better,' she said. 'And by the way,' she continued, her smile widening, 'it's very flattering the way you look at me sometimes – but I'm not much into boys, I'm afraid.'

Despite feeling awkward, I smiled back at her, and I remembered that I had always had some sort of special connection with her – and at the same time I realised I did *not* have such a special connection with Robert.

From that point onwards I never said anything more to Robert King about having feelings for him. But he still occupied a significant place in my day-to-day life. This may have been because he was my key worker on Mrs Causton's shift. But Derek Ball, who had the same role on Mr Taylor's shift, did not seem to loom quite so large in my daily experience.

For whatever reason – and the real reason became clear in the end – Robert was paying quite particular attention to me.

It was on the Wednesday of my sixth week of being back in Oakdale, and my case conference was due to take place that morning. While I was sitting on my bed, shortly before heading off to the morning meeting prior to the start of the school day, Robert came into the dorm and gave me that modern version of the Bible he had previously promised me. It was a large paperback bearing the title *The Living Bible*.

'I don't know what's going to be decided at your case conference today,' he said, 'but whatever happens, you need to keep God's Word close to you.'

I wasn't sure exactly what he meant, and so I didn't say anything in reply.

'Daniel,' he said thoughtfully, 'have you ever actually committed your life to Christ?'

'What does that mean?' I asked.

'So, you haven't, then,' he said. 'You're not really a Christian.'

'Yes, I am,' I told him. 'I was christened when I was a baby.'

'That doesn't make you a Christian. You still need to be saved.'

I didn't understand what he meant. Saved from what? The idea that came into my head was that it was already too late; I needed to have been saved *over a year ago*, saved from ever stepping foot inside Oakdale Children's Unit.

'If you want to be saved from God's judgement,' he explained, 'if you want to be saved from *hell*, you need to commit your life to Jesus.'

I frowned as I tried to make sense of what he was saying. To me it often felt that being in Oakdale was like hell, so it almost sounded as though Robert was suggesting it was God's judgement that I should be here.

'You *want* to be saved, don't you, Daniel?' he asked.

'I suppose so,' I answered uncertainly.

In fact, I certainly *did* want to be saved; I wanted the clock turned back to a time before I had ever been assessed (judged) and found emotionally disturbed (guilty). I wanted to be saved from the condemnation of ever becoming a patient in Oakdale.

'Well, you have a good think about it,' he said, 'and if you decide you *do* want to be saved, come back and talk to me again.'

While I wasn't necessarily dismissive of religious belief – indeed, I was rather curious about it – there was something about Robert's type of faith that struck me as superstitious, as defiant of reason. But regardless of this, I very much felt that I wanted to be saved – desperately so. If there was even only the *faintest* possibility that Robert's way was the answer, then surely that way was worth taking.

'Come on,' he said, interrupting my thoughts, 'we need to get ourselves to morning meeting.'

*　　*　　*

Unlike my pervious case conference, this one did not overrun. I was also rather less preoccupied with it during my morning at school. My expectation was that the powers-that-be would want me to stay in Oakdale, and while that was an uncomfortable thought, the reality of it seemed inevitable. And sure enough, upon leaving the school to make my way back over to the Unit for lunch, I was met by Robert who immediately informed me of the decision: I was to remain at Oakdale.

While I couldn't claim to be shocked by the decision, I was nonetheless upset by it and I fought back the tears as Robert walked with me to the dining room.

We arrived at our table before Greg Peterson and Roger Hampton, and as we sat down I told Robert that I did indeed want to be saved.

'Are you absolutely sure?' he asked me.

Of course I was sure, I thought to myself. My case conference had just condemned me to remaining in the hell of Oakdale for some unknown, indefinite period, so of course I wanted to be saved.

'Yes,' I replied. 'I am absolutely sure.'

'Very well,' he said, as Greg and Roger joined us, 'we'll go in the quiet room after lunch and talk about it.'

'You two want to be alone together in the quiet room again, do you?' Roger sniggered.

I was now more weary than embarrassed by these kinds of comment, and so I would have preferred simply to ignore Roger. But Robert seemed quite angry.

'Roger,' he chided, 'I know what you're implying, and if I find you spreading any malicious rumours, there will be trouble. Do you understand?'

'Yeah,' Roger said, though he was still clearly pleased with his quip, even more so now that it had provoked a defensive response from Robert.

Lunch proceeded uneventfully, and after the distribution of medication and cigarettes was complete, Robert took me into the quiet room.

We sat down on a couple of the vinyl-covered foam chairs, and as we did so it struck me that the yellow-painted walls were the colour of sunshine, an impression that was underlined by the fact the room was overflowing with light from the bright spring day outside the window. It very much felt as though I was in a place of hope. But I was also struck by the irony that this was the place where I had once been beaten almost to the point of unconsciousness – but the terror of that occasion was now gone.

'You do understand what it means to commit yourself to Jesus?' Robert queried.

'I think so,' I responded.

'You need to be sure,' he said. 'It means that you will follow him, be his disciple – even when it gets difficult. It means that you will be promising to be completely loyal to him, no matter what.'

'I understand,' I said.

'And if you love him and trust in him, you will be saved,' Robert said.

I agreed that this was what I wanted.

'Okay,' he said, 'we're going to pray now, and I want you to repeat these words after me...'

I lowered my head, closed my eyes, and carefully echoed Robert's words about being sorry for my sins, asking forgiveness, and thanking Jesus for taking my punishment for me. He then directed me to finish by stating my willingness to receive Jesus as my Saviour.

Although the words were simple, I had to admit to myself that they didn't fully make sense. What did it mean, in concrete terms, to receive Jesus? And wasn't the punishment that Jesus had supposedly taken for me a rather extreme one? But whatever my doubts and questions, I knew that now was not the time to voice them.

Robert was smiling broadly as I opened my eyes and raised my head. 'That's it! You are a Christian now, Daniel – you are saved! Hallelujah!'

I was a bit surprised by Robert's exuberant exclamation, and because it struck me as quite funny, I smiled readily – something which Robert apparently took to be my newfound delight in the Lord.

'So what happens now?' I asked, still grinning.

'Nothing,' he answered. 'That's it – you're saved.'

'But what do I have to *do*?'

'You don't *do* anything,' he said. 'Just have faith in Jesus and be guided by him in all things.'

It was clear to me that there was no point in asking any further questions – and I wasn't sure what to ask in any case, as I was really quite confused by what had just happened.

'There is one thing, though,' Robert said. 'You can't be a Christian all on your own. You need to join a fellowship of your brothers and sisters in Christ, so I strongly suggest you start going to The Living Springs of Zion Church in Horsham.'

There weren't many people who eagerly welcomed the news that I had become a Christian.

Talking to Bridget Fitzpatrick in the hideout after school that day, I learned that many people believed that faith could be understood and expressed in many different ways, and that not all Christians would necessarily have the same approach as did Robert.

'I was brought up Catholic,' Bridget told me, 'and I would be very sceptical about Robert's kind of faith.'

While I was sitting with Bridget to one side of me, Jane was seated to my other side, and it turned out that she had some very strong views on the matter.

'Robert's just been using you, Daniel' she stated.

'Well, I wouldn't go that far,' Bridget said.

'No, he *has*,' Jane insisted. 'It makes him feel good about himself to think he's "saved another soul". He hasn't done this to help you; he's done it for himself.'

'Well, let's not worry too much about who he's done it for,' Bridget responded. 'The question is: has it helped you, Daniel?'

'Well,' I began hesitantly, 'if I've been saved, then yes, that *must* have helped me.'

'Saved from what?' Jane demanded. 'You're still here in this place. You're not in a normal school getting a proper education, you're away from your home and your family, and you're half asleep a lot of the time 'cause of the drugs they give you. You haven't been saved from any of that, have you?'

'Robert says I've been saved from the wrath to come,' I said – though as soon as the words left my lips I recognised how abstract and vague they sounded.

'"The wrath to come"?' Jane mocked. 'What about *now*?'

'Knowing I've been saved means I can *endure happily* what's happening now,' I said, though I wasn't sure I was truly convinced.

'Daniel,' Jane said sharply, 'you're a bigger pillock than Robert is. *He* really *believes* all this stuff, but it's obvious that you don't – and yet you're going along with it anyway.'

'All right! Enough!' Bridget interrupted. 'Why don't we all try and think calmly about what we'd really like to be saved from. And then we can think about what sort of things we could do to help us get saved?'

'Robert says only Jesus can save,' I remarked.

Jane hit me.

Sarah Dawes wasn't greatly impressed by my conversion to Christianity either.

In the period between tea and supper on Thursday afternoon I had decided to take myself off to the boys' dormitory and read from *The Living Bible*. There were a few other kids in the dorm at the time – Jeremy Newton, plus Clester and Greg – who, to varying degrees, were ribbing me for having suddenly 'got religion'. The teasing stopped, however, when Sarah came in and sat down with me on my bed.

'Daniel,' Sarah said, 'don't you think you're taking all this religious business a bit too seriously?'

I closed the Bible and put it on my locker. 'But it *is* serious,' I said.

'Well, yes, I'm sure it is,' she agreed, 'but you look like you're getting obsessed with it.'

She reached over to my locker and picked up my Bible.

'I've heard from some of the other staff,' she said, 'that since yesterday you've been reading this –' she indicated the Bible '– almost constantly.

'Daniel,' Sarah continued, obviously trying to choose her words carefully, 'I know that Robert has become a very big influence on you. He's actually a very good nurse. Although he can be a bit strict, he's very caring and conscientious. But that doesn't mean he's always right about everything. I think you're listening to him far too much, and that you really need to make up your own mind about some things.

'When you come back after half term,' she went on, placing the Bible back on my locker, 'you won't be having quite so much attention from your key workers anymore, so you won't need to spend so much time with Robert. So just you make sure that you start thinking for yourself – don't let him carry on doing it for you.'

For the first time I could remember, I found myself becoming angry with Sarah.

'That's not fair,' I objected. 'I *can* think for myself.'

'I *know* you can, that's why I'm saying this to you.'

'No, it isn't,' I said accusingly. 'It's because you know what the Bible says about people like you.'

There was an unbearable silence, during which I was overwhelmed by regret for what I had said in anger. It also became apparent that Robert and his faith had forced a wedge between myself and Sarah. If this was what being saved meant, then perhaps I had been better off before.

'Is that what you really believe?' Sarah asked unsteadily, evidently fighting back intense emotion.

'I don't know,' I said sheepishly, unable to look her in the eye, 'but I'm sorry I said it.'

'Perhaps we should both just try and forget it,' she said. 'You'll be off home tomorrow for the half-term holidays and the Silver Jubilee celebrations – I hope we can be friends again when you get back.'

CHAPTER ELEVEN

While everyone else seemed to be in the grip of either punk rock or *Star Wars*-fever, the days and weeks following the half-term break were a muddled blur to me in which competing drives vied for my attention. I was uncomfortably stirred by newly inflamed sexual urges, which seemed heightened by the warm weather; and the volatility and irritability I had already been experiencing also appeared greatly amplified.

Set against these forces was my continued adherence to a highly conservative form of Christian faith, which I clung to by suppressing my scepticism – not always with success. Notions of morality and acceptable conduct conflicted powerfully with my other chaotic motivations, leading me to feel, at various moments, more angry, more depressed, more confused and, of course, very guilty.

Predictably, Robert King was pleased to hear that I had started to attend The Living Springs of Zion Church on Sunday evenings, while, just as predictably, Sarah Dawes was not. This contributed to a developing tension between them, but as they served on different shifts this only resulted in a direct face-to-face conflict on one occasion. But the friction between them was frequently evident in comments that one or other of them would make in the other's absence. As I knew myself to be some sort of catalyst behind this friction, I was alternately besieged by feelings of culpability and power, adding to the other internal contradictions I was battling.

One occasion when these intense energies within me exhibited themselves was on a balmy Wednesday afternoon following school. It was then that I made an artless move on Susan Jarman – and over the coming weeks I made similar moves on Louise Bray and Claire Knight.

Susan and I were sitting on the grass close to the Adventure Camp, the sun beating down on us as we watched Mr Jones and John Webber supervising a few kids playing in the tree house and on the death slide. Despite the heat contributing to my perpetual drug-induced sluggishness, I shuffled up a little closer and tentatively slipped my left arm behind Susan to enfold her waist.

She turned her head round sharply to face me. 'What do you think you're doing?' she challenged.

I quickly withdrew my arm. 'Nothing,' I said.

'You're only thirteen,' she said. 'Why the hell do you think I'd be interested in you?'

Susan was fifteen, and I had to concede that maybe I didn't appear to be a particularly appealing prospect to her. But my hormones were raging, and her dismissal of me prompted a desire to prove myself manly.

'Maybe you could have more fun with me than you think,' I said, reaching out to embrace her with both my arms.

I tried to lean in closer to kiss her, but she pushed me away roughly and then slapped my face.

'Get off me!' she exclaimed.

Hearing the commotion, Mr Jones came running over towards us.

'What's going on?' he demanded.

'It's him!' Susan said. 'He had his hands all over me and tried to snog me!'

'Daniel!' Mr Jones bellowed. 'Get up!'

As I got to my feet he grabbed me by the collar and dragged me away from Susan and told me to sit against the trunk of the oak in which the tree house was suspended.

'Stay there where I can keep an eye on you,' he said, before turning his attention back to the other kids.

I looked back over to Susan and saw that she was sniggering to herself, no doubt at my expense, and immediately an enormous sense of rage boiled up within me. I jumped up and stalked furiously back over to her.

'Daniel!' I heard Mr Jones shouting from behind me, 'I told you to stay over here.'

I ignored him, and having marched back over to Susan, I reached down and gave her shoulder a hard shove, knocking her backwards.

'Bitch!' I yelled, before turning and strutting off towards the Unit.

'Daniel Kinsley!' Mr Jones yelled after me. 'Get back here this instant!'

I shot him the best rebellious look I could manage and continued on my way.

Mr Jones didn't pursue me, but confronted me later at suppertime.

'I've seen some very bad reports of you lately, Daniel,' he said, sitting beside me at our table, while Greg Peterson and Roger Hampton tried to hide their amusement.

'And *you've* got nothing to be so pleased about, either,' he spat at them. 'What about that incident with the aspirin, eh, Roger?'

Mr Jones was referring to the large bottle of aspirin that had been discovered in Roger's locker the previous week, presumably intended for the purpose of overdose.

'And as for the last few Cardex entries I've seen for you two –' Mr Jones went on. '"Lively, overactive, badly behaved" and "lively, overactive, *fairly* well behaved".'

He then turned back to me and continued. 'Quite frankly, I'm shocked by what's happened to you lately, Daniel. It's always been annoying the way you were so bloody miserable all the time, but at least you were basically a good kid. But now you're molesting girls and being insolent to staff. If you don't watch your step, young man, you'll find yourself in the time-out room.'

Robert King had been sitting with the kids at the next table, and he obviously overheard what Mr Jones had said to me, as he decided to have a word with me after supper. I had been walking along the corridor, heading for the dormitory, when he stopped me.

'You understand what's happening to you, don't you, Daniel?' Robert said, amidst the corridor traffic.

I looked at him blankly.

'It's the devil attacking you,' he said.

'What?' I responded, rather puzzled.

'Because you're a Christian now,' he stated, 'the devil is testing you. He's making you have lustful desires, making you rebellious and bad tempered.'

I certainly knew that *something* was happening to me, though I wasn't absolutely convinced that this was the explanation. But not really being aware of an alternative I decided to accept what Robert said – whether I really believed it or not.

'You need to do what you *should* be doing *all* the time,' he went on. 'Confess your sin to God, ask for forgiveness, and pray that Jesus will stand with you and strengthen you while you're being tested.'

He patted me on the back and walked off in the other direction, leaving me to resume my journey to the dorm.

Once I arrived at the boys' dormitory, I entered to find John Webber there, and he too wanted to speak to me about my behaviour.

'Ah, Daniel,' he said, as I lowered myself to sit on my bed, 'you're just the person I wanted to see.'

'I can guess what you want to see me about,' I said.

He sat down next to me. 'Everything you did today at the Adventure Camp,' he began, 'is perfectly normal for a boy of your age.'

This wasn't what I'd been expecting.

'But that doesn't make it right, though,' he added. 'We don't allow any amorous activity between kids in the Unit – that's what we call that sort of thing, "amorous activity". If you get yourself a girlfriend while you're home at weekends, that's fine – actually, that would be *great*. But you're not to try anything like that here. And besides, Susan's too old for you; you need to find a girl of your own age.'

I mumbled a vague response.

'And, obviously, it was completely unacceptable for you to shove Susan like you did,' he continued. 'I understand that you were frustrated – that's to be expected – but you really must *control* yourself. And as for disobeying Mr Jones, well, you *know* that was wrong. Again, it's perfectly normal, with all these intense emotions going on, that you might feel defiant, but you've got to *control* these feelings.'

'Robert says it's the devil testing me.'

John swallowed, appearing impatient with that notion. 'Well, I wouldn't know about that,' he said, 'and I'm not sure it makes any difference anyway. The point is: you are growing up, you're going through a lot of changes – physically, emotionally – and you need to learn how to control yourself. Saying that it's the devil's fault isn't going to stop you getting into a lot of trouble, so you need to get a grip and manage your feelings.'

'*Am* I in a lot of trouble?'

'No, not really,' he smiled. 'What happened today – well, what happened to *start* with – isn't really much of a big deal. But just you make sure that you've learnt your lesson.'

'I just can't imagine it,' Mike Kirby was saying to Derek Ball as they stood in the dining room following lunch one Thursday. 'I mean, we've had our share of blackouts during the strikes, but that doesn't come close to what *they're* going through.'

'Yeah, I know,' Derek agreed, 'and they reckon the power won't be back on until later today – and this is one of the biggest cities in the world!'

They were discussing the citywide loss of power in New York, which had started the previous day and was still ongoing.

I was continuing to sit at the table, drowsily half listening to Mike and Derek's conversation. Greg and Roger had gone, leaving me with Sarah Dawes. She was puffing on a Consulate as she suggested to me, not for the first time, that I should take less notice of Robert's inflexible and questionable dogma.

'It isn't doing you any good,' she said. 'You're a teenager, you're having to deal with all kinds of stuff, and Robert's ideas are just confusing you more.'

I no longer felt as relaxed with Sarah as I used to do – in fact, I was just as defensive with her as I was with most of the other staff members. 'He's just trying to help me,' I said, even though I too had some reservations about his approach.

'Daniel,' Sarah said, 'Robert has some very strange and old-fashioned ideas, and –' Sarah was interrupted as Robert himself approached the table, having just come on duty.

'Sarah,' he said sharply, obviously having overheard what she was saying,

'I'd like a word with you.' And turning to me, he said, 'Daniel, go off and find something to occupy yourself with before school.'

I got up and left the table, as Robert sat down opposite Sarah.

Mike and Derek were just leaving the dining room, having finished their conversation on the New York blackout, and I followed them to the door. I didn't follow them through it, however, as – upon glancing back to see that Robert had his back to me – I decided to lean against the wall and see if I could eavesdrop on what he was saying to Sarah.

'Sarah,' Robert was saying, 'you are trying to poison Daniel's mind against another member of staff.'

Sarah could see I was standing there listening, but she didn't let on; but neither did she let my presence stop her from reacting angrily to Robert's accusation. 'I am doing no such thing,' she barked. '*You* are the one who's trying to poison Daniel's mind. You're making him feel guilty for having normal feelings – *and* making him more likely to act inappropriately by encouraging him to *suppress* his feelings.'

'I really don't think you're qualified to discuss "normal feelings",' he retorted.

'And just what is that supposed to mean?' she shot back.

'You *know* what it means,' he said. 'You are a bad moral influence. All the children know about your sordid personal relationships, and that sort of thing can have a harmful effect on an impressionable boy like Daniel.'

Sarah looked absolutely aghast at Robert's words, so much so that she didn't seem able to say anything in reply. She just stared at him for a few seconds, before stubbing out her cigarette and quickly leaving the table.

She stormed past me, and I simply followed slowly in the same direction. I just walked, one foot in front of the other, without looking back to find out whether or not Robert had become aware of my presence.

This was the only time I would see a direct confrontation between Robert and Sarah. But I could never forget the hostility between them, as they would both continue to occasionally make disparaging comments to me about each other. Regrettably, the zeal I was acting out in the name of my faith was leading me to side with Robert, my co-religionist, rather than with Sarah, whose claim on my loyalty was probably the more deserving.

And I was *very* zealous for my faith, regularly praying and reading the Bible as well as defending Christian doctrine against all criticism, whether it came from kids or adults. My strident evangelism during this period was something I would later look back on with great embarrassment.

Despite my faith and its associated moral principles, there was a sense in which I was coming off the rails. Much of my behaviour directly contradicted my declared values. Had my reality not seemed so dreamlike – presumably as a result of the ongoing hypnotic effects of Valium – then I might have attempted to resolve the contradiction.

'You're nothing but a hypocrite,' Jane Sparrow told me over tea one Tuesday after school.

She was giving voice to what I knew many of the other kids were thinking too. And I knew full well that she was right. I was being consistently licentious in my attitude towards many of the girls – though not to Jane, as her anorexia placed her beyond the interest of my libido – and I was frequently giving way to extraordinarily explosive tantrums in which I would lash out at whoever was nearest to hand. This meant that on more than one occasion I had been sedated and confined to the boys' dorm without access to any clothing.

'You claim to be a Christian,' Jane said, 'but you've turned into a lech and a yob.'

'Robert says that the more I try to follow Jesus, the more the devil tries to attack me – that's why all this is happening.'

'Bollocks!' she declared.

'But it's true!' I answered back.

'No it isn't,' she said, 'and you know it. If you *really were* a Christian you'd be interested in the truth, not stupid excuses.'

That conclusion may well have been accurate, but in the midst of all my confusion I didn't actually know what the truth was. I didn't understand the powerful and conflicting drives that seemed to have taken me over, and I didn't know how to stop this turmoil. Things had moved so far beyond my control, that weekends at home had been cut short – or even sacrificed completely – in the face of my volatility. And as the long summer holiday beckoned, it was unclear how much of it I would be able to spend at home and how much of it would have to be endured within the confines of Oakdale.

It was this question that Mrs Fox, the social worker, was to address when she came and interrupted my conversation with Jane and asked to see me in her office.

Mrs Fox informed me that I would not be spending the whole of the six weeks' school break at home. Indeed, my mum and dad, and my brother Mark, would be going on holiday for two weeks to Normandy at the end of July. This would be the first time since my birth that my family would holiday overseas – and I was not going to be allowed to go with them. Apparently, my behaviour was considered unreliable, and so they couldn't risk taking me out of the country.

I was extremely upset at this news, and it hardly encouraged me to work on improving my behaviour.

And so I spent the first few days of the holiday at home in an extremely dejected and irritable state. So much so that I suspected my family were pleased to return me to Oakdale on the Friday evening before sailing to Cherbourg.

The boys' dorm was very quiet on that Friday night. Apart from myself, Mr Köhler had only two other boys to watch over: an eleven-year-old who had only recently arrived at the Unit, called Tony Sparks, and the fourteen-year-old Jeremy Newton. And so, feeling very alone and abandoned, I cried myself to sleep – just as I had done on my first night in Oakdale nearly eighteen months ago.

For two weeks I was incarcerated at Oakdale with Tony and Jeremy, plus four girls – including Jane Sparrow – and three of the younger children. For much of the time we were left with very little to entertain us, although there were a few occasions when either Mike Kirby or Mr Jones would take some of us out for a trip in the minibus. Among the places we were taken were Brighton, Petworth, and the area surrounding Chanctonbury Ring, currently an archaeological excavation site. These were pleasant enough diversions, but they hardly compensated for the family holiday I was missing – and besides, I was often too dozy to get the greatest benefit from them anyway. The self-pity I felt was very much underlined by songs of emptiness and despair which I heard on the Ford Transit's radio: 'So You Win Again', 'Telephone Line', and so on.

Eventually this fortnight in Oakdale came to an end and I returned home for the remainder of the school holiday. I just about managed to keep my temper under control during this period, which certainly improved the experience. But not really having any friends in Horsham – I hadn't maintained contact with the few friends I'd made while at Shelley School – I felt almost as isolated at home as I had done in Oakdale.

When September arrived it was extremely disquieting to discover I was actually *looking forward* to being back among the kids in Oakdale.

I returned to discover that Oakdale was somewhat changed by two particular events. The one with the more enduring impact was the arrival, at last, of a new head at Oakdale School, Mr Barkworth. Although I wasn't immediately aware of him having much effect on me personally, I certainly noticed the relief expressed by the teaching staff at having someone back at the helm.

The other event – and one that was still *relatively* enduring in its impact – had actually happened mid-way through August: the death of Elvis Presley had a major influence on the flavour of Oakdale.

On almost any afternoon after school it was possible to stand at the intersection between the dormitories and hear one Presley song coming from a cassette recorder in the girls' dorm, another from an old record player in the boys' dorm, and yet another from the radio in the nurses' station.

Roger Hampton had returned from the summer break with a mono Dansette record player, which he kept at the side of his bed – it was just a little too large to slip underneath – and he seemed to spend a good deal of time playing about three Presley LPs, one after another.

This was all very well, but I had just begun to start losing myself in reading again – reading books other than the Bible, that is – and wall-to-wall Elvis Presley was fast becoming an unwelcome accompaniment.

It was just as Presley-fever was starting to die down a little – though not by much – that another celebrity death brought back to mind an earlier feature of the Oakdale soundtrack.

I made my way over to the Unit after school one Monday afternoon. I arrived in the dining room and, cup of tea in hand, sat down with Jane, as had become my usual practice. I don't suppose I'd thought of Jane as a particularly close friend until now, but we had both been patients in the Unit for quite some time and there was a sense in which we had come to know each other quite well.

'Do you remember Michael Davey?' she asked me. 'I bet he's very upset now.'

Michael used to constantly play the same T. Rex tape over and over again in the boys' dorm, usually when I was trying to read. It was very similar to the situation now with Roger playing Presley all the time. Marc Bolan, the singer from T. Rex, had died in a car crash on Friday, and like Jane, I too had thought of Michael when I heard the news.

'He must be devastated,' I said. 'But it's a good job he's not here now, or we'd have T. Rex constantly battling it out with Elvis in the dorm – and it's hard enough to hear yourself think with just Elvis.'

'So,' Jane said, changing the subject, 'I expect you've got your eye on that new girl.'

She was referring to Karen Webb, who was fourteen and came from Petersfield, just over the county border in Hampshire.

'I don't think so,' I said, knowing that she was mocking me.

It was true that I found Karen's appearance very stimulating, and I had certainly imagined trying my luck. But I was sure she was well beyond my reach, and I had no wish to face certain humiliation.

'Why not?' Jane teased me, grinning thinly.

I shrugged my shoulders.

'You might have a chance with her,' she said, apparently contradicting my own assessment – though I knew what she *really* meant.

Fully understanding her implication, I couldn't help but give a small laugh. 'That's not very nice,' I said, still chuckling. 'Besides, she definitely wouldn't go for a thirteen-year-old.'

This was the only time I could remember seeing Jane laugh. It wasn't a pleasant sight, given her overly-lean appearance, but I chose to see it as a positive thing.

What lay behind our amusement was a rather unpleasant situation, and one that we shouldn't really have laughed about. The fact was – as far as I could make out – Karen had been admitted to Oakdale as a consequence of an older man having unlawful sexual relations with her. Someone, possibly Karen's parents, had made a complaint against this man, and he had been arrested and charged, and he was currently awaiting trial.

For the moment, however, a certain prurient interest in the matter, along with a rather judgemental attitude derived from my supposedly Christian morality, prevented me from recognising another case of Oakdale injustice. Fortunately, this situation would be rectified a few weeks later when that injustice was spelt out more plainly for me.

It was another Monday. We were all back in the dining room again for morning break, and I was sitting at a table with Jane Sparrow, Louise Bray and Mrs Causton – whose presence was rather inhibiting us.

Karen was late returning to the Unit following the weekend, but all of a sudden she came striding into the dining room carrying a copy of *The East Hampshire Post*. She put the paper down on a table immediately adjacent to ours, where Michelle Newbold and Mrs Sampson were discussing Cardex entries.

'It's in the paper,' I heard Karen say to them excitedly.

'What is?' Mrs Sampson asked.

Karen sat down with them and quickly leafed through the pages until she found the article she wanted.

I couldn't see the headline from where I was sitting, but it soon became apparent that the paper was reporting the sentence handed down to the man found guilty of having sex with a minor.

Mrs Causton, aware of what was happening at the next table, got up and went over to Karen.

'I'll take that, if you don't mind,' she said a little abruptly, folding the paper shut, then folding it again, and putting it under her arm. 'This isn't a subject we want broadcast all over the Unit.'

Mrs Causton turned on her heal and stalked out.

My first thought was that Mrs Causton was quite right. Through the eyes of my inflexible morals, I considered Karen to be guilty of sexual sin, and I was concerned that she seemed to be *celebrating* her indecent behaviour.

But I could also tell that Karen was upset by Mrs Causton's severe reaction, and in spite of my instinct to condemn, I was pleased that Michelle and Mrs Sampson were trying to comfort her – not that they did so for very long before leaving to attend to some, unspecified, duties.

As soon as they were gone, Karen came over and joined us at our table.

She was indeed an attractive girl, and she looked quite a bit older than fourteen – so it was at least possible that the convicted man had been mistaken about her age.

'They've sent Ian to prison,' she told us, 'but when I last saw him, he said he still loves me. He said he wants to be with me when he gets out – and I'll be old enough by then.'

'Do *you* want to be with *him*?' Louise asked her.

'Oh, yes,' she said, becoming more animated. 'He's lovely!'

I hadn't really had very much to do with Karen, so I hadn't previously noticed how the effect of her appearance was challenged by her unsophisticated manner. Though older than me, she was – unlikely as it seemed – less mature. And so it was now obvious that this man, Ian, couldn't possibly have been unaware that she was underage; if anything, he might have thought her even younger than her years.

'He can't be that lovely,' Jane remarked, 'or he wouldn't have taken advantage of an underage girl.'

'But he *didn't* take advantage of me,' Karen maintained, 'I was willing.'

'Exactly how old is he?' I asked.

'He's forty-three,' she said. 'But he looks a lot younger,' she added hurriedly.

'Forty-three!' Jane exclaimed. 'He's probably married with grown-up kids of his own.'

'Oh yes, he is,' Karen said, still speaking with naïve excitement, 'but he's giving all that up for me.'

I hadn't been aware of Mr Jones coming up from behind me, and so hearing him suddenly yell at Karen made me jump.

'Karen!' he said angrily. 'You could *at least* keep your voice down. Everyone can hear you revelling in what you've done to that poor man. He's in jail because of you; he's lost his wife and family because of you – and you just sit there having a good laugh about it.'

Karen started to cry. 'I'm not laughing about it,' she wept. 'I love him – and he loves me.'

'I've never heard anything so ridiculous in all my life,' Mr Jones snarled. 'It's disgusting. And as for you –' he looked from Jane to Louise and then to me '– you should be ashamed of yourselves for encouraging her.'

*   *   *

Given my age, it was only natural to be very preoccupied with matters relating to sex and sexuality. In spite of my often-insensible listlessness, I remained as interested as anyone in these staples of adolescent fascination. However, I would later come to see that, on occasions when the subject didn't directly concern me, things would have been far better if I had just kept out of it. Thankfully, I didn't do or say anything I would come to regret in the case of Karen and her imprisoned suitor – I merely followed her story with interest. But there was another matter where I foolishly and heartlessly involved myself.

It was now the beginning of November – just a few days before my fourteenth birthday. The half-term break was over and Greenwich Meantime had resumed just over a week earlier, and so the evenings were now much darker. It was on one of these dark evenings, at around eight o'clock, that I had somehow ended up in the company of Clester Henry, now sixteen, and Jeremy Newton, now fifteen. We were lurking near the foyer where the doors leading out towards the school were situated. The lights were dimmed, and it was easy to hide in the shadows without being detected by anyone.

While the majority of staff members going off duty would leave by an exit at the other end of the Unit – leading directly to the car park – it was not unknown for some of them to leave via this foyer. By exiting through the doors we associated with going to school, it was possible to take a sharp left, soon followed by another, and leave the Oakdale compound through a side gate. One could then follow a path through the grounds of the main building leading to other car parks and a bus stop, and there were some individuals who would occasionally leave via this route.

From our darkened corner we had already seen Mike Kirby and Tracy Grafton leave this way. But shortly after they had gone we saw a youngish woman we didn't know enter through those same doors. She stood in the foyer leaning against the wall, apparently waiting to meet someone.

After a few minutes, Sarah Dawes came along the corridor, and she went straight over to the woman.

'Carla,' Sarah greeted her warmly, taking the woman's hand in hers, 'I got a bit held up. Have you been waiting long?'

'No,' Carla responded with a smile, 'not long.'

The two of them then left the building, hand-in-hand.

Emerging from our place in the shadows, Clester, Jeremy and I burst out laughing.

'That must be Sarah's lezzy friend,' Jeremy tittered.

'Yeah,' Clester grinned idiotically. 'I wonder what *they're* gonna get up to tonight.'

All three of us collapsed into foolish fits of giggles again, as we made our way back along the corridor to the heart of the Unit.

Not surprisingly, what we had just witnessed became gossip to share with the other kids. But we didn't just share it as we'd seen it – we embroidered our story. Instead of saying we'd seen Sarah and her friend Carla leave holding hands, we said that we saw them kiss – and kiss passionately.

All three of us were equally guilty in spreading our manufactured rumour. I, no less than the others, positively wallowed in publicising the tale. Indeed, my behaviour was probably worse that than that of either Clester or Jeremy, as I further embellished the story with cruel 'moral' condemnation. Sarah, who had been my most faithful advocate and friend from among the staff, was now the subject of my self-righteous and dishonest bigotry. That night, I enthusiastically told my story to anyone who would listen – and there was no one who *wouldn't* listen – and so I utterly betrayed Sarah Dawes.

By the following morning, the story had circulated widely among the staff as well as the kids, and so Robert King took me aside after breakfast to ascertain exactly what I had seen.

He and I sat down in the quiet room, and I repeated my lies to him.

'Well,' he said, 'I'm sure you realise that Sarah's behaviour was completely unacceptable. What she does in her private life is her own business, but when she commits squalid unnatural acts right here in the Unit, that's another matter. I will make sure that Miss Bishop knows about what has happened, and I'm sure Sarah will be disciplined.'

'What will happen?' I asked, suddenly feeling very concerned.

'Hopefully,' Robert replied, 'she will be dismissed. You and I both know that she's a bad moral influence on the children in her care. And now we've got eye-witness evidence of Sarah's disgraceful activities, I'm sure Miss Bishop will do the right thing.' He smiled in way that must have been intended to reassure. 'Daniel, you should be very pleased with yourself,' he said, 'you've done exactly the right thing.

He then led me out of the quiet room and locked the door behind us. As he went off to waylay Miss Bishop as soon as she arrived in time for the morning meeting, I was left standing in the corridor feeling quite nauseous; I knew that, this time, *someone else* was to suffer the 'consequences of my actions'.

When Sarah came on duty that afternoon, she cannot have failed to notice that everyone was reacting to her strangely.

I was just walking by the doors to the – currently unused – art room when I saw, further down the corridor, Sarah coming towards me. Quite apart from feeling extremely guilty at the sight of her, I noticed a couple of kids giggle quite openly as she passed them, while Mr Jones, whom she also passed, gave her an extremely disapproving look.

As she drew level with me, she smiled – clearly not yet knowing what was happening, nor that I was the cause of it. I couldn't bring myself to smile back; I couldn't even look her in the eye – I just looked down at my feet, quickening my pace to get away from her.

After an afternoon of unbearable anxiety at school as I tried, and failed, to concentrate on maths, I was back over in the Unit for tea.

Sitting at a table with Louise and Jane, I was largely oblivious to everything they said; my thoughts were elsewhere. Every so often my eyes would dart around the dining room, trying to catch sight of Sarah, but she wasn't there.

'What's the matter with you, Daniel?' Jane asked.

I only half heard her, so I responded with a vague, 'Uh?'

'You look very pale,' Louise said. 'What's wrong?'

'Nothing,' I answered irritably. 'Nothing's wrong.'

I quickly got up from the table, walking swiftly out of the room without even remembering to take my cup and saucer back to the trolley.

I was heading for the boys' dormitory, but as I made my way through the passageway connecting one section of the Unit with the other, I saw Sarah moving very slowly in the other direction, her gaze fixed on the floor as she walked. As we drew closer to each other, she looked up and saw me. She stopped, and I too was halted in my tracks.

She simply stared at me, and as she did so, I saw tears welling up in her eyes. I opened my mouth to speak, but I couldn't say anything. A feeling of incredible self-loathing came over me, and – like an arrow piercing its target – it occurred to me that I wished myself dead.

We both stood there, as though frozen. And then Sarah wiped away her tears with the back of her hand, and briskly marched past me.

I was now the one to move forward slowly with my eyes fixed to the floor.

Turning the corner into the corridor which led to the dormitories, I decided that I needed to admit to what I had done. On my left, just before the door to Mrs Fox's room, was Miss Bishop's office. I knew she wasn't there at the moment, as I'd just seen her in the dining room having tea. But I needed to confess. And so I sat down on the floor opposite her door, just below a window looking out onto a grassy courtyard.

Time moved very slowly as I waited there quietly sobbing. A few kids passed by – Roger kicked at me and asked, rather sarcastically, if I was depressed. He then moved on as Derek Ball rounded the corner.

'What are you doing, Daniel?' Derek asked. 'Is everything all right?'

'I'm waiting to see Miss Bishop,' I explained.

'I don't think she'll want to see you,' he said, not unkindly. 'She's very

163

busy; whatever it is, I'm sure she'd prefer it if you talked to someone else instead. You can talk to me, if you like.'

'No,' I replied, wiping my eyes. 'Thanks anyway, but I need to see Miss Bishop.'

'Okay, then,' he said, before walking away.

Eventually, Miss Bishop rounded the corner and approached the door to her office. I got up to meet her.

'What do you want, Daniel?' she asked.

'I need to see you,' I said, shaking.

'Daniel,' she said firmly, 'you know perfectly well that you should take any problems you've got to your key worker.'

'No,' I said, swallowing hard. 'I need to see *you*.'

'Oh, all right,' she said in a tone of resignation. 'Come in.'

She unlocked her door and led me into her office.

Her room was slightly smaller than Mrs Fox's and lacked the heavily-laden bookshelves. Indeed, there was very little furniture in Miss Bishop's office apart from her desk, a filing cabinet, a low coffee table, and a few chairs.

She seated herself behind her desk.

'I won't invite you to sit down,' she said, 'as I can't spare you very much time. Now, what is it you want to see me about?'

I gathered up all the courage I could and hurriedly spewed out the necessary words as simply and efficiently as I could. 'I lied about Sarah Dawes. Jeremy, Clester and me – we all lied.'

Miss Bishop looked at me for a few seconds before saying anything in reply.

'Are you saying,' she began eventually, 'that you didn't see her leave the Unit last night with, er, a friend?'

'No,' I said carefully. 'I saw her meet someone in the foyer, and then they left together. And that's it. That's *all* I saw.'

I thought it best not to mention that Sarah and her friend, Carla, were holding hands as they left.

'Are you telling me that you did not see Miss Dawes do anything, er, improper?'

'That's right,' I answered hoarsely. 'I just saw her meet someone in the foyer, and then they left.'

Miss Bishop was clearly very angry. 'Because of you, I've now got to call Miss Dawes back in here and apologise to her – I'm going to have to back down before a member of my staff. Do you have *any* idea what you've done?'

'I'm sorry,' I said. 'I'm very sorry.'

'You *will* be,' she said. 'I'm going to have you, and Jeremy and Clester, all confined to your beds, and your clothes taken away. And you will not be allowed up again until I say so.'

CHAPTER TWELVE

Clester Henry, Jeremy Newton and I remained confined to our dormitory for the remainder of the week – and I had to endure the cutting fury of my fellow conspirators for having broken ranks and admitted the truth. And then, as a further 'consequence of my actions', I was not allowed home for the weekend – although my family did come to visit me on the Saturday.

As always, a weekend spent in Oakdale was a tedious and desolate experience, one that was made all the more difficult by the knowledge that this was no more than I deserved.

When Monday arrived, I had to face Sarah Dawes again. I saw her in the dining room as I arrived with all the other kids streaming in for breakfast. She was about to take her place at table with Susan Jarman, Louise Bray and Karen Webb. Before sitting down at my own table, I nervously made my way over to her. I knew I had to say something, and the sooner I did it the better.

'Sarah,' I said rather croakily.

She stood and looked at me.

'Sarah,' I tried again, 'I wanted to say, er, I wanted to say that –'

'Daniel,' she cut me off, 'I suppose I should thank you. I don't really *want* to thank you – not after what you put me through – but I suppose I should. Miss Bishop suspended me; she said I had behaved with gross impropriety in the presence of children. But because you went and told her the truth –'

'I really am very sorry,' I said, starting to cry. 'If I could go back, have another chance, I'd never do it again.'

She slowly shook her head. 'You can't go back,' she said. 'None of us can go back.'

With nothing more to be said, I turned and made my way to my own table.

Autumn gave way to winter, and I grimly went about the task of surviving from day-to-day while keeping out of trouble. Where possible, I submersed myself in the limited school curriculum of English and maths, and when Mrs Sutton interrupted my concentration to tell of her late husband's wartime exploits, I listened politely.

I even participated – albeit reluctantly and self-consciously – in preparations for the Oakdale Christmas revue. This was to be a rather peculiar event on the evening of the last day of term. Staging was being set up in the hall for kids to perform an incongruous selection of sketches and musical items before an audience of parents – who would then take their kids home for the holiday. No doubt the event was just as excruciating to watch as it was to perform.

My job was to feign the role of a ventriloquist while Tony Sparks – the twelve-year-old who had been admitted back in the summer – was to sit on my knee pretending to be my dummy. This was to represent Tony's last experience as an Oakdale patient, as he would be returning home permanently that night. It occurred to me, without any trace of amusement, that to spend one's last few moments at Oakdale dressed as a ventriloquist's dummy summed-up quite a lot about the nature of the place.

And Tony wasn't the only kid who would be leaving the Unit this Christmas. Susan Jarman and Claire Knight were both returning to their homes, as were Roger Hampton and Clester Henry, while Greg Peterson was going to foster parents. And, very sadly, Julie Wilson was being transferred to St Anselm's, as her age no longer qualified her to remain in a children's unit. Surely this was the worst possible Christmas present the system could bestow on anyone in its charge.

The first few weeks of the New Year were cold and miserable. It seemed there was little to be thankful for at Oakdale, other than the fact that February didn't see us snowed in – which it would have done had we been situated further towards the west.

I was also less fanatical about my faith, having grown tired and irritated with The Living Springs of Zion Church. I ceased attending there and began going, occasionally, to Holy Trinity Church in Rushams Road, where I encountered a more moderate form of Christianity. I was no longer 'on fire' with religious fervour, but the odd visit to Holy Trinity – often accompanied by my family – provided me with a safe maintenance dose of religiosity.

Not surprisingly, Robert King was not impressed with my shift to mainstream Anglicanism – though he did concede that God could do great things, *even* in the Church of England.

Before the winter weather reached its height, mid-January saw the arrival at Oakdale of a new girl of around my age. My first sight of her was on a Thursday morning when she was shown into Mrs Sutton's class by the head, Mr Barkworth.

'You must be Beverley Kemp,' Mrs Sutton said, getting up to meet her as she was guided in.

'Beverley comes to us from Tideway School in Newhaven,' Mr Barkworth said, 'and they've sent some work over for her to be getting on with while she's here.'

Mr Barkworth handed Mrs Sutton a weighty stack of textbooks.

'Good gracious!' Mrs Sutton exclaimed, taking the pile of books.

'I trust you'll be able to keep Beverley up-to-date, Mrs Sutton,' Mr Barkworth said.

'We'll do our best.'

'Then I'll leave Beverley in your capable hands.'

The head gave Beverley a supportive smile and then left.

Mrs Sutton placed the books on her desk, and then directed Beverley to sit down at a vacant table.

'I really don't know what some of these schools are playing at,' Mrs Sutton said, as she pulled up a chair and sat next to Beverley. 'All those books! All those subjects!'

Beverley clearly didn't know how to respond.

'Of course,' Mrs Sutton continued, 'I'll do my best to keep you going with that lot, but generally we try to concentrate on the *important* things here, English and maths. The rest doesn't really matter that much.'

'I think it does,' Beverley replied faintly.

'Well,' Mrs Sutton responded, 'when you're as experienced as I am you might think differently.'

Mrs Sutton proceeded to bombard Beverley with her views on education and employment, after which she then voiced her opinions on current affairs.

She expressed her irritation on the subject of the European Court of Human Rights, and particularly vented her anger concerning its finding against Britain in connection with the mistreatment of prisoners in Northern Ireland.

'We've treated them far better than they deserve!' she held forth. 'I don't know what my late husband would have made of all this. He fought for this country, and now we're letting foreigners dictate how we run our affairs!'

I could tell from Beverley's face that she was uncomfortable with Mrs Sutton's attitude, but – very wisely – she didn't voice any objections.

Although I was attempting to stay focussed on *Ahead in English*, I couldn't help but watch Beverley as she silently endured Mrs Sutton's barrage of opinions and prejudices. For some reason, I was already very taken with Beverley – and I hadn't even had any personal contact with her yet. I found her very attractive, and her softly-spoken reticence somehow fascinated me. But, obviously, I didn't actually *know* her, and yet I urgently wanted to reach out, to find comfort and affection in getting close to her.

After school that day, over tea, I talked to Jane Sparrow about Beverley.

'Just don't,' Jane said. 'Whatever you've got in mind: *just don't.*'

'But she seems really nice,' I said, 'and I really fancy her.'

'Daniel,' Jane warned, 'you've managed to stay out of trouble for quite some time now, so don't spoil it. And besides, she's new here – *you* must remember what *that's* like – and she's hardly had an easy start with Mrs Sutton lecturing her; the last thing she needs is you trying it on.'

'But I could *help* her,' I said. 'I'd be her friend, and I'd look after her.'

'Yeah, right,' Jane said sarcastically.

I should have listened to Jane, but my impulsive and all-consuming enthusiasm for Beverley would not accept any challenge, however reasonable.

And my enthusiasm really was all-consuming. Over the weekend at home I was absolutely aching to be back at Oakdale so that I could be near to Beverley.

But when I returned to the Unit on Monday morning, I was too nervous even to approach her. And so, during breaktime, I wrote Beverley a note, in which I said I had noticed her and that I thought she was very good-looking. I also said that I wanted to get to know her.

I tried to persuade Jane to pass the note on to Beverley for me, but she refused. So I then approached Louise, who agreed.

The remainder of that morning was spent in Mrs Sutton's classroom with me anxiously wondering if Beverley had read my note yet. I tried very hard not to look over in her direction, but every so often my eyes alighted on her despite my best efforts. Each time this happened, however, all I saw was Beverley deeply engrossed in her schoolwork; she never once looked up to acknowledge me.

Following lunch, just as I was about to leave the dining room, Louise accompanied Beverley on her way over to me.

'*This* is Daniel,' Louise told Beverley.

'Thank you for the message,' Beverley said to me diffidently. 'It was very sweet. But I hope I won't be here long, so there won't be *time* for you to get to know me.'

I nodded and smiled, too overcome by the fact she was actually talking to me to say anything useful in return.

After she and Louise had gone, I was furious with myself. I had successfully created an opportunity for real contact with Beverley, but I had wasted it. The only thing I could do, or so I thought, was to write her another note.

Over the next couple of days I wrote Beverley a succession of notes. At first she would either come and speak to me, or write me a note in return, each time politely discouraging my interest.

On Thursday afternoon, following lunch, I was sitting on my bed in the boys' dormitory writing Beverley yet another note. Although there were a couple of other boys in the dorm, it was fairly quiet, and so my attention was immediately captured by the sound of the double-doors swinging open. I looked up to see Beverley coming in, with Jane and Louise either side of her.

'I was just writing to you,' I stammered. 'I suppose I don't need to now, as you're here.'

As I put my pencil and paper down, Beverley said, 'No, don't stop. Finish it.'

I was a little surprised by her response, as I thought she might be losing patience with me. But I picked up the pencil and paper, and with her standing there, I quickly finished the note and then handed it straight to her.

She took my note, and without looking at it, she tore it in two and let the pieces fall to the floor.

By the time I had properly registered what had happened, Beverley, Louise and Jane had marched out of the boys' dorm.

My first instinct was to hide my head in my pillow and sob. But I was aware of the two other boys in the dorm, and I didn't want to appear weak and stupid in front of them. And so I drew upon the energy of my despair, and turned it into an act of resolve – my fear of embarrassment leading me to commit what would possibly be the most shameful act of my entire life.

I jumped to my feet, and barked at the other boys, 'Let's get her!'

Both these boys were relatively new to the Unit. At thirteen, Luke Hadleigh was the younger of the two, while the other, Kevin Hall, was fifteen.

They both followed me as I thundered out of the dorm with a dramatic flourish, intent on hunting Beverley. I hadn't considered what I was going to do when I found her, but I charged through the corridors, Luke and Kevin behind me, determined to play the part of a warrior pursuing his foe.

'Spread out,' I ordered Luke and Kevin.

I didn't look to see where they went, but their acceptance of my command gave me a great sense of power. I stomped through the Unit with enhanced vigour, looking through doors – into the dining room, the TV room, the playroom, and so on – in search of my prey.

'What are you up to, Daniel?' came the voice of Derek Ball, standing near the door to the hideout.

I ignored him, continuing my purposeful search.

Eventually I found Beverley in the hall, still in the company of Louise and Jane.

'Sod off, Daniel!' Jane yelled at me. 'Leave Beverley alone.'

Aware that Luke and Kevin were behind me again, I felt compelled to continue my show of strength. And so I advanced towards Beverley with affected determination.

'Daniel! Stop it!' Louise shrieked, as Beverley started backing away from me.

I didn't stop. I kept advancing until Beverley was unable to retreat any further, her back having come into contact with a wall.

I wasn't thinking. I wasn't reasoning. I was just acting out a role.

As if expecting some hidden film director to shout 'cut!' at any moment, I raised my hands to Beverley's throat as I closed in on her. I began to squeeze my fingers around her neck.

And then I saw the look on her face. Never before had I seen such a look of terror. All the colour drained from her, the black pinpricks of her pupils staring at me with unspeakable fear.

The moment I saw that look, I let go of her and stepped away, thoroughly sickened by what I had done. For me, this may have been a senseless acting role, but for her it was real – she must have thought this insane teenage boy was on the brink of taking her life.

I could never be exactly sure what happened next. There was a lot of shouting, a lot of rushing about, and I found myself face down on the hall floor, securely restrained by brawny masculine arms.

Presumably, a powerful sedative was administered to me – though I wasn't aware of it happening – because the world around me suddenly bled away into nothingness.

I awoke alone in the nighttime darkness of the time-out room. I was at once panicked and puzzled by this. From what I could remember, kids were not normally left in here overnight, as it was inconvenient for staff to cover this end of the Unit while also supervising the dormitories. Perhaps they had simply abandoned me, for here I was, alone, nauseous, light-headed – and very cold. I was completely naked, with nothing but a thin sheet to cover me, and my body ached from lying on the hard, freezing linoleum floor.

Various desperate needs begged for my attention: I needed to get warm; I needed to get more comfortable; and I needed to relieve my bladder.

Groggily, I looked around the room, straining to see. With only minimal light entering the room through a small frosted-glass window, it was some time before I was able to discern the outline of a bucket. But as soon as I saw it, I struggled to my feet – I was so unsteady I thought I might fall – and I used the bucket as my lavatory.

With one need having been met, I set about fashioning some sort of mattress from the foam-filled bolsters and wedges, so that I wouldn't have to lie against the unyielding and unforgiving lino. With that done, only one need remained – but there was nothing I could do to bring warmth to my body.

I lay there, enveloped as tightly as possible in my sheet, shivering violently from the bitterness. I must have slipped back into unconsciousness, as the next thing I knew, bleak winter daylight was seeping in through the window.

It also appeared that the heating system had come on, as warm air was flowing in via the grills of the wall-mounted radiators. The room was still cold, but it was bearable now.

Waves of giddiness assaulted me as I clambered to my feet and tried testing the door. As expected it was locked. I banged my fists against it and called out, but no one seemed to hear – or if they did, they certainly didn't respond.

I flopped back down onto the wedges and bolsters, pulling the sheet up to my chin.

Eventually – I had no idea how much time had elapsed – the door opened, and in came Mr Jones and John Webber.

'Ah, the bully-boy has woken up,' Mr Jones remarked.

'How are you feeling, Daniel?' John asked impassively. 'You've been out for a long time.'

I started to speak, but my words came out slurred.

John sat down cross-legged next to me, while Mr Jones looked down from his standing position.

'Feeling a bit rough, are we?' Mr Jones said callously.

'Yes,' I mumbled.

'Good,' Mr Jones commented.

'Do you think you could manage some breakfast?' John asked me.

I was feeling rather sick, but I was also quite hungry. 'I'm not sure,' I said. 'I think so.'

'I suppose you expect us to bring it to you,' Mr Jones complained.

'Bill,' John said, standing up, 'perhaps we should let him have his clothes back so he can eat in the dining room.'

Mr Jones shrugged his shoulders. 'If you say so,' he grumbled, 'but if it was up to me, I'd leave him locked up in here and throw away the key.'

Up and dressed, I had to lean heavily on John Webber for support as he guided me to the dining room. But upon arriving, I was shocked to see the tables arranged in a central block – they were in their weekend formation.

'What day is it?' I asked John as he helped me to a seat.

'It's Saturday,' he said. 'Don't worry – you've only lost *one* whole day.'

I started to look around the table to see who else had been left behind in the Unit this weekend, but I gave up trying to take in their faces; it was such an enormous effort to keep my eyes focussed.

Remaining in place for breakfast was a terrible struggle, and there were several times when I was so sleepy I nearly slipped off my chair. I was therefore very grateful when the meal was over and I was allowed to find my bed in the boys' dormitory.

I spent most of Saturday asleep, only really getting up for meals, and I didn't start to properly feel myself again until Monday.

At this stage, no one from among the staff was saying anything to me about Beverley or about the dreadful thing I had done. And Beverley herself was nowhere to be seen.

At Monday morning breaktime, I sat – very sheepishly – with Jane and Louise.

'Is Beverley all right?' I asked them wearily.

'She's gone,' Jane replied matter-of-factly. 'After what happened, her parents came and got her out of here.'

'I wanted –' I said, struggling '– I wanted to tell her I was sorry, and to tell her that I'd never go anywhere near her again.'

'Well,' Louise said, 'you certainly *won't* be going anywhere near her again.'

'But she'll never know how sorry I am,' I said tearfully.

'I don't think she cares,' Jane replied. 'She's just glad to be out of here – and well away from you.'

'I would never have really harmed her,' I said, trying to justify myself. 'It was just an act.'

'We know that, Daniel,' Louise said. 'You're an idiot – not a killer.'

I looked up. 'You *know* it was just an act?'

'Of course,' Jane answered. 'You don't think we'd let you sit here with us if we really thought you were dangerous, do you?'

Although I felt thoroughly wretched, I was comforted by the knowledge that Jane and Louise were still my friends. They had seen me at my very worst, and yet they still accepted me.

That afternoon, after school, the three of us sat together in the TV room half-watching *Clapperboard* followed by *The Flockton Flyer*. Robert King was there, keeping an eye on us.

Robert had now adopted an extremely icy attitude towards me, no doubt because I had so spectacularly failed the expectations he had of a staunch Christian convert. But due to the apparent willingness of Louise and Jane to continue associating with me, Robert's disdainful demeanour spilled over into his attitude towards them.

'Be quiet, you three,' he told us as we chatted. 'This is the TV room – people come in here to watch television in peace.'

This was a very odd thing for him to have said, as we were the only kids in the room. Unless Robert himself was particularly hooked on a children's adventure series, there was no possible reason for this rebuke – unless he was just looking for an excuse to air his displeasure with us.

We did as we were told and stopped chatting, and began viewing the television more intently. But it wasn't long before we started talking again.

'I told you to be quiet,' he said.

Jane answered back in an uncharacteristically cheeky way. 'What's the matter, Robert?' she quipped. 'Are you a huge fan of *The Flockton Flyer*? Are we spoiling it for you?'

At that point I noticed for the first time that Jane must have been getting a little better. Although she was still very thin, she was hardly the emaciated bag of bones that she used to be. Her skin was less dry, her hair looked fuller and more healthy, and her eyes were much brighter. This improvement in her condition must have been taking place over quite some time, but I just hadn't noticed it happening. But now, thanks to that flash of brashness at Robert's expense, I could see that Jane was recovering.

This came as quite a revelation to me. Although I had seen several kids come and go during my time at the Unit, I was never really convinced that anyone actually got any better at Oakdale. And yet, here was Jane, a girl who had once seemed on the verge of starvation, growing healthier and stronger.

Robert, however, obviously didn't share my revelation – he was probably only sensitive to the more supernatural variety – and he responded to Jane with annoyance rather than surprised satisfaction.

'Right, that's it!' he declared. 'I'm switching the TV off.'

He got up, unlocked the door giving access to the TV compartment, and shut the set off. As soon as he'd done this Mrs Sampson came in, wanting to watch *Crossroads* – apparently having forgotten that Monday was the only weekday when it didn't run. In any case, the TV got switched back on again.

The weeks went by, and apart from a talking-to from the social worker, Mrs Fox, no one said anything more to me about the incident involving Beverley. The guilt still clung to me, however, although it eventually started to recede somewhat with the arrival of spring.

March saw the enactment of a decision to set Wednesday afternoons aside for sporting activities. Rumour had it that someone at the Local Education Authority had noticed that Oakdale School wasn't fulfilling its obligation to provide physical education. And so, the teaching staff, with the support of the Unit staff, had acted to rectify this problem.

The result was that the majority of kids – of both sexes – together with several members of staff, ended up out on the field every Wednesday afternoon. Usually we would play some vague semblance of football, although an occasional game of rounders was not unknown. Somehow, all the teachers – with the exception of Mr Barkworth and Miss Evesham – managed to avoid the 'Wednesday Games', thus making this more of a Unit event than a school event.

I was less than pleased at this new development, especially as the weather was still fairly cold for the first couple of weeks. And, apart from the exception of swimming, I had no interest in sport whatsoever. Team sports, in particular, were rather problematic for me, as I simply didn't seem to have sufficiently good coordination. And so, when playing football, my teammates would often become exasperated with my poor performance on the pitch. One attempted solution was to put me in goal, but as I never really noticed the ball coming towards me until it was too late, that didn't really help matters.

But I was still required to partake in the Wednesday Games. To avoid the misery of football, I would sometimes join one or two other kids and staff members in running round the circumference of the field. I wasn't really much of a runner either – although I was reasonably good at short sprints – but this alternative activity was certainly preferable to football.

While there were various levels of interest in the Wednesday Games among the kids, there were a few members of staff who suddenly seemed to become quite dedicated to physical exercise. This keenness wasn't confined to Wednesday afternoons, as some of them would arrive at Oakdale early, before coming on duty, so that they go for a run around the field. On Mrs Causton's shift, John Webber and Colin Goodman made a particular effort to get out on the field most days, while on Mr Taylor's shift, Sarah Dawes was the primary enthusiast.

On a Tuesday in early April, soon after the Easter break, I arrived in the boys' dormitory following lunch and just happened to glance out through the sash window above my bed. Across the field, on the far side to my extreme right, I could make out a tracksuited figure lying on the grass. The figure wasn't moving. I strained my eyes to see if I could make out who it was. It was Sarah!

Knowing that something was obviously wrong, I launched myself towards the fire door at the end of the dorm. I pushed hard on the bar to open it, and ran frantically across the field in Sarah's direction. Behind me I could hear the sound of an alarm, activated by my unauthorised departure through an emergency exit. But I ignored it and kept running, until I reached the spot where Sarah was lying.

With my heart thumping, I knelt down beside her and saw that she was conscious but fighting to breathe.

'Sarah,' I panted, 'I'll get help.'

She grunted an acknowledgement, and I ran back towards the open fire door. As I drew closer, I saw Mr Taylor and Mike Kirby emerging from the boys' dorm, obviously responding to the alarm.

'Get back in here this instant!' Mr Taylor shouted at me.

174

'It's Sarah,' I gasped. 'She needs help.'

Neither of them seemed to hear me, and they looked very angry as I approached them. It appeared I had no choice but to turn around and run back to Sarah, knowing that they would chase after me. I could only hope that I'd be able to run well ahead, far enough for them to notice where I was going.

I was already struggling to maintain speed, and so I had to call on all my reserves of strength in order to continue powering my legs, pushing myself well beyond my normal limits as I fought to get back over to Sarah.

I fell in a heap by her side as Mr Taylor and Mike finally caught up with me.

'What the hell have you done, Daniel?' Mike said, horrified at the sight of Sarah collapsed on the grass. 'What have you *done* to her?'

'This time you've gone too far, Daniel,' Mr Taylor snapped as he bent down to assess Sarah's condition. 'We'll probably have to bring the police in.'

I couldn't say a word in my defence, as I was completely shattered from my exertion. But I had led them to Sarah, and that was all that mattered.

More staff were summoned to the scene, mainly to attend to Sarah, but Derek Ball and Gerry Binstead, the auxiliary, escorted me back to the boys' dorm.

'I didn't do anything,' I protested, having caught my breath. 'I saw Sarah collapsed on the grass and I went to help.'

'And you expect us to believe that, do you?' Derek spat at me as we entered through the open fire door. 'Just get your clothes off and get into bed. I don't want to hear another word from you, you sadistic little bastard – I don't even want to *look* at you.'

He shut the fire door behind us. And then, as soon as I was in bed, he and Gerry seized all my clothes, including the pyjamas under my pillow and everything in my locker. Having done this, they left the dorm with all my possessions bundled up in a laundry bag. And so I was left alone, lying naked beneath my sheet and quilt, desperate to know what was happening with Sarah.

By now, most of the kids had gone back over to school, and so the dorm was very quiet apart from sound of the radio in the nurses' station, muffled by closed doors. This meant I could hear, albeit faintly, something of what was going on outside in the field. The sound of some sort of engine reached my ears, and so I sat myself up and looked out of the window above my bed. I saw an ambulance driving across the field and coming to a halt where Sarah lay, and I continued watching as two uniformed men transferred her to a stretcher before lifting her into the back of the vehicle. As the ambulance drove off again, I lay back down on my bed and wept.

CHAPTER THIRTEEN

I had lain there in my bed for some hours, quietly sobbing. School had ended, and various kids had come and gone from the dorm. Some, including Luke Hadleigh and Kevin Hall, had sworn and spat at me for what I had supposedly done to Sarah Dawes.

A little after five o'clock, the double-doors swung open and a few clear bars of 'Knowing Me, Knowing You' infiltrated the dorm from the radio in the nurses' station. Derek Ball had entered, carrying the laundry bag containing my possessions.

Placing it beside my bed, he said, 'We're all so sorry, Daniel; we misjudged you.'

I sat myself up in bed.

'I've been told that Sarah just about managed to say that it wasn't your fault,' he said. 'In fact, it seems that you're quite the hero; because of you, we got to Sarah just in time.'

'Is she going to be all right?' I asked.

'Hopefully – but she may be off work for a while.'

I closed my eyes and exhaled some of my tension, comforted by the knowledge that Sarah would recover.

I then asked what exactly had happened to Sarah, but Derek's response was vague at best.

'Anyway,' Derek said brightly, 'we don't keep heroes confined to the dormitory – I've brought all your things back, so you're free to get up and dressed.'

'Thanks,' I smiled, as Derek made his exit.

Later that week I learned that Jane Sparrow would soon be leaving the Unit.

'I won't be coming back after half term,' she told Louise Bray and me as we sat together in the quiet room on Wednesday evening.

Louise and I both looked at Jane in surprise, and then we looked at each other. It was obvious that Jane had made a significant recovery, but she had been a patient in the Unit long before either of us had arrived, and so it seemed difficult to imagine the place without her.

'You're going back home?' I asked. 'Permanently?'

'Yes,' she answered. 'I haven't said anything until now as I wasn't sure it was really going to happen. But I saw Mrs Fox this afternoon, and it's definite.'

'So you'll be going back to your old school?' Louise remarked.

'No,' Jane said. 'It's nearly three years since I was last there, and it wouldn't be easy to fit back in now. So my mum is going to educate me at home, and get me ready to sit a few O-levels next year – and that's something I wouldn't be able to do if I stayed in Mrs Sutton's class.'

'Can you take O-levels at home?' I wondered.

'No, I think I'll be going to a school in Havant to sit the actual exams,' Jane explained. 'But I'll be able to do all the studying for them at home.'

I was quite intrigued by the idea of being educated at home, and I began to wonder if this might be a possibility for me. After all, I was completely wasting my time in Oakdale, trapped in a kind of limbo where I couldn't make any real progress. And now, one of my closest friends in the Unit was leaving, and no doubt I would see other friends leave before too long as well. I was filled with horror at the thought that I might be left behind to stagnate while everyone else got out and moved forward.

And so I resolved to make an appointment to see Mrs Fox. But I found that I needed to endure what seemed like a very long wait, as the social worker wasn't free to see me until the following Tuesday afternoon.

When the time of the appointment came I made my way impatiently to Mrs Fox's office and knocked on the door.

It seemed a very long time before she answered; I was almost about to knock again when I finally heard her voice call, 'Come in.'

I entered and was directed to the same chair in which I had sat on so many previous occasions. And, as always, Mrs Fox addressed me from her place to the side of her desk.

'So what is it, Daniel?' she said. 'What is so important that you needed a special appointment to see me?'

'Jane Sparrow told me she will be leaving soon,' I said.

'Yes, that's right,' Mrs Fox replied. 'I know you two are good friends, but I'm sure you'll get by without her.'

'She said that she's going to be educated at home; she's not going back to school.'

'Well, yes. But what's that got to do with you, Daniel?'

'I was wondering,' I began, very nervously, 'if maybe we could do something like that with me.'

Mrs Fox didn't answer for a good few seconds, and the drawn out silence was almost intolerable.

'Well,' she said at last, 'I really wasn't expecting this. I don't quite know what to say. I suppose –' she paused for a moment '– I suppose the first thing I should tell you is that it really isn't very likely.'

I felt very discouraged. 'Why not?'

'Jane is a special case,' Mrs Fox explained. 'She's been here a long time, and she's only got one more year left after this one before she finishes her secondary education. Your situation is quite different.'

'But I'm not learning anything in Mrs Sutton's class,' I complained, 'and I want to go back home.'

'Daniel,' Mrs Fox said with exaggerated patience, 'if you want to get out of here, you *know* what you have to do?'

This threw me, as I *didn't* know what I had to do.

'Daniel,' she began again, 'if you want to get away from here, you will have to do two things. Firstly, you will have to convince us that you can control your reckless emotions – one minute you're in a rage, the next you're in despair. Until we see that you can control yourself, there's no chance of you leaving here. And secondly, you will need to commit yourself to going back to your old school – Shelley School, wasn't it? – and that's if they agree to have you back.'

I looked at her, not bothering to hide my disappointment.

'Look, Daniel,' she said, 'I'll have a think about what you've said. But I also want you to go away and think about what *I've* said.'

The next day, all the kids and staff were seated in a circle, as usual, for the morning meeting.

A few rather routine and uninteresting matters had been discussed when Miss Bishop suddenly looked over towards me.

'Now, Daniel,' she said. 'I understand that you've been asking if you can leave here and be schooled at home.'

I was horrified that she had chosen to bring this up in front of everyone, and I felt very self-conscious as all the eyes in the room were now on me. I was also deeply embarrassed that everyone would think I wanted to copy Jane – which, of course, I did.

'Well, let me tell you,' she said, 'that is *not* going to happen. You're not getting away from here that easily. If you want to leave us, then you're going to have to put in the effort to make it happen.'

Before I could think what to say, Miss Bishop had moved on to the next topic.

The meeting continued, the attention that had been focussed on me having passed very rapidly. But the anguish it left behind was more slow to dissipate, my thoughts for the remainder of the meeting all revolving around how Miss Bishop had summarily dashed my hopes and publicly humiliated me.

Inevitably, Jane and Louise were to question me later about my notional plan of following in Jane's footsteps. Though uncomfortable, fearing Jane might possibly be offended that I had appropriated something from her, I found them both very sympathetic.

'You can't trust them,' Jane said to me during morning break. 'You say something to one of them in confidence, but you never know whether that confidence is going to be kept. You just can't expect them to treat you with any kind of respect; Miss Bishop used what you said to put you in your place. You might not have been able to predict that, but you shouldn't be surprised by it either.'

I knew she was right; like her, I had been the Unit long enough to recognise the pattern, albeit it only with hindsight.

After lunch on the Monday prior to the first ever May Day bank holiday, Mr Taylor's shift came on duty, and with it came the return of Sarah Dawes.

In the corridor outside the dining room, a number of kids and staff crowded round her, all eagerly enquiring after her well-being.

'I'm fine,' Sarah assured them.

Some of the younger boys wanted to know graphic details of the procedure in which, apparently, air had been drained from her chest cavity and one of her lungs reinflated. She wasn't too forthcoming on this topic.

'But one good thing has come out of this,' she told the assembled gathering, 'I've given up smoking.'

I stood at the periphery of the crowd, and so Sarah didn't notice me until people began to disperse.

'Daniel,' Sarah smiled once she saw me, 'what would I have done without you?'

She came towards me and gave me a hug, and I remembered the special friendship that I used to have with her.

'You may have saved my life,' she said, releasing me.

'Do you think so?'

'Oh, yes, definitely,' she said.

I followed Sarah as she walked into the dining room, and I sat down with her at one of the tables.

'Sarah,' I said carefully, 'I really want to say I am so very sorry for what I did to you last year. You've always been very good to me, and I've always trusted you. But what I did was –'

'Daniel,' she interrupted, 'all that is over with now. We're friends again. But there's something I have to tell you. Although I've come back to work, I'm not going to stay. I've handed in my resignation.'

I was stunned. 'When do you leave?'

'At the end of May, at half term,' she said.

I wasn't sure how to respond to this. I had missed Sarah's friendship greatly since my rather ill-advised relationship with Robert King had led me away from her. And, of course, I had virtually destroyed what was left of this friendship by spreading false gossip about her. And now, no sooner had the friendship been restored, than I learned that she would soon be gone.

'Why?' I asked. 'Why are you leaving?'

'Because I'm a coward,' she said with a humourless laugh.

I frowned, unable to understand.

'I'm fed up with this place,' she said. 'I can't bear seeing what happens here anymore. I can't stand seeing the abuse anymore. And I'm sick of the prejudice against me from some of my colleagues.'

I looked at her with a terrible sense of sadness.

'Oakdale is a bad place,' she continued. 'Just look at what it's done to you. You probably shouldn't have been sent here in the first place. But since you've been here, you've seen and learnt terrible things. No one has ever really tried to help you, and the same is true for quite a few of the kids, especially Dr Rajasimha's patients.'

Sarah's candidness was unexpected, and naturally I wanted to know more, and so I asked her exactly what she meant.

'Has Dr Rajasimha ever checked up on you while you've been in Oakdale?' she asked me.

I shook my head.

'Dr Collins checks up on his patients from time-to-time,' she said, 'but Dr Rajasimha forgets about his as soon as they're admitted here.'

Although I hadn't been aware of this, the news hardly came as a shock.

'That git Rajasimha,' she went on, 'just recommends kids for admission to Oakdale when he can't be bothered to try anything else. Most parents just say no. No one wants their kids coming to a place like this unless there's no other choice. But some parents – like yours, probably – go along with what Dr Rajasimha says because they think he's the expert.'

'But surely it's very expensive to send kids here,' I said. 'Why would Dr Rajasimha waste all that money?'

'You're right about the expense, Daniel,' she answered. 'Last I heard, the cost of keeping a child in Oakdale was about £80 per week. But you've got to remember, it isn't the consultant psychiatrists who have to pay it; it's taxpayers like your dad who have to pay.'

'And I really shouldn't have been sent here,' I said, slightly astonished.

'All this money is being wasted on me.'

'Yes. You should *not* have been sent here,' she said. 'It's true that you weren't very well when you first came. You were very depressed, but you didn't have major behavioural problems and you weren't psychotic, or anything like that. And all Oakdale has done for you is to *teach* you how to have problems. Public money is being spent on *making* you ill.'

It was a selfish thing for me to ask, but I went ahead and did it anyway: 'You're the only one who's really on my side; what am I going to do once you're gone?'

'Daniel,' she said, 'I'm getting out of here because I can't stand it anymore. *You* shouldn't stand it anymore, either. You've got to get yourself out of here.'

I had, of course, tried to convince Mrs Fox that I should leave the Unit and be educated at home, but she and Miss Bishop had quashed that idea no sooner than I had voiced it. I knew, therefore, that what Sarah was suggesting would not be easy; it might not even be possible.

'I don't know that I *can* get out of here,' I said.

'Daniel,' she said in a hushed but urgent tone, 'just do whatever they want. Cooperate with them completely, even if you know they're wrong. Do whatever it takes, because as soon as you're out of here you'll be free of them.'

If I had needed any further persuading that I had to find some way out of Oakdale, it came on a late afternoon in May.

Mr Barkworth, the school head, had decided that there should be a parents' evening. As far as I was aware, nothing like this had ever happened before at Oakdale School, and given that the place didn't really compare with any mainstream educational establishment, I couldn't imagine what form this might take.

As it was, there weren't all that many parents able to attend. Some lived too far away to come in just for the sake of a few minutes with their child's teacher, while others, it seemed, didn't care. And as for those children who were in Oakdale by court order, it appeared as though there was no one in their lives to act as substitute parent.

I managed to count five sets of parents, including my own, being shown around the small school building, while a handful of us kids trailed behind. Mr Barkworth mainly showed them displays of children's artwork, and spoke about the quality of the school's (limited) facilities and the dedication of his teaching staff.

After this brief tour, each set of parents was given some time with their child's class teacher. If I hadn't been present in the classroom when my mum and dad had their session with Mrs Sutton, I don't think I would have believed what happened.

'Daniel is one of my best pupils,' Mrs Sutton enthused. 'He excels in every subject.'

This seemed rather faint praise, given that I only studied English and maths.

'His geography cannot be faulted,' Mrs Sutton went on, 'and he has a very good understanding of history.'

My first impulse was to burst out laughing, and I had to fight very hard to suppress my amusement. What Mrs Sutton was saying was so obviously absurd that it felt as though I was in the middle of an ironic comedy.

'His grasp of science is improving all the time,' she continued, 'and although we don't have any lab facilities here, Daniel definitely has a good theoretical grounding.'

The feelings that had made me want to laugh had now transformed into absolute astonishment. I couldn't believe that Mrs Sutton seriously expected my parents to accept that I was receiving such a thorough education and that I was such a good academic all-rounder. And I actually felt somewhat offended, given that Mrs Sutton generally seemed opposed to the teaching of anything other than the basics; she was wilfully misrepresenting herself as well as me.

'And,' Mrs Sutton added, 'our day-to-day life in class has really been enhanced by this new machine.'

She was vaguely waving towards the surface above some drawers and cupboards behind her desk, but I had no idea what 'machine' she was referring to.

'I mean *this*,' she eventually started to explain, walking over to the surface and resting her hand, in a bizarrely affectionate way, on the board of a rotary paper trimmer. 'This really is the envy of the whole school,' she expounded. 'Mr Baker and Mrs Conway often send children in from their classes to trim the edges of their drawings, and so on. We use it all the time for various things – I just don't know how we managed without it.'

By now my experience of the parents' evening had drifted so far off into the surreal that I no longer felt any inclination towards laughter; all I could do was stand there and stare incredulously at this preposterous farce.

'And there you have it,' Mrs Sutton finally announced to my mum and dad. 'Daniel is doing extremely well, and we're all doing everything we can to nurture his abilities.'

For a moment I thought she was going say something about how the paper trimmer would contribute to this nurturing, and I almost wished she had, because then my parents would have been left in no doubt about the nature of my 'educational' environment.

                    *   *   *

After supper that evening I sat with Jane and Louise in the quiet room.
Jane's mum hadn't made it to the parents' evening, partly because there was
some distance involved, and partly because Jane was soon to be leaving in any
case. Louise's parents, however, had both attended (even though they were
separated).

'Mr Baker was okay, actually,' Louise said. 'He just described where I
was up to, and what he was doing to keep my progress up-to-date.'

'Mrs Sutton talked complete crap,' I said. 'She just made it all up. And
then she spent ages going on about how amazing the paper trimmer was!'

Louise laughed, but Jane just looked at me grimly.

'You know that Sutton's ruining your future, don't you, Daniel?' Jane said.

'Maybe,' I answered cautiously. 'But I just don't get it. Why is she saying
all this stuff?'

At this point, Sarah Dawes walked into the room, apparently having stood
in the doorway unnoticed for a few minutes.

'You remember what I told you, Daniel?' she said, sitting down on a foam
chair.

I knew she was referring to the need for me to get out of Oakdale.

'And it applies to you too, Louise,' Sarah said. 'You both need to get
yourselves out of this place.'

'Yeah, it's true,' Jane nodded. '*I'm* getting out of here at last, and you both
need to get out of here as well.'

Louise seemed to shiver at the prospect. I couldn't imagine that she feared
going back home, so I could only guess that it was the prospect of returning
to a normal school that frightened her.

'And you all know *I'm* leaving,' Sarah said. 'I may be on the nursing staff
here, but this place has become as much a prison for me as it is for you.'

'Sarah!' came an assertive voice from the doorway. It was Mr Taylor.
'Could I have a word with you, please?'

'I know, Ross, I know,' Sarah answered, 'I shouldn't be talking to the kids
like this.'

'Perhaps it would be better if you and I talked about this in private,' he said.

'There's no need,' Sarah said. 'I know what you'll say. But it doesn't
matter, because I will be gone in two weeks.'

I thought for a moment that Mr Taylor was going to say something more,
but instead he just stood there for a moment before turning and walking off.

'No doubt I shall be in trouble over that,' Sarah said, 'but I just don't care
anymore.'

                    *   *   *

The half-term break came and went, and with it went Sarah Dawes and Jane Sparrow. A couple of new children arrived at the Unit, but otherwise, life just went on, alternating between the routine, the bizarre and the extreme. But I was now very aware that I was in such a rut that nothing could make much of an impact on me anymore. So while things were happening around me, sometimes very unpleasant things, it was boredom rather than dismay that was pressing me to move forward.

With Jane having now left, the friendship between Louise and I became more important. I suppose there was a sense in which we had almost become dependent on each other. This was not because we had a great deal in common, it was just that we had both been in the Unit for a long time, and there weren't really any other long-termers with whom either of us were particularly friendly.

It was on a sunny afternoon in early June, following school, that Louise and I sat together discussing our lot. Almost in defiance of the good weather, we were remaining indoors, sitting in a corner of the TV room away from the small group of children watching the screen.

'I've just remembered something someone said to me when I was first here,' I told her. 'There was this girl called Wendy Cole – Jane knew her too. She left here a long time ago, probably about two years ago.' I paused. 'I think she committed suicide very soon after she left,' I added matter-of-factly. 'But I remember her saying that if you stay here too long you just get used to all the madness. She said that the things that shock you when you're first here just become normal after a while.'

'Yes,' Louise said, 'that sounds about right.'

'Well,' I said, 'I am really sick of it all now. I don't *want* this to seem normal.'

'Jane and Sarah both said that you and me need to get out of here,' Louise said, 'but I don't know if I *can* get out of here; I'm too scared.'

'What are you scared of?'

'Going back to school,' she answered. 'It's all so big. There are hundreds and hundreds of kids everywhere, and there are so many floors and different classrooms. I'd just get completely lost if I went back.'

'Yes, normal schools are big and scary,' I said. '*I'd* be very frightened about going back, but I think I've got to try.'

Louise shook her head. 'I don't think I'll ever be able to go back.'

'Don't you think it would be good if we could both leave here at the same time?'

'Yes,' she said, 'but I don't think I can.'

Louise's fear made me feel very sad, but this was partly due to my own self-interest. I was nervous about approaching Mrs Fox in order to get the ball rolling; what I wanted was the assurance that someone else would be going through the same thing. But clearly Louise was not prepared to follow the same path. While I was now ready to do whatever was necessary to leave Oakdale, Louise was going to settle for being left behind.

Mrs Fox's initial response to my desire to give Shelley School another try was predictably cool.

We were not in her office this time, but our conversation was taking place over cups of tea. Having made my way into the dining room following the end of the school day, I had immediately sought out Mrs Fox in the midst of the busy room and zeroed in on her to ask for an urgent appointment. She didn't appear able to offer me one, but she agreed to join me at an unoccupied table, right there and then, in order to discuss whatever was on my mind.

I wasn't happy with this arrangement, as I would have much preferred the privacy of her office. As it was, there were kids and adults constantly wandering by, and our conversation was frequently being interrupted by staff members who made casual conversational comments to Mrs Fox as they passed her.

'Are you sure you can cope with returning to school, Daniel?' she asked me.

'I need to try before it's too late,' I said.

'You may be right,' she said. 'But you have to realise that it won't be easy. You'd be returning just when it's time to start your O-levels or CSEs, and you've been away for a long time. When was it you were readmitted here?'

'The April before last,' I answered. 'Just over a year ago.'

'So you might find it hard catching up,' Mrs Fox cautioned.

'It would be even harder if I left it any longer,' I argued.

'Mmm,' Mrs Fox said thoughtfully.

'One thing, though,' I added, 'I think I would need my medication to be reduced before going back to Shelley, so that I'd find it easier to stay awake and concentrate.'

'That's a matter for Dr Rajasimha,' Mrs Fox said.

'I know,' I replied, 'but I never get to see him myself.'

'Well,' she said, 'if we decide to pursue the possibility of you returning to school, Dr Rajasimha would have to be involved, along with the whole team. And I'm sure he would look into the matter of your medication.'

'So,' I said, 'do you agree that I should go back to school and back home?'

'Not necessarily,' she answered, 'but I agree to discuss the possibility with my colleagues.'

*   *   *

'That fool Mulley is a complete incompetent, just like Mason before him,' Mrs Sutton was saying, 'and Sunny Jim is a disgrace for letting Mulley keep his job.'

I had no idea what Mrs Sutton was talking about. All I had done was to take my maths exercise book up to her for marking, but as soon as she had my attention she had suddenly launched into a major rant about politics.

'If I were Fred Mulley,' she said, 'I'd send in all the troops we've got and sort out those Irish traitors once and for all. And I'd send troops south of the boarder too; I'd have Cosgrave booted out and I'd close down the Dáil.'

At last I had some idea of what she was on about, albeit a rather hazy one. I had vaguely heard a news report about a shoot-out the previous day between the British Army and the Provisional IRA at a Belfast postal depot. But it sounded to me as though Mrs Sutton's solution to the troubles in Northern Ireland would be to declare war on the Republic, and though I was ill-informed about such matters, this idea struck me as sickening.

'But wouldn't that lead to loads more people being killed?' I asked, feeling that for once I had to voice some sort of objection.

'Yes, it might well do,' she said, 'but it would certainly sort out those Nationalists once and for all, either by killing them or by making sure they stayed put in the back of beyond with all the other bogtrotters.'

I had very little interest in politics at that time, but I found Mrs Sutton's attitude utterly repulsive. The only opinion I had was that killing should be avoided, not revelled in, and for that reason I found myself at odds with my teacher.

'I don't think I agree with you,' I said apprehensively.

Suddenly, and for the first time, Mrs Sutton was very angry with me.

'You don't know what you're talking about,' she barked, attracting the interest of all the kids in the room. 'These people are animals and violence is the only language they understand,' she seethed. 'Now go and sit down, and keep out of things you don't understand.'

She thrust my exercise book back in my hand, unmarked, and I sloped off back to my place, knowing I was being watched by everyone in the class. But although I felt awkward and uncomfortable, I was neither embarrassed nor ashamed, because I had at last recovered the sense of justice I knew when I had first come to Oakdale nearly two and a half years earlier. I knew that Mrs Sutton was in the wrong, and though she told me to keep out of what I didn't understand, I had gained a definite impression that she had no real understanding of the situation either. And so this incident provided me with certain confirmation that there was nothing about Oakdale that I was prepared to accept anymore, and I consoled myself with the thought that, with any luck, I would soon hear from Mrs Fox that arrangements had been made for me to leave.

*   *   *

'That went quite well, Daniel. Well done!'

I was in Mrs Fox's office and we were both in the places so familiar to me. We had returned from a visit to Shelley School, accompanied by my parents, where we had had a long and encouraging meeting with the headmaster.

'It would seem that Shelley School is more than willing to have you back,' Mrs Fox continued. 'I have to admit, I'm a little surprised at how easy it was to persuade them, but you made quite an impression on the headmaster, and he definitely wants to take you back.'

I allowed myself a smile, feeling as though I had just negotiated an arduous series of hurdles, but had emerged at the other end with flying colours.

'So when do I leave here?' I asked. 'And when do I start back at Shelley?'

'You will leave Oakdale at the end of this term,' Mrs Fox said, 'and I'm told that during the summer break your dosage of diazepam will be reduced to a lower level. And then, on Tuesday, the fifth of September, you will have you first day back at Shelley School.'

CHAPTER FOURTEEN

It was so unfair. And it seemed so unnecessary too; an utterly dispropor-tionate consequence to a minor setback. But here I was, aged fifteen, back in Oakdale yet again.

I awoke on a Monday morning in March, in the new bed assigned to me in the boys' dormitory. I was suffering the familiar after effects of having been administered a large dose of some type of barbiturate or benzodiazepine the previous night. I was groggy and could barely move, and my eyes opened unwillingly to see surroundings that didn't really want to pull into focus. And then insult was added to injury when Mr Taylor came over and shook me briskly, urging me to get up.

'Come on, Daniel,' he said. 'If you hurry, we can put you on a bus, and you can go to school from here.'

It seemed that maybe all was not lost.

With the hope that this readmission to Oakdale might only be a very minor interruption to my life, I tried dragging myself out of bed. But I immediately fell to the floor, too weak to support myself.

'Come on, come on!' Mr Taylor said impatiently. 'You need to get going. This is your last chance. If you don't get yourself on that bus, you won't be going back to that school ever again.'

Tears of frustration and despair percolated up through my eyes as I tried to pull myself to my feet.

After an almighty struggle, I was standing, albeit very unsteadily. I then carefully negotiated my way through the crowd of boys queuing to get washed, successfully making it to one of the cubicles just outside the dorm.

But after making my way back, I was so fatigued by the exertion that I collapsed on my bed and consciousness slipped away from me.

How had this happened? How was it that I had ended up so utterly powerless once again?

From September last year through to the beginning of March I had been doing very well at Shelley School. It hadn't always been easy, of course, but I had put every effort into making it work this time. And as a result of sheer willpower, I had managed to catch up academically, renew old friendships and establish some new ones, and maintain a near-perfect attendance record. So how come I had been whisked back to Oakdale as though in the blink of an eye?

The fact was that sustaining my attendance at Shelley while holding out against the day-to-day stresses and anxieties of school-life had taken it out of me. I had become tired and somewhat depressed. It really wasn't anything very much; it was nothing that I couldn't have recovered from. But after having spent Saturday in a withdrawn state, I had retreated into myself even further on the Sunday. I had been aware of things going on around me, of my seven-year old brother, Mark, running around while my parents tried to draw me out of myself. But I was simply too tired, and I couldn't be bothered to respond.

Eventually, Mrs Fox, the social worker, had arrived on the scene, my parents obviously having decided that the situation was so serious that it warranted disturbing her on a Sunday.

We all sat there in the living room as Mrs Fox talked at me. But I didn't want to concern myself with her; I just wanted to be left alone to get some rest and reenergise myself.

'Daniel,' said Mrs Fox, her voice coming to me as though through a heavy fog, 'if you don't say something, I will have to assume that you are very seriously ill, far more ill than I have ever seen you before. And if that is the case, I will have to call out a doctor, and he will probably make arrangements for you to be detained. Neither you, nor your mum and dad, will have any say in this. And you'll probably end up in St Anselm's rather than in Oakdale. Is that what you want?'

Her words horrified me, and I struggled hard to claw myself up towards full engagement so that I could protest.

'No,' I grunted. 'I just want to rest. That's all.'

'In that case,' Mrs Fox replied, 'I think it would be best if I took you back to Oakdale tonight, and you'll be able to get all the rest you need there.'

'No,' I said, a little more strongly this time. 'There's nothing wrong with me. I'm just very tired. But I'll be all right.'

'You don't look all right to me,' Mrs Fox said.

'But I will be if I get some rest,' I said, now much more involved in the interaction.

'I will give you a choice, Daniel,' Mrs Fox said. 'Either you come back with me to Oakdale now, as a voluntary patient, or we can call out the duty doctor from your GP's surgery and see what he has to say.'

I made my choice almost immediately. 'Okay,' I said. 'Call out the duty doctor.'

There was a long and uncomfortable silence.

'Daniel, I don't think you realise the implications of what you're saying,'

Mrs Fox said. 'If the doctor comes out and sees you as you are now, he will almost certainly decide to have you detained. He'll make an emergency application and get you detained for an initial period of seventy-two hours.'

Not that I would have known it at the time, but she was suggesting that Section 29 of the Mental Health Act would be invoked.

'You'll almost certainly be sent to St Anselm's,' she continued, 'and once you're there a further application will probably be made to have you detained for longer – *much* longer. Who knows when you'll get out again. Or even *if* you'll get out again. I don't think you know how serious this is.'

I didn't believe her. I couldn't imagine that any doctor would take such extreme action just because I was a bit tired and withdrawn.

'Call out the duty doctor,' I repeated.

There was another silence.

'I have a confession to make, Daniel,' Mrs Fox said eventually. 'I'm very sorry, but I really didn't think that was what you would decide. So I'm afraid I'm going to have to make the decision for you. I can't risk you ending up in St Anselm's. Therefore, I must insist that you come back to Oakdale with me now; that way you can submit to treatment voluntarily, rather than having it forced on you.'

There was no longer any point objecting. I had lost. And clearly the distinction between voluntary and involuntary was far too subtle to be understood by my adolescent mind.

Consciousness returned to me when four boys came running nosily into the dorm at morning break. Awakening, I became aware of a male nurse I didn't know sitting beside my bed on a foam chair. He was probably in his mid-thirties, and his attention was currently taken by the boys who had just entered the room.

'Quiet, you lot,' he said. 'Daniel is sleeping.'

'No, he isn't,' said one of them, a boy of about fourteen called Lee.

'Ah, you're awake,' the nurse said, turning to me. 'We haven't met before; my name's Chris Nicholas.'

I nodded at him a little blearily.

'I don't suppose you know any of these guys,' Chris said, gesturing to the four boys in the dorm; they were now sitting on the floor playing cards near one of the beds.

I shook my head.

Chris introduced me to them, telling me they were called Lee Reid, Neil Buckley, Martin Boyce and Clayton Winter. I didn't immediately take in which boy was which, nor was I sure of their ages until sometime later.

191

'I hear you've been with us before,' Chris said to me.

'Yes,' I answered despondently. 'I've been here twice before.'

'So you know how it all works,' he said. 'You know that you'll have two key workers, one on this shift and one on Mrs Causton's. Well, you're lumbered with me on this shift, but I'm sure we'll get along fine.'

'I really don't need to be back here,' I said miserably. 'There's nothing wrong with me. I want to go back to Shelley School and back home.'

'I'm very sorry,' Chris said, 'but you had a chance to go back to school this morning, and you weren't well enough. As I understand it, the idea was that you'd stay in Oakdale for just a week or two, but that you would continue going your usual school from here. And then, all being well, you'd go back home. But I think they've now decided that that isn't going to work.'

'There was no way I could go today,' I complained resentfully. 'When Mrs Fox brought me in last night they drugged me up so much that I just wasn't able to get up normally this morning'

'Maybe,' Chris answered, 'but I think that, had you been well, you'd have been able to shake off the effects of the sedation better. At least, that's what I've been told. The fact that you're still so groggy, even now, just confirms that you're very run down and depressed. I'm afraid you're just not well enough to go back to your old school, and so you're going to have to put up with us again.'

I swallowed hard. And as I was very sceptical of the explanation Chris had given me, I found myself torn between the twin demands of controlling my anger and fighting back tears.

'This isn't fair,' I whined.

'No, it probably isn't,' Chris shrugged. 'Being ill hardly ever is.'

I sighed in frustration.

'I suggest you stay in bed for the rest of the morning,' he said, 'and then, if you're feeling strong enough, you can get up for lunch, and this afternoon you can go over with the others to school – *our* school, that is.'

The thought that I might find myself back in the abyss of Mrs Sutton's class filled me dread, and I found myself desperately hoping that, this time, they would either put me in with Mr Baker again, or in Mrs Conway's class.

By lunchtime I was indeed up and dressed, and Chris Nicholas showed me to my new place in the dining room, sitting at a table next to the one I had sat at when I first arrived at Oakdale three years earlier.

Chris took his place sitting opposite me, just as hoards of children came rushing in following school. We were joined at our table by the fourteen-year-old Lee, and by Jeremy Newton, who was now sixteen. And we were also joined by Martin, who was fifteen.

'You just couldn't keep away, then?' Jeremy said to me.

I simply looked at him, feeling too grim to make a response.

'So, you knew Daniel when he was here before, Jeremy?' Chris asked him.

'Yeah,' he replied. 'I've been here the longest of anyone, so of course I remember Daniel.'

'I was here before Jeremy was, though,' I told Chris.

'But *I've* been here the *longest*,' Jeremy repeated competitively.

I merely shrugged my shoulders, as I couldn't see anything to be gained from contesting who had the greater claim on being Oakdale's most established patient.

'I've only been here a few weeks,' Martin said, 'and I hope I won't be here much longer.'

'I've not been here long, either,' Lee added.

'You don't *want* to be here long,' I remarked. 'Kids like Jeremy and me are failures for being here so long.'

'Fuck off!' Jeremy barked. '*You're* a failure; not me.'

'Jeremy,' Chris said firmly, 'mind your language. And Daniel,' he said, turning to me, 'neither of you are failures.'

Before I could say anything more, Barbara Heaton, the auxiliary, came by telling us to join the queue for soup. And so I got in line, as I had done so very many times before, as if I had never been away.

Returning to my place, I slurped my anaemic tomato soup with disinterest, thinking that almost everything I needed to do in Oakdale could be done on autopilot. The faces of most of the kids around me may have changed, but very little else had. I knew the Unit so very well it was as though it had warn a groove in my brain which I could simply drift in without paying any conscious attention.

Having finished my soup, I quickly glanced around the dining room in order to take in the new faces. Across the room, however, I spotted a table occupied by three girls, along with Tracy Grafton, and saw one very familiar face: that of Louise Bray. I was at once pleased to see that I still had an old friend here, but I was also sad to see she had never managed to master her fear and leave this place. The thought struck me that both she and I would be here till the bitter end.

And then I saw, sitting next to Louise, a flame-haired girl of about my age whom I would later learn was called Caroline Holmes. Without realising it, I was staring at her, and she soon looked up and saw me, and so I looked away self-consciously. For some reason I had been mesmerised by the colour of her hair set against the royal blue of her top, and it took me a few seconds to realise that someone was speaking to me.

'Were you in Mrs Sutton's class when you were here before?' asked Martin.

'Yes, I was,' I answered once I'd shifted my attention back to my own table. 'Is she still here?'

'Yeah,' Martin giggled. 'I'm in her class. She's really crap. But it's a good laugh trying to set her off. All you've got to do is ask her about the war; she'll go on for ages about what a hero her husband was, and how he practically defeated the Germans all on his own.'

Lee was chuckling. 'And another thing that gets her going is if you ask her what trains were like when she was young.'

Even Jeremy was grinning.

'Come on, fellas,' Chris said. 'I don't think you should be talking about your teacher like this.'

'But that's exactly what she was like when I was here before,' I said, smiling a little despite my unhappiness. But my smile faded as I remembered how her shortcomings as a teacher were failing her pupils. 'She really isn't a very good teacher,' I said seriously. 'It's very entertaining getting her to talk endlessly about almost anything, but it doesn't actually teach us what we should be learning.'

'She can't be that bad,' Chris commented.

'Haven't you heard?' Martin said. 'Everyone says exactly the same things about her. We all like her because it's really funny hearing her go on and on, but she's a useless teacher, and she's really prejudiced too.'

I nodded my agreement.

'I'm sure,' Chris said, 'that she wouldn't have been in her job all these years if that was true.'

Once again, Barbara passed by our table, this time calling us to queue up for our main course.

By the time I returned to the table, the topic of conversation had moved on, but I had been left fearing the likelihood that I would again find myself back with Mrs Sutton.

The afternoon shift had come on duty, and I discovered that Glenys Dawson was the nurse assigned as my key worker under Mrs Causton. Although I already knew Glenys, I didn't actually know her all that well. And so I wasn't quite sure what to expect of her, and I really didn't have much opportunity to find out before it was time to head over to school.

'It's time to switch that off,' Glenys said to girl carrying a small radio as we walked through the corridor in the direction of school.

The song 'Oliver's Army' was suddenly silenced as the girl did as she was told.

'I'll just take you in and leave you with Mr Barkworth,' Glenys said to me, 'and I'm sure he will sort you out.'

We made our way through the double-doors leading out to the grassy play area and onwards to the school building, where we found Mr Barkworth waiting.

'Welcome back, Daniel,' he said to me as we stepped inside the school entrance. 'I'll take you into Mrs Sutton.'

'See you at teatime, Daniel,' said Glenys, leaving me with Mr Barkworth.

Having learnt what I had been expecting anyway, that I was to be in Mrs Sutton's class again, I felt a tremendous sense of futility rushing in on me. But I tried to fight it, and so I questioned Mr Barkworth about my class allocation as he led me along the short passageway.

'Is there a particular reason why I'm back with Mrs Sutton?' I asked.

'It's mainly because she already knows you,' he answered.

'But so does Mr Baker,' I argued.

'Don't worry about it, Daniel,' he said, patting me on the back as we reached the classroom. 'You'll be okay with Mrs Sutton.'

As we were now at the classroom door there was no opportunity to say anything further.

'Mrs Sutton,' Mr Barkworth called out as we entered, 'we've got an old friend of yours back.'

'Daniel,' Mrs Sutton smiled as she came over to meet us, 'it's good to have you back.'

This seemed to me to be an extraordinary thing to say, given that my return was a sign of defeat, and I was very tempted to say that it wasn't at all good to *be* back.

'Come and sit down, Daniel,' Mrs Sutton invited.

'I'll leave you to it, then,' said Mr Barkworth as he left the room.

Mrs Sutton directed me to a vacant table, and as I remembered her doing on previous occasions, she drew up a chair of her own to join me.

It seemed that, besides myself, there were six other kids in Mrs Sutton's class at present: there was Jeremy, Lee, Neil and Martin, plus a thirteen-year-old girl called Dawn Cross. And there was Caroline, the girl with the fiery-red hair.

'I can't pretend I'm not pleased to see you back,' Mrs Sutton said. 'I know it's a shame for you to be back in Oakdale again, but you were always one of my best pupils, and it's personally gratifying for me to have you back again.

'Of course,' she continued, 'I haven't got a completely useless class at the moment. Martin's a good lad, and Caroline is very conscientious. Dawn's not too bad either. But Lee can be very disruptive, and Neil isn't much better – and Jeremy's just as insolent as ever.'

I just sat and listened to her, as I neither felt like speaking nor had anything to say in any case.

'Right,' Mrs Sutton said at last. 'Let's get you started on some maths this afternoon.'

She briefly went over to her desk and rummaged through her drawers before returning with a textbook and exercise book.

'There you go,' she said, pushing the books across the table towards me.

Seeing that she had assigned me another *Beta Mathematics* book, I voiced an objection.

'Mrs Sutton,' I said, 'I'm a bit beyond this now. When I went back to Shelley School, they put me in Set 4 for maths to start with, but I was soon moved up to Set 2. I'll be going backwards if I have to return to the *Beta* books.'

'Daniel, Daniel, Daniel,' Mrs Sutton said with affected patience. 'It will do you no harm at all to concentrate on the basics. You just work your way through that, and then we'll see about moving you on to something more advanced.'

I knew there was no point arguing, and so I just did what I was told, knowing that I would probably complete all the exercises in the textbook within a very short space of time.

After school I returned to the Unit, queued up for a cup of tea, and sat down at an empty table, where I was soon joined by Glenys Dawson and Louise.

'I'm sorry to see you back,' Louise said, 'especially after everything we talked about before you went.'

'I know,' I said. 'I'm probably here for good now.'

'Not necessarily,' Glenys said. 'After all, you can't stay here forever.'

'But I guess this is it until I finish school,' I said.

'You haven't been back for a whole day yet,' Glenys said. 'It's a bit early for you to be writing off the rest of your school days.'

'What about you, Louise?' I asked. 'Are you ever getting out of here?'

'Nothing's changed,' she answered. 'I'm probably stuck here now.'

'Look, you two,' Glenys said, 'you mustn't think like that; neither of you are hopeless cases.'

I eyed her doubtfully.

'I suggest,' Glenys offered, 'that you both go and see Bridget in the hideout as soon as she opens up in there. You two need goals, and I can't think of anyone better than Bridget to help sort you out.'

As we were talking, I saw Caroline walk past us on her way out of the dining room. Seeing that vibrant head of hair disappear through the door as she stepped into the corridor, I thought to myself that the only goal I had was strictly short term: I wanted to find out about Caroline.

*   *   *

Despite my sense of defeat in connection with planning anything more long term, I agreed to Glenys's suggestion and went along with Louise to see the occupational therapist in the hideout.

Together, Louise and I wandered through the open door leading into the hideout's outer room. There was one boy of about five playing on the floor by the low table, while on the other side of the partition, in the darker inner room, I could see Bridget Fitzpatrick being 'entertained' by Lee, who was standing in the centre of the room performing an outrageous, and very funny, hula dance coupled with some sort of Elvis Presley parody.

'Can we come in?' Louise asked.

'Of course,' Bridget replied, and so Louise and I made our way past the highly animated Lee to sit down on the foam chairs with the OT.

'Okay, Lee,' Bridget called to him above the din of his extraordinary takeoff, 'Elvis Presley has now left the building.'

'Oh, all right,' he said grudgingly, 'but can I just do my imitation of Paul McCartney being James Cagney?'

'No,' Bridget laughed, 'not now. Save it for another time.'

Louise was quietly giggling next to me, while I just stared at Lee, completely thrown by the concept behind the proposed impersonation.

'All right, I'll see you later,' Lee said, as he hurriedly exited the hideout.

'Sorry to see you back with us again, Daniel,' Bridget said to me.

'I'm sorry to be here,' I answered.

'Aren't we all,' Louise remarked.

'Let me guess,' Bridget began, 'someone has noticed you two encouraging each other's pessimism, and they've sent you to me. Am I right?'

'Sort of,' Louise said.

We spent an hour or so with Bridget, during which time other kids came and went. By the time we came to leave, however, we were no nearer to having anything in particular to aim for than we were to start with. But at least I hadn't descended completely into passive apathy; I was still highly motivated to become acquainted with Caroline. After all, with nothing else on the horizon, there was no reason not to concentrate my energy on pursuing her.

The nightshift had come on duty, and Carrie Hancock was being DJ for the kids assembled in the hall for a makeshift disco. She was taking record requests from her place behind the hatch in the hall's end wall, and as I walked in she had just begun playing 'Rockin' All Over the World'.

I had hardly ever participated in any of these Oakdale discos before, and not being especially confident about my dancing ability, this occasion was no exception. But I planted myself in one of three foam chairs that were resting against one of the longer walls. As I sat and watched the others dancing, I couldn't help but see Caroline leaning against the wall opposite. Just as I began to wish I had the confidence to go up and ask her to dance, Lee came and sat next to me.

'All right, Daniel?' he said affably.

I had gained the impression that Lee was a rather over-active fourteen-year-old, someone who might be described as 'boisterous', to use polite understatement. But he also seemed friendly and good-natured, rather than threatening, and so I was not unhappy to have him join me – not that I expected him to stay for long.

'I saw you looking at Caroline,' he said. 'You fancy her, don't you?'

'I suppose,' I answered. 'What's she like?'

'She's all right,' he said. 'She's a bit quiet, but she's all right.'

Just then, Carrie changed the record, and a slow song came on.

'Go and ask her to dance,' Lee said.

'No, I don't think so,' I replied.

'Go on,' he insisted, trying to push me up from my seat.

I was feeling extremely embarrassed by now, but to avoid Lee making me any more of a spectacle, I got up and made my way over to Caroline.

'I'm Daniel,' I said to her very nervously.

'I know,' she replied bashfully. 'I'm Caroline.'

I didn't know what to say next, so, rather abruptly, I said, 'Would you like to dance?'

Much to my surprise, she said that she did, and she joined me in the centre of the hall in a slightly awkward intimate dance.

Aware that 'amorous associations' between kids in the Unit were not allowed, and that a slow dance probably constituted such an association, I gently manoeuvred Caroline out of Carrie's line-of-sight towards a corner away from the hatch.

My arms were around her as we shuffled vaguely to 'How Deep is Your Love', and though the warmth of her closeness was pleasing, my heart was hammering away uncomfortably in my chest and my mind was racing ahead to what I should do next.

With her face close to mine I could feel her soft, warm breath against my skin, and so, turned on by this, I looked her in the eyes and said, 'I'd like to kiss you.'

I knew this was a rather graceless move on my part, and that I had arrived at it in an unseemly rush, but despite my clumsiness I was not facing rejection.

'All right,' she said.

I lent in closer and kissed her lightly on the lips.

By now I had become aware that a group of spectators had gathered around us, and so I further accelerated my already rapid progress.

'Shall we go somewhere where we can be alone?' I asked her.

She gave a faint shrug and said, 'All right.'

I led her out of the hall towards the TV room, which was currently unoccupied.

The television was switched off and there was no one in the room. The chairs were scattered about haphazardly, and we made our way to a couple of seats about a third of the way into the room, just adjacent to the glazed door leading into the other corridor.

As we sank into our chairs, I enfolded her in my arms again.

'I've never really done anything like this before,' I confessed to her.

'Nor me,' she said.

I held her close to me and kissed her.

By now I was feeling extremely aroused, but at the forefront of my mind was a sense of anxiety. I had got Caroline alone, but I was worried about whether my kissing was satisfactory and whether I should attempt to go any further.

'Have you ever French kissed before?' I asked her.

'No,' she replied.

'Would you like to try?'

'All right,' she answered.

Our kissing became more passionate, and we slipped to the floor as the foam chairs fell away from us in response to our movement.

We both giggled.

I was just beginning to worry about what my next move should be when I became aware that there were now several kids on the other side of the glazed door, their faces pressed up against the glass. They were watching us with mischievous amusement.

Caroline had also become aware that our moment of privacy was over, and she pushed me away from her. As she did so, Carrie Hancock emerged from behind the crowd of kids in the corridor, pushing her way through them and opening the door. As she strode in, Caroline leapt to her feet, and sprinted out of the room via the other door, leaving me to face Carrie on my own.

'That kind of behaviour is not acceptable, as well you know,' Carrie said sharply. 'You've only been back here one day, and already you're up to your old tricks.'

Although I was extremely flustered, I had sufficient presence of mind to challenge Carrie's implication. 'Old tricks?' I said. 'I've never done anything like this before.'

'But you've wanted to,' Carrie countered.

Although I felt guilty, having been caught out, I was also righteously angry at being condemned for what I *might* have done on previous occasions, but actually hadn't.

'Daniel,' Carrie continued sternly, 'you don't just get *yourself* into trouble with this sort of thing; you're getting *Caroline* into trouble too.'

Although I very much felt as though I was in the wrong, I did my best to look Carrie in the eye and sound confident. 'I've done nothing to be ashamed of,' I insisted, 'and neither has Caroline.'

'Well,' Carrie responded, 'I don't suppose that *Caroline* has done anything wrong. *You're* the one who led her on; *you're* the one who's responsible.'

'I'm not listening to anymore of this,' I said, exasperated, turning my back on Carrie and walking out of the room.

As I made my way along the corridors, heading for the dormitory and bed, Lee caught up with me.

'Daniel,' Lee said spiritedly, 'that was fast work! Well done!'

I stopped and turned to him, bemused by his enthusiasm.

'What?' I said.

'Caroline's a quiet, shy girl,' he said. 'But you just went up to her, and before anyone knew what was happening, you were snogging her! That's amazing!'

Lee had made me stop and realise that amidst my feelings of culpability and fury, I was also highly elated. I had successfully approached a beautiful girl and experienced my first real kiss.

'What was it like?' he asked me.

'It was great,' I said.

The truth was, however, that I didn't really *know* what it was like, as I had been so busy worrying about getting it right and looking ahead to the next stage that I hadn't been fully present in the moment itself. But it did feel good to have done it.

CHAPTER FIFTEEN

The following day I discovered that Caroline Holmes was avoiding me. I wanted to speak to her; I wanted to achieve something of the 'getting to know you' phase which I had overlooked the previous evening. But Caroline seemed completely determined to evade my every attempt at approaching her.

'Silly cow,' said Louise Bray with uncharacteristic severity, as we sat drinking our tea in the dining room following school. 'Caroline wasn't exactly avoiding you last night, was she?'

'I don't know what to *do*,' I said.

'Ignore her; if she's going to be like that, why bother?'

This wasn't really a reaction I had foreseen. Louise and Caroline were friends, and so I had been expecting to be condemned for my conduct rather than simply dismissed for wasting my time.

'But it doesn't seem right,' I complained. 'We should at least talk about what happened last night. Even if she doesn't want anything more to do with me, we should at least discuss it.'

Louise gave a small laugh. 'Daniel,' she said, 'you don't need to discuss and analyse *everything* that happens. Just let go and forget it.'

'But I don't want to,' I objected. 'I really *like* Caroline.'

'But you've admitted that you don't really know her,' Louise said. 'It's not as if you did much talking last night, is it?'

It was obvious from Louise's grin that she was not taking me very seriously.

I sighed in frustration. To me this seemed like something quite major. I had just had my first experience of a particular kind of intimacy, and now the girl in question had completely severed any contact between us. It was as though I had climbed a hill, congratulated myself on the accomplishment, and then been sent tumbling back down by a sudden storm.

Over the coming days and weeks I kept trying to reinitialise some sort of contact with Caroline. And Louise continued to surprise me by regarding my efforts as nothing more than foolish. Given her friendship with Caroline, coupled with my own sense of awkwardness, I had half-expected Louise to see me as guilty of harassment.

Eventually, Caroline's attitude towards me began to change slightly. She stopped avoiding me completely and started to at least acknowledge my existence, albeit rather formally.

One Tuesday evening in late April, after we had all returned to the Unit from the Easter holidays, I was sitting with Louise and Caroline in the quiet room.

Caroline seemed a little more relaxed in my presence than she had done previously. But if Louise hadn't been there I'm sure Caroline and I would not have interacted.

'I knew about this place before I came here,' Caroline said. 'A friend of mine in Newhaven was sent here.'

An instant alarm bell went off in my head, informing me in one sudden, horrible flash where this was going to lead.

'Who was that?' Louise asked, not that the question was really necessary.

'Beverley Kemp,' Caroline answered, confirming what we had already realised.

For a moment it felt as though my heart had stopped, and I was very much aware that I was trembling.

Louise lowered her eyes to the floor, evidently uncomfortable at this inevitable verification of an already-known fact.

Although Louise was Caroline's friend, she had clearly been oblivious to the fact that Caroline knew Beverley, and it was obvious that she was acutely aware of potential trouble.

'So you both knew Beverley, then?' said Caroline, obviously having noticed the way we had reacted. 'And I suppose you know what happened to her when she was here.'

Louise and I both nodded uneasily.

'I was terrified of coming here knowing what had happened to Bev,' said Caroline.

'How was Beverley when you last saw her?' I rasped, my throat having suddenly gone dry.

'That was quite a long time ago now,' Caroline said. 'When she came back home she was a lot quieter than she used to be, far worse than she was before. And she was very jumpy; she seemed frightened of everything. I suppose that's not surprising after what happened here.

'Anyway,' Caroline continued, 'she wasn't back at our school for very long. Her parents decided to move away. I think they went to somewhere in North Wales.'

'Was that because of what had happened here?' Louise asked.

'I'm not sure,' Caroline said. 'It might have been. She was certainly looking forward to getting away and starting again somewhere else.'

Louise gave me a look that I couldn't make out. It may have been accusing or it may have been sympathetic; I just couldn't tell.

'So I suppose,' Caroline began again, 'that you both knew the boy who tried to kill her.'

I closed my eyes and swallowed hard. And then I summoned up all the nerve I could manage and looked Caroline directly in the eye.

'It was me,' I said unsteadily, hastily adding that I hadn't actually meant her any real harm. 'I'm not sure what I was trying to do,' I said. 'But I would never have really hurt her.'

Caroline stared at me for a moment, and I thought she may have paled slightly.

'What I did was terrible – absolutely disgusting,' I said. 'But it was only an act. I would never really do anything to hurt *anyone*.'

Caroline's eyes narrowed. 'Bev more-or-less had a complete breakdown because of you,' she said in a low cold voice. 'And you made her family move away.'

'Hang on,' Louise interjected. 'I thought you said you *weren't sure* why they'd moved away.'

'I'm sure enough,' Caroline answered. And turning to me, she said, 'I lost my best friend because of you.'

'I'm sorry,' I spluttered. 'I'm *desperately* sorry.' I tried my best to control my need to cry, but I couldn't stop the tears from forming. 'It was all an act,' I tried to explain, 'but I never stopped to think about what it would do to Beverley. I am so very sorry. There's nothing else I can say.'

'No,' she said frostily. 'There's nothing you *can* say.'

Caroline got up and ran from the room, just as she had run from me when we had been discovered kissing.

I made to run after her, but Louise called me back before I reached the door.

'Leave her,' she said. 'There's nothing you can do. Not tonight, anyway.'

I sank back down in my seat and rubbed my eyes. 'I've got *no* chance with Caroline now,' I said dejectedly.

'Daniel,' Louise said, 'she'll calm down eventually. But I don't think you had much of a chance with her anyway.'

I sat and stared into empty space.

'Come on,' Louise said, 'let's go and see what's on the telly.'

And so we moved into the TV room next door, joining the small group of kids half-heartedly watching the last few minutes of *The Good Old Days*, before the room completely emptied for an election broadcast by the Workers' Revolutionary Party.

*   *   *

On the Monday of the following week I learned that Dr Rajasimha was moving on to take up a position in a Child Guidance Clinic in another part of the country. This brought to mind what Sarah Dawes had said to me about Dr Rajasimha almost exactly a year ago. She had just tendered her resignation from the nursing post she held at the Unit, and she had clearly felt more free to express her opinions, and her opinion of Dr Rajasimha had not been favourable. She had commented on how he recommended children for admission to Oakdale when he couldn't be bothered to do anything else, and how he never checked up on his patients following their admission. And so I now found myself wondering if there might be a change for the better when Dr Rajasimha left.

I had heard of Dr Rajasimha's impending departure from John Webber, as he was one of the staff on Mrs Causton's shift who made it his business to pass on the news to the kids. And so, when the official announcement came during the morning meeting the following day, the matter was already common knowledge.

As usual, we were all seated in a circle in the TV room as Miss Bishop orchestrated the matters for discussion. Quite appropriately, this was one of the occasions when Dr Rajasimha himself was in attendance.

'Some of you may have heard,' Miss Bishop said, 'that Dr Rajasimha will be leaving us very soon. He has been an important part of our team at Oakdale for many years, and I'm sure we will all miss him.'

Dr Rajasimha nodded and smiled in acknowledgement.

'Many of you have a lot to thank Dr Rajasimha for,' Miss Bishop continued. 'He has shown great care and concern for every one of his patients, and has worked tirelessly to deal with each one personally, despite his very heavy workload.'

This was another one of those reality-defying moments that were a characteristic part of the Oakdale brand, and so I just sat there and accepted it, knowing full well that everyone in the room recognised Miss Bishop's words as fiction. And, no doubt, Miss Bishop herself realised her words were being received in that spirit.

Dr Rajasimha, however, was clearly delighted with Miss Bishop's invention, and he responded in kind.

'Thank you, Miss Bishop,' he beamed. 'And may I say what an honour it has been to serve here these last eight years. I could not have wished for a more dedicated team of colleagues. In fact,' he went on, glancing around at us all, 'you kids don't know how fortunate you are to have someone like Miss Bishop at the helm. She really has all your best interests close to her heart.'

I was starting to find this extended pretence rather tedious when Lee Reid suddenly piped up with a typically cheeky comment.

'Well done, Dr Rajasimha!' he declared. 'We all think you're marvellous! You're the finest shrink who ever lived!'

I felt a powerful need to giggle hysterically, and so I affected a coughing fit to overcome this urge. Meanwhile, a ripple of laughter spread around the room, and even a few members of the nursing staff were forced to raise hands to mouths to hide their smiles.

It was apparent that neither Miss Bishop nor Dr Rajasimha was amused by Lee's remark, nor by the general reaction it provoked. On the one hand, Dr Rajasimha looked a little confused and shaken, while on the other, Miss Bishop was obviously very angry.

'That's enough, everyone!' Miss Bishop barked at us. 'And as for you, Lee, you need to learn some respect. In fact, you *all* need to learn some respect.'

The meeting returned to order just in time for us to be sent on our way to school.

By Thursday, speculation as to who might replace Dr Rajasimha had given way to election fever.

'I hope we'll be rid of that Sunny Jim once and for all after today,' I heard Mr Jones saying to Glenys Dawson as I queued for tea following school.

'Mmm,' Glenys replied doubtfully. 'I'm not sure I want "Margaret Thatcher, milk snatcher" running things, though.'

'Oh, I don't know,' Mr Jones said. 'What this country needs is a bit of sensible house-keeping, and I reckon Mrs Thatcher fits the bill perfectly.'

'If you say so,' Glenys said.

I didn't hear any more, as I had now collected my cup of tea from Rose Boyd, the auxiliary, and seated myself at a table with Louise.

Much to my surprise, Caroline soon joined us at our table.

'Everyone's going on about the election,' Caroline said as she sat down.

'Yeah, I know,' Louise said. 'Who would you vote for? – if you were allowed to vote, that is.'

'I think I'd probably vote Liberal,' Caroline answered.

'Me too,' said Louise. 'How about you, Daniel?'

I still didn't really know too much about politics at that time, but I had started to develop a passing interest in the environment, so I said I'd vote for the Ecology Party.

'Oh, right,' Louise remarked.

'Still,' I went on, 'it'll be interesting if we end up with our first woman prime minister after today.'

'Oh, God, I hope not,' Caroline said. 'Not Thatcher; she's awful!'

I was pleased, if not a bit puzzled, that Caroline was now talking to me. Ten days ago I had reached the conclusion that she absolutely hated me, but now, while not being overly friendly, she was at least prepared to engage with me in conversation.

Taking something of a risk, I decided to change the subject and ask Caroline a question that might possibly have been construed as personal.

'Caroline,' I said, 'which doctor are you under? Dr Collins or Dr Rajasimha?'

I was encouraged to hear her answer quite willingly and without hesitation. 'Dr Collins,' she said.

'You're lucky,' I commented. 'I hear he's a lot better than Dr Rajasimha.'

'He's okay,' she said, rather neutrally.

'He's *definitely* better than Dr Rajasimha,' Louise said. 'Daniel and I both come under Rajasimha, and he's a complete disaster.'

'So you're glad he's going then?' Caroline said.

'You can say that again!' I exclaimed.

'Knowing our luck,' Louise said, 'we'll end up with someone even worse.'

At breaktime on the following Monday morning, I was sitting alone at one of the dining room tables wondering where Louise was, when John Webber came over to me.

'Daniel,' he said, standing beside the table. 'Have you heard? Your old friend Jane is back with us. She was admitted this morning.'

This was something I had not been expecting, and I wasn't immediately sure how I should feel about it. On the one hand, I was glad that a good friend of mine had returned, but on the other, I knew very well that returning to Oakdale indicated some kind of catastrophe.

'How is she?' I asked.

'She's a bit thin,' John answered. 'She's up in the girls' dormitory now; why don't you go and see her?'

I hastily took my cup back to the trolley, and then walked briskly in the direction of the girls' dorm.

As I passed the nurses' station and approached the open doors leading into the dorm, I found I already had a good view of the interior. I could see about three girls, including Louise, gathered around one of the beds. Drawing closer, I saw Jane Sparrow lying in the bed, looking extremely frail and wasted.

I stopped when I reached the doorway. Jane feebly turned her head on her pillow to look at me with grotesquely sunken eyes. I was so horrified and sickened by the sight of her that I just couldn't force myself to go in. All I could do was raise my hand and wave to her, before turning and walking away.

As I made my way to the boys' dorm, I heard John Webber's words echoing in my mind: 'She's a bit thin.' This was the only time in my life that understatement acted upon me as an instrument of torture.

I threw myself down on my bed. Somehow I couldn't bring myself to cry, but I felt physically sick. Burnt into my brain was a gruesome image of Jane's skull, scarcely covered by a thin layer of skin, with the dim light of her eyes barely glimmering from the darkness of her eye-sockets. And as I lay there, my face buried in the bedding, I knew I had to find the courage to face that image again in reality. Jane was my friend; I had a responsibility to her.

The remainder of the morning was spent at school with me staring vacantly at my rudimentary *Ahead in English* textbook. I was completely unable to do any work, as all I could think about was the horror of Jane's current condition. And if any further evidence was required of Mrs Sutton's incompetence as a teacher, it was provided by her complete failure to notice that I was sitting in her class doing absolutely nothing.

When twelve o'clock came, I wandered out of the class with the others as we made our way back over to the Unit for lunch. Caroline caught up with me just as we left the school building. I was surprised to feel her put a hand on my shoulder as we walked.

'You knew Jane when she was here before, didn't you?' she said. 'You knew her very well.'

I nodded silently.

'I've never seen anyone look like that before,' Caroline continued as we passed through the doors into the Unit. 'It's horrible.'

'When she left here,' I said shakily, 'she was better. She was fine; there was nothing wrong with her.'

Caroline's hand shifted from my near shoulder to my other one, and she briefly pulled me towards her in a semi-hug. And then, just as we reached the dining room, she released me.

I sat myself down in my place at table with Lee Reid and Jeremy Newton, and we were soon joined by Mr Jones. Of all the members of staff who could have come over to sit with us for lunch, we ended up with the least sympathetic one.

'Have you seen the state of that Jane Sparrow?' he said. 'I really don't know why we bother with her. If she's so insistent on starving herself to death, then I reckon we should let her.'

Jeremy laughed coldly in agreement, but Lee protested.

'I think that's a terrible thing to say,' Lee remarked, revealing that some genuine concern lay behind his often-wayward behaviour.

'She's a waste of Health Service resources,' Mr Jones argued back.

'There's no point trying to help people who don't even want to help themselves.'

'She's ill,' I said with precariously contained anger. 'She *can't* help herself.'

'Really?' Mr Jones said sarcastically. 'And when did *you* qualify as a psychiatric nurse, Daniel?'

Lunch spent in Mr Jones' company proved to be excruciatingly uncomfortable, and it wasn't helped by the knowledge that there would be no immediate relief once it was over. I knew that as soon as we were given leave to exit the dining room, I had a duty to visit the girls' dorm, suppress my shock and revulsion, and talk to Jane.

Upon leaving the table, I found I was shaking as I timidly made my way to Jane's dormitory. This time, however, I didn't stop at the doorway, but walked straight in towards the bed where Jane was lying.

I sat down on a bed adjacent to Jane's, and through an effort of the will I made myself to look at her.

'Daniel,' she acknowledged me weakly.

'Hello,' I said, rather inadequately.

'Do you know what they've just put me through?'

I guessed that Jane may well have been force fed. And knowing Jane, I realised that she would have put up a fight, not that she could possibly have had much strength in her.

'I'm sorry to see you back here,' I said, deciding not to answer her question.

'Why are you looking at me like that?' she asked.

I had tried to keep my face as impassive as possible, so I was disturbed to think that maybe I wasn't being wholly successful.

'What do you mean?' I said.

'You're looking at me as if I've got a huge blotch on my face,' she answered.

'No,' I replied, knowing very well that my denial would not be convincing. 'It's just that I thought you'd gone for good; I wasn't expecting to see you back.'

The conversation continued awkwardly for a few minutes before I found the strain too overwhelming to continue. And so I quickly came up with a vague excuse and left.

Later in the day, after school, I told Bridget Fitzpatrick, the occupational therapist, about my encounter with Jane.

Sitting next to Bridget in the inner room of the hideout, I mentioned how Jane had asked me why I was looking at her as if she had a blotch on her face.

'You should have told her the truth,' Bridget said.

'But I didn't want to upset her,' I argued.

'Daniel,' Bridget said, 'Jane doesn't really *know* how bad she looks; she doesn't know how *ill* she is. Her view of herself is distorted. She needs someone like you to tell her that she looks bloody awful. If she says anything like that to you again, just tell her straight. Don't try and be nice, just be as brutally honest as you can – it's the only way anyone will get through to her.'

Later that evening, about three hours or so after supper, I found my way into the dining room and sat down alone. The lights were out, and the only illumination came from the failing daylight reluctantly bleeding through windows. I nestled my head in my arms as they rested on the table, and I let the gloom envelope me as I thought about how I should deal with the issue of my friend Jane.

After a while, I heard the sound of the chair next to me being pulled out, and I felt the presence of someone sitting down next to me. Then there came the soft touch of a hand resting on my back. The hand slowly moved upwards to my neck, and then fingers gently found their way into my hair and began to caress me.

'It's all right, Daniel,' a voice whispered in my ear. The voice belonged to Caroline.

Though utterly astounded, I was very grateful for her attention. But with my thoughts so firmly focussed on Jane, all I could do was murmur my thanks without actually looking up.

Caroline continued to lightly fondle my hair while also stroking my arm with her other hand. And so in the midst of grief over the present state of a close friend I found myself becoming powerfully aroused. Eventually, I sluggishly looked up to meet Caroline's lips as she leant in closer and kissed me. I kissed her back, lifting my right hand to touch her face while using my left to pull her towards me in an embrace.

Finding such tender affection in an occasion of anguish was deeply moving, and though highly stimulated, I felt no pressing demand to worry about what I was to do next. Instead, I lost myself in the moment, inhaling the fragrance of her warmth and enjoying the touch and taste of her lips on mine.

It almost seemed as if this moment would go on forever, but it was brought to an abrupt holt when the dining room's florescent lighting came flickering on to bathe us in a cold accusing light.

'Right, that's enough!' came the voice of Carrie Hancock as she came striding towards us. 'I've told you about this before, Daniel.'

Caroline and I separated ourselves from each other, but remained seated.

'Your behaviour is not acceptable, Daniel,' Carrie continued. 'It's not fair that you should keep on bothering Caroline.'

At this, Caroline stood up. I thought she was going to run from me, as she had done previously, but she didn't. Instead she stood facing Carrie.

'Daniel is *not* bothering me,' Caroline said in a slow and measured voice, 'and his behaviour is *perfectly* acceptable.'

Carrie seemed nonplussed for a moment. But then she regained her sense of authority and marched us out of the room, accompanying us on the journey to our respective dormitories.

We reached the nurses' station and Carrie directed Caroline and I to part company. But before we did, I reached out a hand to touch Caroline's arm and thank her – which prompted Carrie to slap my arm away – while Caroline gave me a demonstrative but graceful smile.

Though forced to bed slightly early, I soon drifted into a curiously pleasant sleep. This was the first time in Oakdale that the night had greeted me with anything other than bleak hopelessness.

As the weeks went by my relationship with Caroline adopted an 'on again, off again' character. There were times when we were able to easily enjoy each other's company, not to mention each other's physicality, and there were other times when we were very awkward around each other. There appeared to be no pattern to this situation, and neither was there any obvious explanation for it – apart, that is, from the fact that neither of us would have been in Oakdale had we not been somewhat unstable.

Of those various Unit staff members aware of the haphazard relationship between us, two alternative approaches were adopted. Some stuck rigidly to the party line with regard to 'amorous associations' and did everything they could to keep us separate; others, however, were prepared to turn a blind eye, adopting the view that we were teenagers behaving naturally, albeit in an unnatural setting.

While this was going on, Jane was starting to put on a small amount of weight and become stronger, and as she was now up and about it became possible for my friendship with her to gradually re-establish itself. As this happened, something that really should have been apparent for quite some time became more obvious to me: most of my major friendships were with girls. Every morning breaktime, and every afternoon after school, I would sit in the dining room drinking tea with Louise, Jane and Caroline. There was almost never any exception, and if it hadn't been for the fact that a friendship had developed between Lee and myself, I would have felt very self-conscious about this state of affairs.

My initial impression of Lee had been that he was trouble. He was boisterous to the point of being unruly, and I was vaguely aware that the police had apprehended him on more than one occasion for vandalism and even violence. But his sense of fun appealed to me, as expressed in the absurd satire of his mimicry. And more recently I had learned of his compassion, as apparent in his challenge to Mr Jones over Jane's condition. The truth was, that despite surface appearances, Lee was no lout; he was actually an intelligent, witty and caring individual who somehow just happened to have a rather tenuous capacity for self-control.

After school one Wednesday afternoon, Lee and I were playing in the Adventure Camp with a handful of other kids, including Clayton Winter and Neil Buckley, under the watchful eyes of Colin Goodman and Julian Perry. It was a fine spring day, the penetrating light of the sun piercing through air still imbued with an element of crispness, and so we were making the most of being outside.

Between us, Lee and I must have taken the death slide from the tree house to the wooden platform opposite at least a dozen times, but now we were sitting breathlessly in the improvised pirate galleon.

'So,' Lee said. 'You're getting on all right with Caroline now, aren't you?'

'Yeah,' I said.

'Come on then,' he urged, 'tell us.'

'What?'

'How far have you gone with her?'

Being greatly enthused by my relationship with Caroline, I was as keen to brag about my exploits as any other teenage boy would have been, but I realised that in the small community of Oakdale, whatever I said would not remain a secret, especially if Lee was involved. And I knew only too well that Caroline would not react well to any indiscretion on my part.

'A gentleman doesn't talk about such things,' I said, laughing off Lee's question with affected irony.

I was, of course, trying to imply that I'd gone quite a long way with Caroline, but without actually saying so. However, the truth was that any intimacy between us had mostly been quite modest.

'You are *not* a gentleman,' Lee giggled, indicating he had understood my inference.

We both sat there sniggering childishly, immaturely revelling in our indirect allusions to sexual activity.

Then, all of a sudden, Lee completely changed the subject and the mood.

'You've heard that the new doctor's starting soon, haven't you?' he said.

As it happened, I hadn't heard any such thing; it was often the case that I was slow to pick up on news unless it was brought directly to my attention.

'He's starting after half-term,' Lee said.

'What else do you know about him?' I asked.

211

'Not very much, but I think he's called Dr Vonderspeek.'

The new consultant psychiatrist, as it turned out, was actually called Dr Vanderspeigle.

We were all introduced to him at the Tuesday morning meeting following the end of half-term break. Looking around, I very much noticed that Dr Vanderspeigle's was not the only new face in the meeting. About three or four children had been discharged just before the brief holiday, and their places had now been taken by new admissions. But it was the arrival of Dr Vanderspeigle that was receiving all Miss Bishop's attention.

'I am sure,' Miss Bishop began, 'that you would all like to join me in welcoming our new member of staff, Dr Vanderspeigle, to Oakdale Children's Unit.'

As one, we all turned to look at the seated figure of a suited and rather plump middle-aged man sitting next to the other Oakdale psychiatrist, Dr Collins.

'Dr Vanderspeigle is a leading expert in child psychiatry,' Miss Bishop continued, 'and he comes to us from Leiden in the Netherlands, from one of the world's best psychiatric research centres. So all of you who were former patients of Dr Rajasimha, you're now very fortunate indeed to be in the care Dr Vanderspeigle.'

At this point Lee chimed in with a coda to his comments about Dr Rajasimha in a previous morning meeting. 'Hurray for Dr Vonderspeek!' he gushed. 'The finest shrink who ever lived!'

Just as before, a wave of laughter lapped around the room, and even Dr Vanderspeigle himself seemed mildly amused. The only person who didn't seem at all entertained by Lee's intervention was Miss Bishop, who glared furiously at him. But before she could reprimand him, Dr Vanderspeigle responded.

'Thank you, young man,' he said. 'I hope I can live up to your high expectations. And by the way,' he added, 'my name is Vanderspeigle, not Vonderspeek.'

He then went on to say that he was looking forward to meeting each of his patients individually over the next few weeks and discovering their particular needs.

This all sounded very positive, but I had learnt long ago that hopes and expectations were easily dashed in Oakdale, and that it was not wise to rely on promises made, even if they appeared to be sincerely meant.

*   *   *

212

Roughly coinciding with the arrival of Dr Vanderspeigle came news of another impending departure. Later that same week, in school assembly, Mr Barkworth, the headteacher, informed us that Mrs Sutton would be retiring at the end of term.

As always, all the pupils, with the exception of the very young ones, were gathered for assembly in Mr Baker's classroom. In recent weeks I had found myself sitting with Lee for assembly, and today was no exception. This, of course, meant that he was able to whisper occasional irreverent comments, and the news that Mrs Sutton would soon be leaving provided him with a rich vein of raw material. It was all I could do to keep my attention seriously focussed on Mr Barkworth, standing at the front with the other teachers seated either side of him.

'As you all know,' Mr Barkworth said, 'Mrs Sutton has been a teacher here at Oakdale for many years.' He paused for a moment, and then turned to Mrs Sutton. 'How long have you been here exactly, Mrs Sutton?'

'I started here in 1968,' she answered.

'So that's eleven years,' Mr Barkworth said, turning back to address the assembly. 'In that time Mrs Sutton will have seen many children come and go, but now the time is fast approaching for *her* to go.' Then, glancing back at Mrs Sutton, he added, 'This place just won't be the same without you.'

Mrs Sutton said something in response, but I didn't quite catch it as Lee made a comment about how the school would probably be a lot better without her.

And then Mr Barkworth went on to announce the hymn we were to sing (Number 43: 'All things bright and beautiful'), and Mrs Conway struck up with the piano introduction.

During the singing of the hymn, Lee continued to make remarks about Mrs Sutton's retirement; although these were all rather impolite, they were, in my view, reasonably accurate.

'You know what's going to happen though,' Lee murmured softly. 'There'll be a new teacher who will expect us to get on with some work.'

I smiled a little at this, and then tried to ignore Lee and focus on the hymn.

Looking back, it surprises me that neither of us ever thought to comment on the fact that Mrs Sutton *hadn't quite reached retirement age*, and so she was actually leaving her job one or two years early. Had she been persuaded to take early retirement to make way for someone more competent? This was a question I was never to hear asked, let alone answered, and so this phase of my experience in Oakdale simply limped towards its end without explanation. But then, very little of what happened at Oakdale came with an explanation.

*   *   *

By the latter part of June there were various crude jokes circulating among the older kids at the expense of Jeremy Thorpe, the former leader of the Liberal Party, who had just been cleared at the Old Bailey of conspiracy to murder. The jokes, however, were focussed on Thorpe's sexuality, not his alleged involvement in a failed homicide.

Perhaps surprisingly, Lee, who often generated much humour at the expense of authority figures, chose not to participate in these gags. Whether this was out of sympathy for Thorpe (unlikely) or disinterest in politics (more probable), was uncertain.

Lee joined Louise, Jane, Caroline and myself in our Thorpe-free zone after school on Thursday. The five of us were crammed around a dining room table nursing cups of tea.

'Thank God Sutton's going,' Jane said. 'Not that it's going to do *me* any good.'

'What do you mean?' Louise asked her.

'I finish school at the end of this term,' she said. 'I'll still be in the Unit next year, but I'll have nothing to do during the day.'

'Can't you still come over to school?' I asked.

'No,' she answered. 'Once you're over sixteen and have come to the end of the final year of compulsory education, the Local Authority no longer has any obligation to do anything with you.'

'But lots of kids stay on in education longer,' Caroline said.

'Yes, at sixth forms or colleges, once they've done their O-levels,' Jane answered. 'But I didn't get to do any O-levels, and Oakdale School hasn't got a sixth form.'

I was starting to contemplate how grim this sounded when Glenys Dawson entered the dining room and came over towards us.

'Daniel,' she said, 'Dr Vanderspeigle wants to see you. Come with me.'

Glenys led me through the Unit's familiar corridors, and then through some double doors into another corridor, one I had never previously entered. I was amazed to find that, after more than three years since my first admission to Oakdale, there were still parts of the Unit that were unknown to me.

We stopped by a door which still bore the name 'Dr G Rajasimha, MD, FRCPsych'. Glenys knocked at the door, and when an acknowledgement came from behind it, she opened it to let me through.

As I entered the room, the door closed behind me, leaving me alone with Dr Vanderspeigle.

What followed, once I had seated myself, was not an overly long consultation, but it was still far more than I had ever had previously at Oakdale. Furthermore, Dr Vanderspeigle managed to cover a good deal of ground in this short meeting, reviewing my time in Oakdale, my home and school life, and my medication (which he decided to reduce). Somehow it felt reassuring to know that someone was at last paying some attention to the nature of the treatment I was receiving. Though I wasn't expecting anything to change significantly, I now had the impression that whatever might befall me during the remainder of my time at the Unit, it was at least possible that it would happen by considered intention rather than by accident.

Shortly after we entered the second half of July, there was much enthusiastic talk about Sebastian Coe having run a mile in record time in Oslo. This event brought us very close to the end of term, and therefore to the beginning of the long six-week holiday.

I knew that when I returned to Oakdale in September, Mrs Sutton would be gone, and I would be beginning my final school year with the prospect of eventually being turned out into the world with no qualifications and no prospects. This filled me with dread, but my more immediate concern was with being parted from Caroline. My relationship with her had become much more firmly established, but as she lived in Newhaven, and I was in Horsham, I realised there was little prospect of meeting up with her during the summer break.

And so we exchanged addresses, promising to send each other postcards. And then, out of sight in the quiet room, we kissed dolefully in anticipation of our temporary but extended separation.

CHAPTER SIXTEEN

Somehow I lost Caroline's address early on in the summer holidays, and so I never actually sent her a postcard. However, I did receive one from her, which made me feel very guilty, given my inability to reciprocate.

My sense of guilt was intensified somewhat by the fact that, while parted, I was beginning to have second thoughts about our relationship. My doubts had been prompted by the realisation that, although I was missing her, our separation had not resulted in an aching void. I still liked her, but my desire to see her again fell a long way short of desperate. And so, upon returning to Oakdale in September, my reunion with Caroline was accompanied by an uncomfortable feeling of uncertainty. And, as always, there was a song in the soundtrack to this period to accompany the moment; 'We Don't Talk Anymore' seemed to be venting constantly from every radio.

It was definitely the case that, once back, there were changes that needed to be faced. Of rather more long-term significance than my shifting feelings concerning Caroline, were the changed circumstances over at the school. The installation of Mrs Sutton's replacement, Mr Brendon, brought with it a dramatic transformation in the momentum and purpose of daily school attendance. Relatively young and energetic, he was an entirely different kind of teacher from the one he had replaced. Moreover, in collaboration with the head, Mr Barkworth, he had hatched some quite definite plans in connection with the older kids, and not just those in his own class.

This was actually a very positive development, as far as it went. The decision had been taken that those of us in our final year of secondary education would be given crash courses in the necessary materials to enable us to sit some exams the following spring. The opportunity this afforded was, however, rather limited, as only three subjects were on offer – English, arithmetic and art – and participants would only be entered for the lesser-status Certificate of Secondary Education.

On the first day back, following school assembly, all the final year pupils were ushered into Mr Brendon's class, while his younger pupils were temporarily handed into the care of either Mr Baker or Mrs Conway. Upon entering what had once been Mrs Sutton's classroom, Mr Brendon directed us to sit down at newly, and more formally, arranged tables.

'Good morning,' Mr Brendon said purposefully. 'My name, as you will have heard Mr Barkworth tell you during assembly, is Mr Brendon. I won't bother getting you to introduce yourselves to me now, but I will make sure I get to know who you all are as we go along.

'Now,' he continued, 'let me tell you what we're going to be doing from now on. As you know, you are all in your final year at Oakdale School, and it is my hope that everyone who isn't going to be returning to some other school before the year is out, will be able to sit at least one CSE before leaving us.

'Mr Barkworth has been working hard over the summer to come to an arrangement whereby you can go and sit your exams at Bourne Comprehensive School.

'Now, whether you actually sit the final exams or not,' he went on, 'you will each be required to follow three CSE courses. You will be studying English with Mr Baker, arithmetic with Mrs Conway, and I will be taking you for art. Does anyone have any questions?'

Martin Boyce, who was due to turn sixteen by the end of the week, spoke up. 'Are we going to –?' he began, before Mr Brendon cut him off.

'I don't know what things were like when Mrs Sutton was here,' Mr Brendon said, 'but *I* expect anyone who wants to ask a question to raise their hand first. Now, let's try again. Does anyone have any questions?'

There was silence.

'Doesn't *anyone* have any questions?' he asked.

The silence continued.

'You,' Mr Brendon said to Martin, 'I thought *you* wanted to ask a question?'

'No,' Martin mumbled, 'it doesn't matter,'

'Very well, then, if no one has any questions, perhaps we should get started. Your first lesson today is English, so I want you all to make your way quickly and quietly to Mr Baker's classroom.'

Somewhat startled by this dramatic change in style, we all got up rather sheepishly and shuffled our way out of the room.

On Wednesday, after school had finished for the day, I sat in the TV room with Jane Sparrow, Louise Bray, Caroline Holmes and Lee Reid, just by the open French doors leading out into the play area. We were sharing with each other our ambivalence about the new arrangements at school.

'You should consider yourselves lucky,' Jane said. 'I've *left* school now and I've come away with nothing. At least you'll all come out with two or three CSEs.'

'That's if I can even *get* to the exams,' Louise said. 'I don't think I've got the nerve to go into a huge crowded school.'

'It'll only be for two or three hours a time,' I said.

'I know,' Louise answered, 'but I still don't think I've got the nerve.'

'It's ages till the exams,' Caroline remarked. 'You'll be all right by then, Louise.'

'And I won't have to do mine for another year,' chirped Lee.

'Well,' Jane said, 'if you've got any sense, Lee, you'll get yourself out of here and into a proper school before then.'

As we were talking, I noticed for the first time since our return after the break that Caroline wasn't really looking too well. She was slightly pale and her expression appeared strained. Also – and I wasn't exactly sure about this – there was a moment when she briefly rolled up one of her sleeves, and I thought I spotted evidence of recent cuts on her forearm. But before I really registered what I'd seen, she hastily rolled the sleeve back down. Given that I was now considering breaking-up with her, this troubled me; how could I possibly end it with her at a time when something was obviously wrong?

Before I could think about this any further, Lee changed the subject. 'It's Wednesday!' he announced, as if this was somehow newsworthy. 'That means *Star Trek* is on tonight.'

That immediately made me think back to my first time as a patient in the Unit, when my friend Andrew Ramsey had been here. Back then, Miss Bishop had recently introduced a rule which required all kids to be in their dormitories during the changeover between the afternoon and night shifts, but Andrew had somehow managed to secure a concession. *Star Trek* had been showing on Monday evenings, but Miss Bishop's rule would have meant us missing all but a few minutes of it; Andrew, however, had somehow pulled off the impressive coup of negotiating an exemption from the ruling.

I was just starting to think that I'd probably join Lee in front of the television that evening, when Jane corrected him.

'No,' she said, 'it's not on tonight. They're showing Lord Mountbatten's funeral service.'

'Oh, well,' I said. 'I suppose that's more important, really.'

'I'm going outside,' Lee resolved grumpily, getting up and going out through the French doors.

I felt a wave of mild discomfort, having been prompted to remember something of my first stay in Oakdale. It all seemed such a long time ago now, and I was aware that, apart from Jane, I was the only patient from that time who was still here. I briefly wondered about the kids I used to know – like Gary Jameson and Sean Townsend, as well as Andrew – all of whom had been able to leave and, to their credit, had never returned. It occurred to me that by still being here, Jane and myself – and perhaps Louise too – were 'lost ones', possibly condemned to live the rest of our lives inhibited by inadequacy.

With Lee having stepped outside, we all decided to rise and wander off in separate directions.

I followed Caroline as she wandered across the TV room and opened the internal glazed door leading into the corridor.

'Are you all right?' I asked her as we walked in the direction the foyer.

'Yes, I'm okay,' she said.

I had no idea where Caroline was intending to go, but we ended up stopping just a short distance from the time-out room.

'Why didn't you send me a postcard or anything?' Caroline said, turning to face me.

'I'm sorry,' I said, feeling embarrassed. 'I lost your address – honestly. I looked for it everywhere.'

'I suppose you got *my* card,' she said.

'Yes,' I answered. 'Thank you. It was great hearing from you. I felt really bad that I couldn't send you one back.'

'I missed you,' she said, 'and I thought maybe you weren't interested in me anymore.'

'I missed you too,' I said, which was only partially true.

As there was no one in sight, Caroline obviously felt free to put her arms around my shoulders and draw me towards her. Though I now had reservations about our relationship, I felt no scruples about responding, placing my arms around her waist and kissing her lips fervently.

Slowly I eased her around so that her back was against a wall, and I pressed my body in against hers, enjoying the sensual provocation of her closeness. The warmth of her breath on my skin was enthralling, and inhaling her natural aroma seemed to intoxicate me.

'I thought perhaps you'd gone off me,' Caroline said on one of the occasions when our lips parted.

'Of course not,' I replied, before our mouths connected again.

Over the next four weeks I continued to agonise over what to do about Caroline. The fact was that I liked her and still found her attractive, but somehow she no longer occupied such an important place in my imagination. Furthermore, there was something clearly the matter with her. As the days went by she was becoming more and more morose, while she also continued to appear unhealthily pallid. She was no longer the same dynamic flame-haired girl I had first met some nine months earlier. Not only had her face become somewhat ashen, but her hair also seemed drained of colour; although this was a comparatively superficial concern, it had been the vibrant redness of her hair that had caught my attention in the first place. And, of course, I had the now very definite suspicion that she was self-harming.

Following the end of the school day one Monday afternoon, Caroline was sitting with me in the dining room, as was usual, along with Louise and Jane. It was the first day of October, and the general atmosphere in Oakdale suggested there was some substantial and disturbing malady afflicting the Unit.

Sure enough, a member of the nursing staff came over to confirm this impression to us while we were drinking our tea.

'As soon as you've finished,' John Webber said to us, 'go through to the TV room and find a seat; there's going to be a meeting.'

John then moved to the next table to pass on the same instructions.

Jane sighed. 'I wonder what we're all in trouble for this time.'

We drained our cups, returned them to the trolley, and then made our way through to the TV room, where I sank down into a foam chair, with Jane to one side of me and Caroline to the other.

I got the impression that some of the kids already had some inkling about the seriousness of what we were about to be told, even if they didn't actually know precisely what it was. The clue was in the eerie silence pervading the room; normally there would be *some* chatter passing between kids, even with the suspicion of impending trouble.

The room gradually filled as staff and children gravely funnelled in. Eventually, Miss Bishop arrived and took her place, and with everyone now seated, the meeting was ready to start.

Miss Bishop looked intently at each one of us as her eyes scanned the circle, presumably ensuring that everyone was present. Needless to say, a couple of staff members, Mrs Sampson and Jill Cooper, had redirected the very youngest kids to the playroom. Despite these two staff absences, I gained the impression that the adults were as much subject to this three line whip as were the kids.

Even after Miss Bishop had carefully cast her eye around the room, she continued to hold the silence. Although it could only have been for a matter of seconds, it felt as though it was going to stretch out indefinitely. It almost seemed to me that, by doing this, she was deliberately building-up the level of anxiety, perhaps already administering to us a 'consequence of our actions' before most of us even knew what those actions had been.

'This is what is going to happen,' she said at last, her stern voice slicing through the quiet like a freshly sharpened blade. 'I am going to talk and *you* are going to listen. No one apart from me is going to say a word, except for those directly involved, and then only if I request it. Do you all understand?'

Taking Miss Bishop's directions very literally, no one gave a response.

'*Do you understand?*' she repeated, obviously angered by our excessively strict interpretation of her instructions.

A few murmuring voices from around the room indicated that we did indeed comprehend what she had said.

'Very well,' she continued in a more level tone. 'No doubt, some of you will already know about what happened in the boys' dormitory last night.'

I had no idea what she was referring to, and I had the impression that very few others did either. Having arrived back from weekend leave that morning, I was not present for whatever events had taken place on Sunday evening. I also knew that the Unit was only sparsely populated at weekends, and while the previous night may have seen one or two children return early from their weekends at home, it was likely that there were very few witnesses, if any, to whatever it was that had happened.

'Perhaps *you* would like to tell us what went on last night, Jeremy,' Miss Bishop said, looking at the sixteen-year-old almost directly facing her.

Jeremy Newton, of course, sat at the same table as me at mealtimes, but despite having had lunch in his company some four hours earlier, I had not received any hint that he'd been involved in some noteworthy controversy. It was true that he had been unusually quiet at lunch, but for some reason I hadn't considered that particularly remarkable. Derek Ball had been the staff member sitting with us during that meal, but as far as I could remember, he hadn't said anything especially notable to Jeremy, and so I'd had no reason to suppose anything was amiss with him. Therefore, it simply hadn't occurred to me, until now, that Jeremy was at the eye of a tumultuous storm.

Jeremy said nothing. He just sat there looking extremely uneasy, something which made him almost unrecognisable. This boy had always had a conspicuously aggressive demeanour, and as he was usually very quick to answer back when challenged by an authority figure, the sight of him cowed before Miss Bishop was totally perplexing.

'So,' Miss Bishop said, 'you've got nothing to say for yourself. That's not like you, is it? I suppose *I'll* just have to tell everyone about last night.'

Jeremy looked positively stricken.

'Yesterday evening,' Miss Bishop began, 'while the reduced weekend staff were occupied by the changeover between shifts, Jeremy Newton invited Adrian Jordan into the boys' dormitory.'

Naturally, my eyes darted around the room until they alighted on the figure of Adrian, an eight-year-old boy who slept in the younger children's dorm. I hadn't really taken much notice of Adrian previously, but I certainly noticed him now: he looked absolutely petrified.

'And then,' Miss Bishop said, 'when Mr Köhler came into the dorm, he found Jeremy and Adrian performing a lewd act.'

Miss Bishop then went on to describe this 'lewd act' in considerably more detail. I was shocked by what I heard, but it occurred to me much later that perhaps I should have been more shocked by the fact Miss Bishop considered it appropriate to air such information so publicly.

I could see that Adrian was shaking, but that didn't stop Miss Bishop from then turning on him.

'And Adrian isn't blameless, of course,' she said. 'He encouraged Jeremy; he got his weapon out.'

There was a faint sound of strangled laughter from around the circle, and shamefully, I let out an awkward giggle myself.

'Please,' came Adrian's voice, so obviously desperate despite being almost inaudible, 'don't tell my dad; he'd *kill* me.'

'Well,' Miss Bishop replied condescendingly, 'we'll have to see about that.'

Somehow I failed to notice what should have been so obvious: Miss Bishop was further traumatising a young boy who had just been sexually abused. Indeed, she was actually *contributing* to his abuse by placing half the responsibility for the incident on his shoulders. I also failed to consider that when the incident took place, Adrian was supposed to be in the care of the Oakdale nursing staff – as, indeed, was Jeremy. What happened was surely as much the responsibility of the staff on duty as it was Jeremy's – and surely Adrian was far too young to bear *any* responsibility.

'And what about you, Jeremy?' Miss Bishop said, turning her attention back to the sixteen-year-old. 'Do you have an explanation for what you did?'

'I –' he began with an uncharacteristic hesitation '– I was pissed off because I didn't have a girlfriend.'

'Really?' Miss Bishop said flatly. And then, addressing us as a whole, she said, 'I want you all to be absolutely clear about this: any amorous or sexual activity between any of you is absolutely forbidden. It doesn't matter whether it's homosexual or heterosexual –'

'What's *hetero*sexual?' I whispered to Jane, not having heard the word before.

'It's normal,' she whispered back, explaining it in a fairly usual way for the time.

'It simply will not be tolerated,' Miss Bishop finished.

Once again, it wouldn't be until quite some time later that it would dawn upon me how appalling Miss Bishop's words were; she was equating a case of child abuse with the consensual and unremarkable activity engaged in by teenagers such as Caroline and myself.

'It has been decided,' Miss Bishop finally declared, 'that Jeremy and Adrian will now both be confined to their separate dormitories without access to their clothing until we can determine appropriate consequences. That is all.'

And the meeting was over.

Stunned and quiescent, we all edged out of the room, barely noticing as Jeremy and Adrian were frogmarched to their respective dorms by Mr Jones and Robert King, with some assistance from other male staff members.

*   *   *

Days passed and some semblance of normality returned to the Unit. As it happened, there were no further punitive consequences for either Jeremy or Adrian – at least, none that I was aware of. Neither was *any* kind of further action taken: Adrian received no supportive therapy, and Jeremy received no remedial therapy. And needless to say, there was no question of the duty staff at the time of the incident being disciplined. It seemed that child abuse was a matter to be brushed under the carpet.

Jeremy, however, was left with a certain legacy from the incident: he would no longer enjoy the same tough reputation that he once had. Although it was imagined by many of the kids that he must have callously pressurised Adrian, the fact it had been a *boy* that he'd abused called into question his masculinity. After all, this had all happened in an age where homosexual behaviour was still commonly regarded as a legitimate target for ridicule; and so Jeremy came to be seen as ridiculous.

With issues to do with sex and sexuality having been foregrounded in this particular way, the matter of my relationship with Caroline began to appear rather trivial by comparison. It therefore became a less daunting task to finally face her and tell her that I no longer wished to 'go out' with her.

On a Thursday afternoon, shortly before supper, I found Caroline in the TV room and asked her to step out into the corridor with me. Rather insensitively, I led her to the foyer where we had kissed on a number of recent occasions.

Wearing a gentle smile, she started to advance towards me, no doubt expecting us to share a moment of intimacy. But I stood there coldly, and before she could reach out to me, I spoke.

'Caroline,' I said, 'I've been thinking. I think I would like it better if we were just friends.'

Her smile faded in response to my indelicate brush-off. She then rapidly turned from me, and ran very quickly towards the doors leading outside.

'Caroline!' I called after her. 'Let's talk about this.'

But she was gone, having darted off into the greyness of that October afternoon.

Inevitably I reflected upon the fact that, yet again, Caroline had run away from me.

In the remaining two weeks leading up to half-term, I observed Caroline from a distance, noticing that her descent into gloom was continuing and that she appeared to be becoming physically more fragile.

As I watched this painful and inexplicable process, I half wished that I hadn't split up with her. I still cared about her, and I wanted to know what was wrong; I wanted to offer her my friendship and support. But the trust between us had been broken, and she was completely resistant to my every attempt at approaching her.

'I'm sick of that girl,' Jane said, as I sat with her and Louise in the quiet room one evening. 'She's always moping about and whining.'

'I don't think she can help it,' I said. 'I think it's pretty serious, actually – she's been cutting herself.'

'Well, that's her fault,' Jane said coldly.

It briefly crossed my mind that some would have said the same about Jane when she had been refusing to eat.

'Come on, Daniel,' Jane continued. 'You've had enough of her too; why else would you have split up with her?'

'I sort of wish I hadn't now,' I said.

'You can't mean that,' Louise declared. 'Just *look* at her: she may not be very well, but she's being a complete bloody pain. *No* one wants to spend any time with her now she's like this.'

'I don't think it's her fault,' I said.

'You've both heard what she's saying now, though, haven't you?' Jane said.

'What?' I asked.

'She says that it's Oakdale that's *making* her ill,' Jane revealed. 'And her doctor at home is going to get her out of here.'

'Bloody cheek!' Louise exclaimed.

Suddenly I felt very angry with Caroline. She had managed to convince her GP that Oakdale was doing her harm, and it looked as though he was going to get her discharged. At that moment it no longer mattered to me that Caroline might really be suffering; what mattered was that she had someone in authority on her side, and I was furiously jealous.

By all appearances, Louise and Jane were having similar feelings.

'It isn't fair,' Louise continued. '*We* all have to put up with this place. Why should she be any different?'

Later on I would come to look back on this period with great sadness and remorse, because then I realised that Caroline's condition had been deteriorating, and that we, her closest friends, had turned against her.

The last time I saw Caroline was on the Friday immediately preceding the half-term break. I didn't get to speak to her, and neither did I try. But I saw her at the other end of the corridor as Mrs Fox, the social worker, led her out to the car park.

And so my final view of Caroline, the one that was to become permanently embedded in my mind, was of her looking incredibly weak, like an old woman, resting heavily on the arm of Mrs Fox. I had to fight to remember that this shrunken and frail figure represented a once strong and vital girl who hadn't even yet celebrated her sixteenth birthday.

CHAPTER SEVENTEEN

Weeks passed, my sixteenth birthday came and went and, in time, so did Christmas. The return to Oakdale following the holiday more-or-less coincided with the news that Joy Adamson, the naturalist and author of *Born Free*, had been killed by a lion – or so the initial reports claimed. I thus found myself remembering a time when I'd never even heard of Oakdale, when I and my school friends at Worthing Road Comprehensive used to watch the *Born Free* TV series. That was a lifetime away now, the innocent and sensitive young boy that I had once been having grown into a fatalistic and cynical teenager. Somehow, Adamson's tragic death reminded me of a part of myself that had died, a part of myself that had been delivered unto lions.

A handful of faces at Oakdale had changed in recent weeks, both among kids and staff. But a few significant ones remained, namely those belonging to Jane Sparrow, Louise Bray and Lee Reid. But I was now no longer bothered to note who had gone, the departure of Caroline Holmes having left me numb, and I was only marginally more observant regarding who had arrived.

As it happened, there was one arrival that caught my attention: an extremely elegant-looking black girl called Katie Fofana. Katie was fifteen, and in my immature way I was very attracted by what I saw as her 'exotic otherness'. My impression of her as 'other' was further enhanced by her rather ethereal soft-spoken manner. I therefore worked hard at being friendly towards her, and I found her relatively friendly in return.

'He's at it again,' I heard Clayton Winter say.

It was a Tuesday afternoon, and a group of us were making our way through the passageway connecting the main body of the Unit to the section housing the dormitories.

'Daniel always tries it on whenever there's a new girl,' the thirteen-year-old Clayton continued, making sure that everyone present, including Katie, could hear him.

I was embarrassed and annoyed, and also a little bewildered; Clayton's suggestion didn't really have any basis in reality. It was indeed true that there was a time when I had pursued a succession of girls, but that had all been before Clayton's arrival at the Unit. The only girl with whom he could have seen me 'try it on' would have been Caroline, and she had been my girlfriend for a period of some months.

Naturally, I was concerned about the impression Katie would gain from this remark, but as I watched her, walking a few paces ahead of me, I saw no reaction from her whatsoever. She couldn't have failed to hear him, and I was sure she would realise he was referring to the attention I had been giving her. But she didn't react, and whatever her reasons were for ignoring him, I felt an oddly haunting sense of gratitude.

When we reached the area of the nurses' station, most of the kids wandered off to their own dormitories. I followed Clayton into the boys' dorm, and once the doors had closed behind us, I challenged him.

'What was that about?' I demanded. 'Since when have you seen me try it on whenever there's a new girl?'

'Just joking,' he laughed dismissively.

'But why?' I said, not yet willing to let the matter go.

''Cause I can see you're after Katie, and I wanted to see the look on your face when I showed you up in front of her.'

I stared at him, rather lost for words, as he made his way to his locker and started poking around in the drawers.

My intention while heading for the dorm had been to lie on my bed and start reading the Douglas Adams book that everyone was currently raving about, but I was so exasperated with Clayton that I walked straight back out and retraced my steps to the main body of the Unit.

By now, the small number us who were in our final year at the school were heavily involved in our CSE work. Although we weren't due to actually sit the exams until May, there was coursework to be prepared, and we were beginning to feel rather pressured. Given that we were only studying three subjects, this pressure seemed a little disproportionate; but then, we were trying to fit two years' worth of learning into one. Furthermore, we were having to do all of it in class time during Oakdale's shorter school day – no 'homework' was ever set due to the acknowledged difficulty of attempting such a thing in the environment of the Unit.

It was during one grey afternoon, while Martin Boyce, Louise Bray and myself were attempting screen-printing in our art class, that Mr Brendon came over to me and started talking about work experience.

'Daniel,' he began, 'we've been talking with your social worker, Mrs Fox, and we think it would be a good idea if you started to get some experience of the working world.'

This was something I hadn't anticipated.

'The idea is,' he explained, 'that you take one day a week out from school and get used to working for an employer.'

Although the idea made me feel very anxious, I had the presence of mind to ask whether I would get paid.

'No, of course not!' Mr Brendon laughed. 'It's just work *experience*. The employer would be doing you a favour by having you. But if you're lucky, he might be prepared to pay your bus fare.'

'So what do I need to do?' I asked. 'Do I have to start looking for the kind of work I'd like to try?'

'No,' Mr Brendon said. 'We'll sort all that out for you. In fact, we're already making the arrangements. On Friday afternoon, I'll take you into Horsham, and you can meet the employer we've been negotiating with. And then I can drop you home afterwards.'

Perhaps I should have been a little offended that a decision like this had been made without my knowledge, but I simply accepted that this is what had happened; what I wanted was to know more about it.

'What employer?' I asked.

'He's an old friend of mine: Jack Griffin,' Mr Brendon said. 'He's actually the boss's son. They run a print shop together called Griffin Duplicating. As you live in Horsham, you might well have seen it, it's in Middle Street.'

I had to admit that, although I'd probably walked down Middle Street on a number of occasions, I'd never noticed Griffin Duplicating.

'Not to worry,' he said. 'You'll know all about it after Friday.'

Before I had a chance to ask any further questions, he patted me on the arm and went over to comment on what Martin was doing.

It was approaching half-past three, and so it was time to start packing away and clearing up. I set about completing this task, and then, with thoughts of work experience running around my head, I trailed slowly after the others as they left the school building and headed back to the Unit.

By the time I entered the foyer area, the others were some way along the corridor, well on their way towards the dining room. I was alone, therefore, when I was approached by a smartly dressed middle-aged woman who had followed me in.

'Excuse me,' she said in a cultured voice, 'could you tell me where –?'

The woman had overtaken me, presumably to make sure she had my attention. But despite this, she wasn't able to fully hold it; I failed to hear the rest of her sentence because I was distracted by what I could see behind her.

She was standing with her back to the door of the time-out room, and over her shoulder I could see the door open to reveal a completely naked thirteen-year-old boy. The boy in question was a recent admission to Oakdale by the name of Charlie Flood. I hardly knew Charlie at all, but I was aware that he suffered from what we would later come to describe as severe learning difficulties.

Charlie's disability, coupled with the fact that he had obviously been drugged, must have caused his failure to recognise the inappropriate nature of his undressed state.

I tried to signal to Charlie with my eyes, tried to urge him to retreat back into the time-out room, but it was impossible to communicate with him without alerting the visitor to his presence. And so I hastily tried to refocus on the visitor and act as though there was nothing amiss. The priority I adopted was to protect the reputation of the Unit before an evidently refined individual.

The woman clearly noticed that I seemed distracted, and she gave a quick backwards glance in the direction where I had been looking. But she did not actually turn around, and so to my great relief she never saw the unclad figure of Charlie. She did, however, seem a little perplexed by my manner.

'Did you hear what I said?' she asked.

'Uh, no, sorry,' I answered, more falteringly than I would have liked. 'What did you say?'

'I said, Could you tell me where I might find the nursing officer, Anna Bishop?'

'She'll be in the dining room at this time,' I said. 'Just go to the end of this corridor –' I gestured in the appropriate direction '– and turn right, and the dining room is straight ahead.'

I could, of course, have escorted her to dining room myself, as that was where I was going anyway, but I just felt too flustered.

As soon as the woman had disappeared from sight, I turned on Charlie and expressed my annoyance with him.

'She could have seen you!' I said sharply. 'Get back in the punishment room before anyone else comes along!'

Without waiting to see whether or not Charlie had followed my instruction, I marched off.

As I collected my cup of tea from Barbara Heaton, the auxiliary, I noticed that the visitor had indeed found Miss Bishop, and that the two of them were making their way out of the dining room.

Instead of joining Louise, Jane and Lee, as I usually did, I made my way over to where Katie was sitting – on her own.

'Do you mind if I join you?' I asked, feeling a little uncomfortable with my rather clichéd approach.

'Not at all,' she replied in her characteristically precise way. 'Go ahead.' I sat down.

'Did you notice that woman with Miss Bishop?' I asked. Katie nodded.

'I saw her just a minute ago, when she got here,' I said. 'She came in at the same time as me after school. She asked me for directions.'

'And?'

'Well,' I said awkwardly, 'while she was talking to me, I saw Charlie behind her, coming out of the punishment room – he was stark naked! I was worried that woman might see him and get the wrong idea about this place.'

Katie looked at me thoughtfully, her deep dark eyes seeming to quietly question me. 'If she *had* seen him, she may have got the *right* idea, Daniel,' Katie said eventually.

Suddenly I felt very ashamed. I had been worrying about the wrong thing. And just in case I'd been in any doubt, Katie went on to underline my error.

'Charlie isn't like us,' she said. 'He doesn't understand what he's doing half the time. I don't know why they put him in the punishment room, but whatever he did, I'm sure he couldn't help it. But they've stripped him of his clothes and obviously just left him to be humiliated in front of whoever walks past.'

I looked down at the table. 'You're right,' I said uneasily. 'I should have thought of that. Maybe it would have been better if that woman *had* seen Charlie.'

'Maybe,' Katie replied. 'But I don't think it would have been right if that woman had ended up gawping at him as if he was in a zoo.'

I sighed, uncertain about what I should have done.

'Daniel,' Katie said, 'you worried about what that woman would think of this place, instead of worrying about Charlie.'

I was mortified. I had made a choice without even thinking, and it had been the wrong choice. And if that wasn't bad enough, I was appalled at being so disgraced in front of Katie, the girl I desperately wanted to impress.

'What can I say?' I mumbled, looking up timidly. 'I just didn't think.'

She looked at me with understanding. 'I know,' she said. 'It's easy for me to criticise – I wasn't there. If I had been, I may have done the same as you.'

I smiled slightly, realising that my attraction to this girl would always have been inevitable: quite apart from the impact of first appearances, I could now see that she had compassion and integrity, and that she was very forgiving of others' failings. Perhaps I was placing her on a pedestal, but it seemed that every new thing I learned about her made her appear more perfect.

*   *   *

Friday afternoon arrived, and with my weekend suitcase stowed away in the back of Mr Brendon's red Mazda 323, I was driven to meet Jack Griffin at the print shop in Horsham. My involvement in the meeting was limited to a tour of the rather cramped premises and an introduction to Mr Griffin, Senior, and two of his employees. Apart from answering a few basic questions about myself, I had little opportunity to speak; it seemed that I was there simply to observe as Mr Brendon and Jack Griffin finalised their arrangements concerning me. The end result of the meeting was an agreement whereby I would start to undergo work experience at the print shop following the half-term break. The requirement was that I would attend at Griffin Duplicating on Wednesdays between nine in the morning and four-thirty in the afternoon, thus gaining a taste of a near-to-full working day.

'And that just leaves the question of Daniel's bus fare,' Mr Brendon said.

'I think we can cover that,' said Jack Griffin. 'After all, if he's not worth his bus fare, he's not worth having at all.'

And so, with everything having been decided, the meeting was over. Mr Brendon then took me home, where I discovered that my parents were actually far better informed about my anticipated work experience than I was.

Though I had felt inconsequential during the process of securing the work experience placement, once I actually began setting off on a Wednesday morning for my job of work, such as it was, I began to feel rather empowered. It was as though I had taken a step towards the adult world and that I was no longer simply a kid. And on Wednesday evenings, when I arrived back at the Unit in time for supper, I experienced a sense of seniority – I was now the working man coming in from a hard day of industry.

I was not the only Oakdale patient to be undergoing work experience – Martin had been given a placement at a florist's, of all places – but I certainly felt that I stood apart from the other kids. And this gave a quite significant boost to my confidence, which in turn enabled me to be more self-assured in talking to Katie.

It was after supper one Wednesday that I finally decided to be more explicit about my feelings. I had managed to get Katie on her own in the quiet room, and while we sat together on the foam chairs, under the less-than-conducive light of a florescent tube, I told her how I felt about her.

'I know,' she said. 'But there's something I have to tell you.'

There was an uncomfortable pause.

'I have to tell you,' she began again, 'that I've started "going out" with

Lee.'

I sat there dumbstruck. I hadn't even noticed that Katie and Lee were getting close, and yet they had become an item right under my nose. And to make matters worse, Lee was one of my best friends. How could this have happened?

'I really like you, Daniel,' Katie said. 'But I just don't feel *that* way about you. I should have said something sooner. My dad always says "We should put out fire while it is still small".'

For me, the fire was not small; I was consumed by it, and so my immediate urge was to flee, and that is exactly what I did. Given that I'd only known Katie for a short time, my reaction may have been excessive, but I ran from the quiet room with uncontrollable tears stinging my eyes. I made it to the dorm in a matter of seconds, and threw myself headlong onto my bed. I sobbed convulsively into the bedclothes, and though I tried desperately to regain some control over myself, all I could do was give way to frantic howling accompanied by unrestrained spasms.

Eventually the muscles in my body began to loosen and my explosive bawling transformed into a gentle moan. My thoughts also became more ordered as I began making sense of what had happened. My distress wasn't caused simply by knowing Katie wasn't interested in me, it was the fact she was interested in someone else. And that 'someone else' was my friend Lee. I felt betrayed. Added to this was my sense of embarrassment at my outburst, which I imagined was loud enough to have been heard throughout the Unit.

I don't know how long I spent just resting face down on my bed, but when I turned over, I saw a fourteen-year-old boy, Neil Buckley, standing over me.

'You all right, mate?' Neil asked.

I couldn't quite manage to speak, but I nodded. I then took a deep breath, rubbed my eyes, and got up.

As I made my way out of the dorm through the double doors I was discomforted to see Katie and Lee standing together by the nurses' station. I decided I would just walk away from this section of the Unit without acknowledging them. But Katie came over to meet me. I swallowed hard, thinking to myself that she had never looked more beautiful. Her carefully braided ebony hair hung about her face, accenting the way she seemed almost aglow with mesmerising warmth – but that warmth was not for me.

'I really am sorry, Daniel,' she said.

'And so am I,' Lee added, joining her.

I looked from Katie to Lee and then back again. Somehow I couldn't bring myself to feel badly towards them, which was something that only added to my sense of hopelessness.

'Daniel,' Lee said, 'you've a good friend. The last thing I want to do is upset you like this.'

I muttered something to them, suggesting that I understood, and then went on my way.

Whether it was my preoccupation with Katie and Lee, my work experience placement, or CSE coursework, I had somehow failed to notice that Jane's condition was worsening again.

Four years had passed since I had originally met Jane and witnessed, for the first time, the sight of someone suffering anorexia nervosa. During that time I had seen Jane make progress and I had seen her relapse. Since her readmission to Oakdale the previous spring, when she had been especially frail and emaciated, she had achieved some degree of recovery, but now she was deteriorating once again.

It was on a Thursday evening, after I had been sitting in the TV room with Louise watching *M*A*S*H*, that we made our way into the dining room for a final cup of tea before bedtime.

'Jane looks very poorly again,' said Louise, as soon as we had settled ourselves at a table.

'Where *is* Jane?' I asked. 'I haven't seen her around today.'

'You haven't really seen her at all lately,' Louise said. 'You've been too busy agonising over Katie and Lee.'

I was bit irritated by Louise's remark, but I decided to ignore it. 'Well, where *is* Jane?' I repeated.

'She's been in bed all day,' Louise answered. 'She's too weak to get up, and they're force feeding her again. And there's a rumour that they're going to send her to St Anselm's.'

'They can't do that!' I exclaimed.

'I think that's what they're going to do,' Louise confirmed. 'They're going to transfer her. They think she's too old to stay here. And since she's got sick again they don't want to be bothered with her anymore.'

The news stunned me, even though I must have known there was always a risk of this happening to Jane.

'When?' I asked falteringly. 'When is she going?'

'I don't know,' Louise replied. 'But it's going to be pretty soon.'

As it happened, it was only a few days after this conversation that Jane was transferred from Oakdale Unit to St Anselm's Psychiatric Hospital. It happened on a Wednesday, the day after Robert Mugabe was elected Prime Minister of Zimbabwe. It was also on a day when I was at my work

234

experience placement. As I was busy at Griffin Duplicating operating a photocopier or dyeline machine – while a transistor radio was blaring out 'Brass in Pocket', or some such – Jane was being removed from her bed in the Unit to be escorted the relatively short distance to St Anselm's.

At least I had managed to talk to Jane on the Tuesday before she went. Although no specific information had been forthcoming, I realised that she could be leaving at any time, and so I made a point of going to see her in the girls' dormitory.

Pulling up a foam chair so that I could sit by her bed, I experienced a definite sense of *déjà vu*. This was so like the time when she had accused me of looking at her as though she had a blotch on her face. That was when she had returned to Oakdale looking so hideously gaunt and withered that I couldn't look at her without betraying my horror. While she didn't appear quite so sickly this time, the difference was only marginal. But what made this occasion distinct from that previous one was the knowledge that this was not a time of return but a time of final departure.

'I'm scared,' she said, almost in a whisper.

I thought to myself that if I had been in her position, I would have been *more* than scared. The prospect of leaving for some bleak and forbidding ward in St Anselm's must have felt worse that a death sentence. As Oakdale kids, we hadn't had much experience of the main building, but we had all been taken over there at some time, often to see the dentist or the chiropodist. And when that had happened, we had often found ourselves lurking in grim corridors which often reeked with the overpowering stench of ammonia. It was in such places that we would have to wait for whatever appointments we were there for, observing occasional adult patients wandering by, zombie-like in their ill-fitting dressing gowns. More disturbing still, there had been odd instances when we had heard distant screams, their far-away echoes straying in our direction from situations we could only guess at. This was the world that Jane was now going to have to live in.

Once again I found myself sitting with Jane trying to keep my face as impassive as possible. I knew that on no account must I reveal that I shared her fear.

'They'll help you over there,' I said, knowing that I didn't sound remotely convincing. 'It hasn't done you much good being here. But they've got more doctors at St Anselm's – you'll have a much better chance of getting well again.'

Her sunken eyes looked at me almost contemptuously.

'You can't possibly believe that,' she said.

'Of course I do,' I tried bluffing. 'That's their job; that's what they're there for.'

'Yeah, right,' she answered with muted sarcasm.

I remained with her for a few minutes, taking in the image of the dry and flaking skin that unwillingly wrapped the harsh contours of her skull, and the dull strands of hair that had fallen from their follicles to rest on her pillow. Despite myself, I shivered at the sight, somehow realising that this would be the last I would ever see of my friend.

Time seemed to be moving by very quickly now. Spring arrived, and so did the Easter holidays, following which I realised that this phase of my life was rapidly coming to an end. It was only a matter of weeks before I would sit my CSE exams, and once they were out of the way, I would no longer be required to attend Oakdale School.

Before I really had a chance to contemplate what might happen to me at that point, I discovered that the powers-that-be were planning for me to be discharged from the Unit for the third and final time. Before that could happen, there would be one last case conference, but in truth, decisions had already been made.

I had meetings with the social worker, Mrs Fox, and with my psychiatrist, Dr Vanderspeigle. Both of them talked in rather abstract terms about how I had to make the transition from childhood to adulthood, and how I could best achieve this by returning home. They also talked vaguely about the kind of support I could expect, and what they in turn would expect of me. It was, however, left to my teacher, Mr Brendon, to explain one of the more concrete components of what was to happen.

He took me aside during one of his art classes, and got me to sit next to him at his desk.

'Jack Griffin is very pleased with you,' he told me. 'What's more, he *was* hoping he'd be able to give you a job at the print shop once you'd left Oakdale.'

I started to feel quite encouraged by this prospect, but then Mr Brendon told me that, unfortunately, it wasn't going to be as straightforward as that.

'It seems, though, that Mr Griffin, Senior, isn't quite so impressed with you,' Mr Brendon went on. 'He's not *un*happy with your work, but he thinks you're a bit slow. He's also being very cautious following Geoffrey Howe's budget. *I* thought the Chancellor had done quite a bit to *help* small businesses, but Mr Griffin thinks he's made conditions more unfavourable. These are tough times.

'But,' Mr Brendon went on, 'we've managed to come to an alternative arrangement. Instead of actually being employed by Griffin Duplicating, you'll be able to work there for six months under the government's Youth Opportunities Programme. You'll get £23.50 a week, and it won't cost Mr Griffin a penny as he'll get the money back. And then, after six months, if

236

everything's gone well, Mr Griffin may be in a better position to offer you something permanent.'

Once again, things had been decided for me without my knowledge. I wasn't entirely displeased with the outcome, however, though I was somewhat aggrieved to learn that Griffin Duplicating apparently wanted my labour, but they weren't currently willing to pay for it.

I brushed these thoughts aside and concentrated on the fact that, after leaving Oakdale, I would have a job to go to, even if it was only a placement on a government scheme.

Even now, after a few weeks had passed, it was difficult seeing Katie and Lee together so much of the time. But I was making an effort to stay on good terms with them both, and I tried to affect a cheerful manner when in their presence. Presumably my positive demeanour appeared every bit as artificial as it actually was, but I maintained it because I didn't want Katie and Lee to see I was continuing to feel badly about their relationship. And, of course, they were my friends, and I didn't want them to feel awkward around me.

Regrettably, Katie and Lee's alliance was not to be my last taste of anguish while at Oakdale. As April gave way to May there was another event that was to leave me horribly shaken. Staff chatter, however, completely avoided this matter, preferring instead to focus on what was dominating the radio and television news: the Iranian Embassy Siege in London. While recognising this to be a major ongoing event, the fact was that I had little understanding of what it was about. It was this other event, far closer to home, that was to have the greater impact upon me.

I heard the news from Louise. It was during morning break, and we were sitting together at one of the dining room tables.

Louise appeared traumatised, and as she lifted her teacup to her lips it was apparent that she was shaking.

'Are you all right?' I asked her.

'No,' she wheezed. 'Have you heard about Jane?'

Without knowing why, I experienced a sudden and overwhelming sensation of dread.

Louise visibly shivered as she lowered her cup, her trembling causing it to rattle as she placed it in its saucer. 'Jane is dead.'

I stared.

'They just let her die,' Louise murmured bitterly.

'How do you know?' I managed to ask.

'I overheard Glenys Dawson and John Webber talking,' she explained. 'It was just before the morning meeting. I was up by the nurses' station; I don't think they knew I was there.'

I gulped dryly, grimly trying to ward off the sense that I was about to be buried under the rubble of absolute chaos.

'I've known about this all morning,' Louise said tearfully, 'and I haven't been able to say anything until now.'

Unsteadily, I got up from my chair and walked around the table. I knelt next to Louise and threw my arms around her. She grabbed on to me, and we both wept into each other's shoulders.

'No! No! Stop that!' came the brittle voice of Mrs Causton.

Mrs Causton had come up behind Louise and me, and she was prizing us apart.

I leapt to my feet and turned on Mrs Causton angrily.

'Why didn't you tell us?' I shouted at her.

The dining room went silent as everyone's attention was captured by my raised voice.

'Why didn't you tell us about Jane?' I demanded.

Lee got up from where he had been sitting with Katie, and walked over to where Mrs Causton and I were standing.

'What's happened to Jane?' he asked.

Mrs Causton glanced solemnly around the room, clearly aware that all the kids were listening intently for her answer. She cleared her throat.

'I have some very bad news,' she announced to the room in general. 'Jane Sparrow died yesterday afternoon in St Anselm's Hospital. The doctors there did everything they could, but she was very ill and there was nothing anyone could do to save her.'

With so little time left before I was to leave Oakdale, there was nothing for me to do but to focus on my CSEs. First, I had seen hope lost in Katie, and now I had seen life lost in Jane. But this part of my existence was now closing down; all I had to do was endure the little that remained.

During May, the Oakdale minibus made a few trips to Bourne Comprehensive School so that a handful of us could undergo our English and arithmetic exams in the sports hall. In addition to these, we also had to produce paintings under invigilated conditions in the Bourne Art Department, and I was also subjected to an English oral exam in one of the teachers' offices. It was a test of endurance to get through all of this, and sadly, I was the only one who *did* endure it all. Unfortunately, none of the others succeeded in sitting every CSE exam. Even more regrettable was the fact that Louise was so overcome with anxiety that she failed to take *any* of the exams – much as she has predicted some months earlier.

With the last of my exams having been sat, I could finally let go. I could breathe out the carefully maintained control that had seen me through these last weeks – and I could breathe out my entire experience of Oakdale, good as well as bad. It was now over.

And so it was on a sunny spring afternoon that I wandered into the Oakdale dining room one last time, and found my mum and dad, and my eight-year old brother, Mark, waiting for me. I said my goodbyes to the kids around me – Louise, Lee and Katie – and to a few of the staff – John Webber, Mr Jones, and a couple of others. And then I went with my family to the car park and got into our aging Morris 1100. Whatever difficulties now lay ahead of me, I knew that nothing could ever be so terrible as what I was finally leaving behind.

EPILOGUE

I don't really know how long I've been walking, but I imagine I have now walked the length of Oakdale Drive several times. Feeling a little self-conscious about my behaviour, and how it could be construed as suspicious, I decide to turn left at the end of the road, and after a few paces I see the entrance to an open green space: Hawkins Down Recreation Ground.

Despite the drizzle, I can see a couple of children in the play area, and further off to the right there's a man walking his dog. And then, in the far corner of the park I see my wife looking on as our two teenage sons kick about with a football. I hasten my pace to join them.

'Did you find what you were looking for, Daniel?' my wife asks me.

'Sort of,' I reply.

'I don't know about you,' she says, 'but I'm cold and wet. Can we go now?'

I smile at her. 'Yes, of course.'

My wife calls out to the boys that it's time to go.

Together we make our way out of the park and walk back down Oakdale Drive. Turning onto St Anslem's Road, I glance behind me with sadness at the memory of what happened in this place. And then I look ahead, and I see my two boys running towards the place where we parked the car. I allow myself to smile, because I know that whatever else may happen to my sons, they will never have to suffer the kind of experiences I once had.

Beside me, my wife takes my hand in hers.

'It's all right, Daniel,' she says. 'We can go now. It's over.'

Together we walk towards the car and our waiting sons, and this time I know I will not return. Oakdale will never hurt me again.

Lightning Source UK Ltd.
Milton Keynes UK
05 November 2010

162433UK00001B/85/P